Contemporary Argentinean Women Writers

Edited by Gustavo Fares
and Eliana Cazaubon Hermann
Translated by Linda Britt

CONTEMPORARY
ARGENTINEAN
WOMEN WRITERS

A Critical Anthology

University Press of Florida

Gainesville · Tallahassee · Tampa · Boca Raton

Pensacola · Orlando · Miami · Jacksonville

Spanish Edition Published in 1993 by Peter Lang Publishing, Inc.

03   02   01   00   99   98   6   5   4   3   2   1

Library of Congress Cataloging-in-Publication Data
Escritoras argentinas contemporáneas. English
Contemporary Argentinean women writers: a critical anthology / edited by
Gustavo Fares and Eliana Cazaubon Hermann; translated by Linda Britt.
     p. cm.
Expanded English version of: Escitoras argentinas contemporáneas.
ISBN 0-8130-1553-7 (alk. paper)
1. Argentine fiction—Women authors—Translations into English.
2. Argentine fiction—20th century—Translations into English. 3. Argentine
fiction—20th century—Bio-bibliography. 4. Women authors. Argentine—20th
century—interviews. I. Fares, Gustavo C., 1957–. II. Hermann, Eliana Cazaubon,
1930–. III. Britt, Linda. IV. Title.
PQ7776.2.W65E713   1998
860.9'9287—dc21   97-34995
                                                                              CIP

The University Press of Florida is the scholarly publishing agency for the
State University System of Florida, comprised of Florida A & M University,
Florida Atlantic University, Florida International University, Florida State
University, University of Central Florida, University of Florida, University of
North Florida, University of South Florida, and University of West Florida.

University Press of Florida
15 Northwest 15th Street
Gainesville, FL 32611
http://nersp.nerdc.ufl.edu/~upf

To Lori Ann Williamson Fares, my wife
    —G. F.

To all my family
    —E. H.

Contents

Preface

Since the so-called boom of Latin American literature in the 1960s, the same authors, with only a few new additions, have been read repeatedly by American audiences. The most famous of these Latin American authors are men: Mario Vargas Llosa from Perú, Julio Cortázar from Argentina, Augusto Roa Bastos from Paraguay, José Donoso from Chile, and Juan Rulfo from Mexico, to name a few. More recently Isabel Allende from Chile and Laura Esquivel from Mexico have become well known; however, there are many other women in Latin America producing excellent literature whose work remains unknown.

It was our intention with our book *Escritoras argentinas contemporáneas* (1993) to expand the availability of Latin American literature. In that volume, we focus on thirteen contemporary Argentinean women writers, some very well known and some new and upcoming, including: Estela Canto, María Esther de Miguel, Alina Diaconú, Angélica Gorodischer, Alicia Jurado, Jorgelina Loubet, Martha Mercader, Elvira Orphée, Mabel Pagano, Alicia Régoli de Mullen, Reina Roffé, Noemí Ulla, and María Esther Vázquez.

For the publication of this expanded English version, Linda Britt, from the University of Maine, has translated the original chapters. We have, moreover, added a fourteenth writer, María Rosa Lojo, and revised the introduction. The result is *Contemporary Argentinean Women Writers: A Critical Anthology.*

Each chapter of this book has four sections: the first is a short biography; the second, a bibliography of primary and secondary sources; the third is an interview with the writer; and the fourth is a selection of her work. The selections, either short stories or novel excerpts, were chosen, whenever possible, by the writer herself. We feel that the authors' input makes the selections all the more valuable and significant.

Together, these interviews and excerpts depict the sociopolitical and economic climate of Argentina over the last decades. These authors reveal the ways in which their literary production has been affected by that climate and, in turn, the ways in which their art has helped to mold the country's life and help bring about a resolution to its crises.

Our work is aimed at three audiences: scholars of Latin American literature, university professors and students interested in Latin American literature authored by women, and members of the general public. Ideally, this book will serve as a resource for all three audiences to provide better access to what we think are among the best works of contemporary literature.

We want to thank the writers, whose collaboration was essential for the completion of this volume and whose permission to use selections from their work made all of this possible. Among the many persons we would also like to thank and who have contributed their ideas, encouragement, and suggestions, are Dr. Javier Herrero, from the University of Virginia, and Professor Luis Harss, whose criticism was extremely valuable in the examination of literature authored by women. We are indebted to the reviewers of this manuscript whose comments helped make it a better work, to Dr. George Bedell who was instrumental in the publication of this volume, and to Susana Díaz Vasco whose patient work and collection of data in Buenos Aires proved invaluable in the completion of the manuscript. Finally, our thanks goes to Lynchburg College for granting Dr. Fares the semester-long sabbatical that allowed him to complete the final version of this book.

Contemporary Argentinean Women Writers

Introduction

Gender and History in the Works of
Contemporary Argentinean Women Writers

The writing of fictional texts by contemporary women authors of Argentina can be fruitfully explored to examine a variety of interactions between literature, gender issues, and society at large. In the process of examining those interactions, we propose that the literary fiction produced in Argentina during the last two decades searches for two kinds of identities: that of the individual, and that of the country as a whole. In the first kind of examination of identity, that of the individual, the issues of sex and gender are very important; in the case of the second identity, that of the country as a whole, history plays a fundamental role. Some of the voices Argentinean women writers add to the debate regarding personal and societal identities are presented in this volume. Their works stand witness to the array of relationships that exist between what is personal and societal, intimate and political, that which is individual and that which is historical. They also relate the practice of literature to gender and history and illustrate the ways in which these relations play themselves out, contributing to the shaping of Argentinean culture and society in the last decades.

In the present work we are interested in providing an overview of the fiction produced by contemporary Argentinean women writers and in examining what their texts denote and connote about the state of society and the condition of women therein. Before doing that, however, it will be useful to summarily underline certain aspects of the recent history of the country in

I

order to familiarize the reader with a series of events that will be useful in understanding the interactions and relationships between and among literature, gender, and history in contemporary Argentina.

In the last three decades Argentina has passed from a de facto military government (1966–72), to a brief democratic interregnum (1973–76), to another military government (1976–83), to the current democratic rule, from 1983 to the present. This succession of military and democratic governments began with the coup d'état of 1930 which overthrew Hipólito Hirigoyen (1916–22 and 1928–30), breaking, for the first time, the continuity of democratic rule. Since then, political instability has been endemic to Argentinean political life. The last fifty years of the country's history have been dominated by the presence of Colonel Juan Domingo Perón and of the Peronist movement and party (*Partido Peronista*). Colonel Perón rose to power as minister of labor in 1943, when army officers overthrew the government of Juan Ramón Castillo (1942–43). As minister, Perón strengthened the unions and won the support of the urban workers while a series of generals (Arturo Rawson, Pedro Ramírez, and Edelmiro J. Farrell) served as presidents. The workers' vote was decisive when Perón himself ran for the presidency, which he won in 1945. Perón stayed in power for the next ten years, until he was overthrown in 1955 by the military uprising known as *Revolución Libertadora*.

Following the terms of two military rulers, Eduardo A. Lonardi (1955) and Pedro Eugenio Aramburu (1955–58), democratic elections were called for in 1958. These elections, however, were held with a proscribed Peronist Party. The Radical Party (*Partido Radical*), representing the Argentinean middle class and a coalition of anti-Peronist parties, won the 1958 election, and President Arturo Frondizi (1958–62) was sworn into office. The military, fearing Frondizi would yield to Perón's supporters and restore Peronist economic policies, removed him in a 1962 military uprising that allowed the vice-president, José María Guido (1962–63), to finish the presidential term in office. In 1963 elections were held, once again, with a proscribed Peronist Party and, once again, a Radical Party candidate, Dr. Arturo Illia (1963–66), won. In 1966 General Juan Carlos Onganía commanded a military coup, overthrowing Illia and beginning once more the cycle of military rule. Military power changed hands three times, from Onganía (1966–70), to Roberto Marcelo Levingston (1970–71), to General Alejandro Agustín Lanusse (1971–73).

In the economic arena during the late 1960s and early 1970s, Argentina's situation became increasingly difficult due to poor management in the government and corruption in the military. The economic situation led to strikes, violence, and anti-government protests. Faced with economic failure, the fierce opposition of workers and unions, and radical youth groups waging a campaign of violence and terror, the military allowed the return of Perón and his party to the Argentinean political scene. In 1972 General Lanusse called for democratic elections allowing, for the first time since 1955, the participation of the Peronist Party. The Peronist candidate, however, was not Juan Domingo Perón, but a party loyal, Dr. Héctor J. Cámpora (1973), who won the 1973 elections. His democratic triumph was short lived. Three months after Perón's return to the country, Cámpora resigned his post and called for elections, this time to allow the candidacy of Perón to take place. In 1973 the presidential ticket Perón-Perón, that is, Juan Domingo Perón as president, and his wife, María Estela Martínez de Perón, as vice-president, was elected (1973–74).

The people saw an old and ailing Peron, still popular but surrounded by a highly incompetent and authoritarian group of advisors and facing challenges from the still radical youth. The Peronist Youth (*Juventud Peronista*) faction, also called *Montoneros*, and a number of leftist groups, including the People's Revolutionary Army (ERP or *Ejército Revolucionario del Pueblo*), expressed their discontent and disappointment with the democratic government by going underground and resuming the violent practices they had used against the military government between 1966 and 1972. Montoneros and ERP were two of the groups that, in Buenos Aires and other urban settings, began a series of guerrilla operations which included kidnapping, extortion, murder, bombing, shooting of military officers and their families, and the creation of a state of chaos. Their goal was to force the democratically elected government to suspend constitutional law and respond violently. The response of the government was twofold: on the one hand, it authorized the army to take on the fight against the guerrilla groups; on the other hand, it organized paramilitary groups like the AAA (*Alianza Anticomunista Argentina* or Anticommunist Argentine Alliance) and other death squads.

In 1974, amid this escalation of violence, Juan Perón died. His wife, María Estela, popularly known as Isabel, vice-president up to that point, succeeded him as president (1974–76). By 1975 the failure of her government's economic policies produced a 50 percent devaluation of the currency, rampant hyperinflation, workers' strikes, violence and unrest, and increased military pressure on the government. Democratic process deteriorated, censorship was widely prevalent, and the government and the military intensified their struggle against the radical groups, embarking on the "extermination" of the guerrillas. Government-sponsored kidnappings, known as "disappearances," were used as a routine way of controlling the "enemy," a practice that increased in the years following the March 1976 military coup. This military takeover, coming after years of violence and the radicalization of workers and middle-class students, resulted in the overthrow of the constitutional and democratically elected government of Isabel Perón.

The coup did not come as a surprise to either the people or the government. Many expected the military to take control and restore "order" at any cost. The incompetence, or inaction, of every branch of the government and the failure to identify a solution to the problem of replacing Isabel Perón only speeded the actions that followed. The military junta quickly bestowed power on the army leader General Jorge Rafael Videla (1976–81) and established what was called *Proceso de Reorganización Nacional* (Process of National Reorganization), known as *El Proceso* for short. The policies advanced by El Proceso were authoritarian on the political and cultural fronts and favored a free-market, conservative agenda on the economic front. The government immediately proscribed all political parties and activities, imposed strict censorship, and intensified the campaign of violence against the "enemy" in what was to be known as the *Guerra Sucia* (Dirty War). This "war" was fought with abductions, disappearances, and tortures that were a continuation and an intensification of the methods already used under the democratic government in 1975.

In 1981 Videla was succeeded by General Viola (1981), who was, in turn, replaced by General Leopoldo Fortunato Galtieri (1981–82). Under Galtieri's rule, Argentina went to war with the United Kingdom over the Malvinas (Falkland) Islands in 1982. The defeat Argentina suffered in this military adventure, as well as the revelations that came out of the Dirty War investigations, revealed an exhausted military regime. Galtieri was replaced by General Reynaldo Bignone (1982–83), who called for democratic elections. The military government was succeeded by the administration of Radical Party candidate Dr. Raúl Alfonsín (1983–89). Dr. Alfonsín began a program designed to correct the abuses committed by the military. He appointed the writer Ernesto Sábato to lead a commission to investigate the crimes and the disappearances that had taken place under military rule. The report, entitled *Nunca más*

(Never Again), accounted for about 10,000 disappeared persons, although the actual number is believed to be higher. As a result of these investigations, in 1985 and 1986, three former military leaders and several high-ranking officials were convicted and sentenced to prison for their involvement in crimes of murder and torture. They were later granted a presidential pardon by Dr. Carlos Saúl Menem, Alfonsín's successor.

During the early 1980s Argentina continued to have serious economic problems. High inflation, decreasing production, and heavy government spending contributed to the crisis. By the end of Dr. Alfonsín's mandate, the economic situation had worsened to such an extent that the government accelerated the transfer of power to the Peronist Party's elected candidate, Dr. Carlos Saúl Menem, who has governed Argentina since 1989. Under Menem's rule Argentina has reversed its economic crisis, in part, by privatizing government-run factories and services and by attracting foreign capital and investment. In 1994 the constitution was reformed to allow for presidential re-election. Menem was subsequently re-elected in 1995. The civilian regimes of Dr. Alfonsín and Dr. Menem are responsible for establishing operative democratic institutions and political activity in Argentina, and for stabilizing the country's economy.

Argentina's upheavals and misfortunes are portrayed in different ways by the distinct voices of contemporary Argentinean literature. To better understand those voices and literary works, we propose to use gender and history as categories that interact with ethnicity, race, age, and class, and which can guide our examination of Argentinean women writers' works. The concept of gender allows the critic and the reader to distinguish and appreciate the different voices that form the tapestry of contemporary Argentine literature and to listen more attentively to female accounts. A field dominated by "patriarchal hegemony," literature has only recently begun to recognize the particular voices of women. In the past, women have had to accept and adopt forms and tones defined by the patriarchal order and its language. Even in writing by and about women, women's experiences and bodies were not considered "literary" unless described through a man's eyes and voice. Female writing had to occur, as Lucía Guerra Cunningham states, in a sort of palimpsest, above and between the masculine marks, in the margins and through the subversion of the masculine motifs of the woman as housewife or prostitute (*Splintering*, 7).

Only when women started to represent themselves through their own eyes, languages, and histories, were they able to seriously question the world of the "literary" as a patriarchal domain, to transgress the expectations placed upon them as women writers, and to transform the authoritarian contexts wherein they lived. According to Tierney-Tello, the use of experimental fiction forms, like the one used by Reina Roffé in this volume, makes possible the transgression and transformation of that context. For Tierney-Tello, women writers' experimentation takes place not only at the thematic level but also, and primarily, when questioning the means of expression, namely language. In recognizing language as the basic building block of our social structure, women writers stand as witnesses to the importance of the cultural and symbolic spheres as "prime battlegrounds for the production of meaning" (Tierney-Tello, 212), where social transformations can begin to be conceived. In their search for a voice and an expression, their appropriation and use of language, of the symbolic, is thus of utmost importance and justifies making the literature authored by women a subject of our interest.

The close relationship between language and gender has been examined by feminist research, which has also linked language to power issues, analyzing the origins and mechanism of power in different social and historical moments. Research on women and language began as long ago as the mid-1900s, but the publication of Robin Lakoff's *Language and Women's Place* in 1975 is often considered a turning point. Lakoff was one of the first writers to relate the subordinate role of women to their speech; since then, questions of gender and societal roles have become increasingly complex, especially when intersected with issues of race and social class. In recent years biological accounts of gender have given way to theories that regard it as socially constructed. Catherine MacKinnon, for example, considers gender difference to be the result of a difference in power between men and women. For MacKinnon, "gender" does not convey difference, but rather dominance, and it is in itself a construct of the difference gender makes (Torres, 287). Joan Scott's definition of gender is close to MacKinnon's: "a constitutive element of social relationships based on perceived differences between the sexes . . . a primary way of signifying relationships of power" (1067). As MacKinnon's and Scott's definitions suggest, the issue of gender is intimately linked to that of power and, in that aspect, relates gender, as a personal trait, to societal issues at large.

Besides illuminating the ways in which language is linked to the position of women in modern society, the use of gender as a category of analysis has also helped to make the study of history more inclusive of women, forcing a critical reexamination of existing scholarly work. When studying gender and history, most of the research done since the 1970s has centered around "the task of restoring women in history and history to women" (Lewis, 155), opening the way to a "new history" which includes and accounts for women's experiences (Scott, 1054). For authors such as Fredric Jameson, texts are rendered meaningful by their insertion into history, or their contextualization into a time frame that is not only sequenced, but also layered, and that accounts for nothing less than the ever present conflict between Desire and Necessity. Since history is only present in texts that give accounts about what has happened in the past, historical discourse can be placed at the same level as rhetorical performance. When such "textualization" takes place, history becomes no more authoritative than literature. The question is not whether history exists, because for Jameson it clearly does, but rather, to what extent is it possible to make sense of the Necessity people feel as the result of past actions which history makes manifest.

Hayden White tries to answer this question when he affirms that different aspects of history try to achieve the task of rendering past actions meaningful. Since there are, for White, different aspects of history that constitute almost different histories altogether, it is, in his opinion, a good idea to decide what kind of, or whose, history is being considered. This decision provides the context necessary to make better sense of the past, although, White warns, new interpretations should not to be expected to be univocal or monolithic. In fact, as White sees it, there are bound to be multiple interpretations, all of which will have to exist alongside each other. In the end the history that becomes dominant, or "believed," will become so as a result of power. The question is not which history is more true or best, but who has the power to make his/her history "stick as the one that others will choose to live by or in" (White, 13). As a matter of choice, White says, we can even choose to get "out of history," out of the history that has produced the massacres of the twentieth century and the politics that helped to enable them. White proposes a "post-political age insofar as 'politics' is conceived in its nineteenth-century incarnations" (13) and the move to exit the history that made those "politics" viable. For him, modernism may supply the utopian moment necessary for the recall into consciousness and the escape.

Just as White is leaving, Diana Fuss is entering the scene, and she does not seem in a hurry to discard history as such. Fuss is interested in revisiting some of the feminist criticism that takes into account Marxist theory. Examining Toril Moi's *Sexual/Textual Politics: Feminist Literary Theory*, which signals the failure to study "the historically changing impact of patriarchal discourses on women" (148), Fuss determines the existence of two feminisms: French "theoreticism" and American "empiricism." She wonders about what has led feminist criticism of both kinds to focus almost exclusively on psychoanalytic and deconstruction theories (like those of Derrida, Lacan, and Freud) and not on materialist ones (like those of Gramsci, Adorno, Althusser, White, and Jameson). When taking into account materialist theories, feminist criticism begins to pay attention to the history of women and, more importantly, to perceive, as Denise Riley does, that it is not enough to assimilate women into history, but that it is equally significant "to simultaneously historicize 'women' as a socially constructed category" (Fuss, 105). Following this project, Fuss proposes not only to insert the experience of women into history, but to change the whole discipline as we know it. For her, History is "His story," a master-narrative that accounts for the male experience throughout the ages and that, in all aspects, is a gender-biased narrative. The task at hand is that of debunking "His story" while avoiding the creation of another master-narrative that would only take its place as if it were "Her story." This task can be accomplished if, looking for a destination in history, as White suggests, we begin by drawing new maps of the uncharted territory, creating a "feminist cartography" that would "make possible a more radical historiography" (Fuss, 106).

In the Argentine literature produced during the last three decades, the search for an individual and national identity has been taking place in this "uncharted territory" as it developed in those fictional works that interrogate questions of gender and history. A number of critical works consider the relationship between a nation's politics, as lived and experienced by its people, and the determination of individual and societal identity. Trying to understand a conflictive time in the country's history, Gimbernat González characterizes women's novels written between 1976 and 1983 as a counterpoint to the hegemonic official discourse, as a space of defiance and challenge. Based on "the means of enunciation of the diverse voices" (20), she stresses in recent Argentine literature written by women the importance of three major themes: history, the journey, and marginality. The situation of Argentina in the early eighties imposed the use of fiction to present a history opposed to the official one, and the authors used means associated with a female audience, such as melodrama and poetry, to tell their alternative history. The theme of the journey appears in a series of novels that challenge the patriarchal voice dominating the society through a trip to unknown territories, created by the author's imagination. This new space provides an instance of inner exile where it is possible to question the hegemonic culture. Finally, Gimbernat describes the existence of other marginal spaces in the novels of the eighties, such as the Argentine provinces, the spaces of the home, and those of the body. For his part, Fernando Reati proposes that the main topics of contemporary Argentine literature are related to questions of identity, memory and history, and sex. These themes allow Reati to explain the phenomenon of violence in Argentine society, the attitudes of its perpetrators, and the expressions of both in literary works. In an attempt to understand the phenomenon of violence, Reati rejects the Manichean or authoritarian interpretations that were prevalent in Argentine society of the 1970s and 1980s. Instead, he opposes a plurality of identities, memories and histories, and sexual roles to the hegemonic certainties imposed by the government's official story.

Our own exploration of contemporary Argentinean writing reveals a common preoccupation with identity, both individual and societal. Naturally, the two are closely linked. Identity issues, as manifested in the personal and the societal, have a close relationship to matters of gender and history and are also marked by the presence of power, or by its lack. It is the importance of power and its relation to issues of gender and history in the personal and political life of a country that prompts Francine Masiello to propose that "when the state finds itself in transition from one form of government to another, or from a period of traditionalism to a more modernizing program, we find an alteration in the representation of gender" (*Between Civilization and Barbarism*, 8). This statement reminds us of the connections between the individual and the society, whose fields of representation, articulated through concepts like "woman" and "man," are the results of ideological constructions, historical accounts, and fictions that are often disguised as memories.

Memory certainly plays an important role in the writing of historical fiction, but also in the search for personal identity, namely in autobiography, which relates the individual to his/her times and historical circumstance. As an example of the ways in which autobiography bridges the gap between the individual and the society, Sylvia Molloy talks about a crisis of political authority in nineteenth-century Argentine culture, which was readily reflected and incorporated into autobiographies of the period, and particularly into women's autobiographies. In nineteenth-century Argentina, the received order of the colonial state was being replaced by the created order of the newly independent nation and, contemporaneously, the self entered into a crisis that autobiographical examination was intended to question and understand. Autobiography, then, was a genre cultivated by women writers, and as such it became an important antecedent to the fictions presented in this volume.

In autobiography, memory plays a central role as the mechanism that makes possible the production of texts. The construction of such texts is based, certainly, on an individual account of collective experiences, making evident at the same time, the cultural, social, and historical contexts that allow the author's writings and "fabulation." In an economically and culturally dependent country like Argentina, the fictions writers create are molded and constantly altered by Argentina's past, by the telling of this past, by its remembrance, and not only by history but by historiography as well, by the country's access to modernity, by issues of race, gender, money, prestige, social movements—and by its literature.

The writers collected in this volume call attention to the interconnections between personal and societal identities, and to the role of women in Argentine political and cultural life. Some of the circumstances that most strongly determined the authors' selection of themes and narrative techniques were, among others, the need to register the voices of marginalized or oppressed groups and present their vision of history as an alternative to the official monolithical version; to avoid the prevailing censorship of the military rule in the 1970s and 1980s; and, as Reati notes is common with Argentine writers, to propose symbolic solutions "for social conflicts, synthesized in the case of Argentina, in the opposition between authoritarianism and democracy" (Reati, 14). These goals changed and alternated according to the societal conditions and to the exercise of power by different political players, and we find them in the writings that address the identity of the individual and that of the country.

The search by Argentine women writers to represent a personal identity is also closely related to the notion of gender, a notion that is frequently expressed in sexual motifs. During military rule (1976–83), gender and sexuality were presented in women's texts such as Roffé's *Monte de Venus* (Mount of Venus), as an act of "defiance" to the government's power and to its official morality. At the same time, gender and sexuality also opposed what Gimbernat González calls "the well-known generic oppression" (15). This "well-known" oppression assumes shape as the two powers to which women are subjected: the first, that of law, is experienced not only by them, but ubiquitously; while the second layer of oppressive power, that of gender difference, is suffered particularly by women because they are women. The manifestation of alternative forms of sexuality and re-defined gender roles challenges the value of personal identity as a single referent and its capacity for unifying the individual.

In novels and short stories of the 1970s, 1980s, and 1990s, personal and societal conflicts of power are frequently played out along the thematic axis of sexuality, and often the sexuality is one marked by deviation, aberration, and by its relationship to violence. In the literature of these years, sexual deviation and aberration can be seen as having both positive and negative connotations. Sexual deviation and aberration may be considered positive when they free the character or negative when they are the direct result of the violence that dominated the rest of the social body. Sexuality and gender roles can be sites where struggles and social contracts are negotiated and mediated. This is the case for Tierney-Tello, who examines the fiction written by women under authoritarian conditions in the social, cultural, and political spheres and finds that some women's work resists authoritarianism by portraying sexuality not as a private activity but as a political and social process "where issues of power and control are foregrounded" (8). For Tierney-Tello, authority and power are the central issues that define women as different and marginalize them in patriarchal and, even more so, in authoritarian contexts. She finds that as the fictions authored by women tackle authoritarian oppression, they are inevitably also commenting on patriarchal oppression since, for Tierney-Tello, both orders are contained within one another, that is to say, political authoritarianism is not *like* patriarchal oppression, but an *intensification* of it. In dealing with authoritarianism and patriarchy, she stresses the relation between sexuality and politics, which is "more metonymical than metaphorical, implying contiguity rather than analogy or similarity" (13). Under authoritarian and oppressive conditions, sexuality and politics are not and cannot be separated, but become closely related and contiguous, since "gender cannot be isolated from the sociopolitical context" (219). Their transgression defies textual, sexual, and political conventions. Embodied in sexuality, transgression allows the writers to confront the ways in which sexuality and gender have been constructed, to violate the boundaries of patriarchal discourse, and to break authoritarian structures. This transgression makes possible, in turn, the transformation of the authoritarian context.

Transgressive fiction authored by women disrupts and transforms authoritarian and patriarchal social systems on several counts: first, it contradicts the patriarchal belief that women do not write; second, it challenges the assumption that if women do write they will employ realistic forms congruent with patriarchal attitudes to describe their experience as women; and third, transgressive fiction takes on a political function when it questions dominant conventions and models through aesthetic means.

Tierney-Tello addresses the close relation between the aesthetic and the political, mediated by women's experimental fictions and their accounts of transgressive sexuality. For her, the aesthetics of women's writing becomes politically subversive, criticizing gender politics, denying authoritarianism's role as the sole source of meaning, and confronting the representation crisis "implied by postmodern international literary trends" (215). The transformation sought by women writers is not to be understood as a radical break with the political past or with the hegemonic discourse, but rather as a dynamic, deconstructive, and reconstructive change. Tierney-Tello proposes that such a model for change works *through* and *against* previous forms, reworking the materials used by authoritarian and patriarchal social systems and transforming them "into sources of resistance and creativity" (210) in order for women to attain power, to become subjects of narrative and not simply the objects of it.

The changes taking place at the thematic and symbolic levels in the fictions authored by women are evident not only in the use of sexual themes and symbolism, but also in women writers' handing of history. The Argentine novel of recent decades has depicted many (often contradictory) visions of Argentina's history, all of which stand as alternatives to the single, hegemonic, authoritarian version of "official" history, demystifying it and casting doubts on its veracity and validity.

After ten years of violence in Argentina in which there were no clear winners or losers, literature, not history, became responsible for representing alternative versions of the past. In doing so, literature denied the existence of a single version of history and offered narrative as the receptacle of a collective memory that no longer trusted official versions of history. According to

Gimbernat González, any novel can be read "as a broken fragment which accounts for its times" (23). A wide range of work by Argentine women writers opposes official history and challenges its unitary voice, as does the work of many male writers. However, women's historical fictions differ from their male counterparts in that they attempt to rewrite history not only from a variety of points of view, but specifically from the point of view of women. Moreover, women writers have been more likely to make use of forms associated with the feminine public, like the melodrama, and have been more pointed in their denunciation of authoritarianism as a vehicle of patriarchy. The readings and writings of history proposed by women writers reconstruct personal and societal events from the space of intimacy, a space most often considered irrelevant to the grandiose text of History. These readings re-present the national past, trying to illuminate events that are irrelevant to the official voice, as in Martha Mercader's *Juanamanuela, mucha mujer* (Juanamanuela, a great woman), María Isabel Clucellas' *La última brasa* (The last coal), or Mabel Pagano's *El país del suicidio* (Suicide country).

Martha Mercader, for example, explores the disguise history can assume and demonstrates the ways in which history (in this case Argentine history of the nineteenth century) is also always contemporary. Her reflections on Juana Manuela Gorriti in her novel *Juanamanuela, mucha mujer* (Juanamanuela, a great woman) are as relevant to contemporary Argentine political and social life as they are to the nineteenth-century world she writes about. In that novel, and in the subsequent one, *Belisario en son de guerra* (Belisario in war mood), Mercader deals with issues of national and personal (specifically feminine) identity, and opposes oppression in the form of machismo, militarism, and authoritarianism. In her interview, Mercader says she "wanted to tell our history in a human, not heroic, scale; to cohabit with characters of flesh and blood rather than with names of squares and streets."

During the military rule of the late 1970s and early 1980s, historical fictions were also used as narrative vehicles of disguise to avoid censorship of politically loaded representations of contemporary problems. Reina Roffé states that in a country governed by democratic rule, the population is not only allowed to express their ideas and to participate in political decisions, but it is expected to do it as well. In Argentina between 1976 and 1983, the exercise of those rights and responsibilities was suspended. As Roffé points out, when a population suffers the consequences of political authoritarianism, the writer and the reader also experience authoritarianism in the form of official censorship. The identity of the censor, and oftentimes the censor's source of authority generally remain unknown. In Argentina, a single signature and some rumors were enough to keep a book out of circulation and to lay upon it, and sometimes its author, a veil of silence. The writer was, moreover, subjected not only to such official silencing, but also to a cultural climate that unofficially imposed its own state of censorship. This climate affected the distribution of cultural materials (books, films, paintings) and, in the literary field, the result was that foreign best-sellers became the most widely read books, displacing those works more directly engaged in presenting national problems. This climate of censorship also had its favorite literary figures, among whom were writers whose works, disguised as opposition, in reality justified the political situation.

It is necessary to remember that the military did not act in a social or cultural vacuum; a large segment of the population supported, implicitly or explicitly, the state of affairs imposed by military rule. Thus, it became not only convenient but sometimes necessary for writers with a political agenda to write in disguise, using ellipses, omissions, metaphors, and other tropes in order to be able to be published without being banned. The Argentine critic Saúl Sosnowski underscores the elusive forms that writers had to use in order to fall within the narrow guidelines of what was permissible in Argentina at that time ("La dispersión de las palabras," 957). This elusive writing was used by both male and female writers. Historical fiction of the times authored by women often utilizes Argentina's past as a background in order to explore unexpected ways of telling stories about the country and its people of the present time, stories that had to remain silent due to the hegemonic presence of the official account of facts and of the censorship of alternative views.

In addition to avoiding the hegemony of the official discourse and its censorship by reexamining the past, historical fiction has also been instrumental in using Argentina's past as a way of searching for answers to current problems. This search grew out of the sense of failure that was engendered by the Dirty War (during the mid-1970s and 1980s) as well as by the collapse of the political and economic project of the "república" which had led the country since 1880. This sense of failure and political exhaustion is often present in literature that stresses moments of personal and societal crisis, since the fictional works themselves were written during a time of crisis. The goal of literature in such cases is to propose symbolic solutions "for social conflicts" (Reati, 14) and to look for answers to the country's crisis. Ricardo Piglia's *Respiración artificial* (Artificial breathing, 1980); Jorge Manzur's *Tinta roja* (Red ink, 1981); Andrés Rivera's *Nada que perder* (Nothing to lose, 1981); Carlos Dámaso Martínez's *Hay cenizas en el viento* (There are ashes in the wind, 1982); Juan José Saer's *El entenado* (The stepson, 1982); Tomás Eloy Martínez's *La novela de Perón* (Perón's novel, 1985), and *Santa Evita* (Saint Evita, 1995); or José Pablo Feinman's *El ejército de ceniza* (Army of ashes, 1986) are just a few of the works by male authors that reflect on Argentina's history in order to understand its past and comment on its present. Women's accounts of histories and searches in the past for solutions to the country's problems are numerous and continue to appear as we write. The publication of this book makes available the contribution of other voices—women's voices—to the narration of Argentina's past, present, and future.

Taking into account these and many other women writers' works, it becomes clear that the relationship between literature and history is one of recognition and not one of mirroring or of a faithful reproduction. Literature does not reconstruct an epoch, rather it is part and parcel of its ideological debates; it is an active builder of politics and history and not a passive recorder of either. One of the positive values of Argentine literature of the last decades is its tendency to question, interrogate, doubt, and examine the country's history and that of its peoples, and also, in the process, to examine itself. Avoiding the totalizing vision of master-narrative, Argentinean literature acted (and continues to act) as a conscience whose goal is to resolve the opposition between democracy and totalitarianism. By offering a symbolic resolution to some of the country's conflicts and by contributing to the debate of that society as a whole, Argentinean literature engages itself directly in the country's history and contributes to it.

Currently the challenge is to produce a framework that will allow us to better explore and understand the interactions between literature, gender, and society so as to avoid the building of a newly vitiated space and the re-writing of "His" (or "Her") Story. Such master narratives have already shown their pervasiveness and uselessness. This goal can be achieved by studying the literature of a country such as Argentina and by incorporating different voices into the ongoing dialogue, voices that question accepted traditions and opinions about the gendered roles women have historically held in society, thereby contributing not only to the definition of women's individual identities but to that of the country as a whole. Some of those new voices are presented in this volume. The dominant themes we have identified in contemporary Argentine literature, including the search for personal and societal identity through the questioning of gender issues and the country's history, and the link between the individual and the social offered by memory and autobiography, are present in the fictions we introduce here. In some instances the personal character of the texts and the search for a personal identity dominate the narrative, as in the selections by Canto, Lojo, Loubet, Mercader, Pagano, and Vázquez. In others, the relationship between fiction and Argentine history are explored (explicitly or implicitly), as in the work of de Miguel, Orphée, and Roffé. The autobiographical appears as narrative technique or as sincere confession in the texts of Diaconú, Jurado, Lojo, Orphée, Pagano, Régoli de Mullen, and Roffé. In many instances, the autobiographical account reflects on the moment when the characters realize their personal identity, a realization that takes place as the result of either a physical or psychological journey. Such an event molds the selections of Diaconú, Gorodischer, Lojo, Mercader, Orphée, and Roffé.

These authors and their works present a panorama of present-day fiction by Argentine women writers. Their works witness the array of relations between the personal and the societal, the intimate and the political and individual existence and the country's history. We hope the texts introduced here will provide better access to and knowledge of these authors and their work, as well as a sharper understanding of the relations between and among literature, gender, and history within the context of contemporary Argentina.

Estela Canto

Estela Canto was born in Buenos Aires on September 4, 1920, and attended the Saint Lucy English School. She directed the magazine *Nuestras Mujeres* and collaborated with the journal *Sur* and with several national newspapers. In 1945 she published a collection of stories, *Los espejos de la sombra,* which she herself illustrated. In the same year she won the Imprenta López Prize, important at that time since it allowed the publication of her novel *El muro de mármol.* The jury for that prize consisted of Victoria Ocampo, Leónidas Barletta, Adolfo Bioy Casares, Guillermo de Torre, and Julio Aramburu. The novel was published by Editorial Losada and was also awarded the Municipal Prize for 1945 by the same jury.

In 1950 she published, also with Losada, *El retrato y la imagen,* one of her best novels, in the author's own opinion. Her book *El hombre del crepúsculo* won the Medal of Honor from the Argentine Writers' Society (SADE) in 1953. In 1959, Goyanarte Editors published *La noche y el barro,* which was later translated into Russian and Romanian. Under the pseudonym Alma Canto she published *La ciudad embrujada* with Editorial Abril. Between 1966 and 1978 she published *Isabel entre las plantas, Los otros, las máscaras, La hora detenida,* another novel that the author considered "good," *El jazmín negro,* and *Ronda nocturna.* In 1982, under the pseudonym Evelyn Clift, she published a historical novel, *Detrás de la medialuna,* which takes place in Turkey during the sixteenth century and in which she devotes a devoted and careful investigation of the period's historical characters. Over the years she has translated works from English and French for many publishing houses, including Losada, Goyanarte, Emecé, Sudamericana, Siglo XX, Vergara, and Alvarez. She has also dabbled in journalism and published stories in newspapers and magazines like *La Nación, La Gaceta, Sur, El Hogar,* and others. Espasa-Calpe, of Spain, published her book *Borges a contraluz,* in which she describes her friendship and romantic liaison with Jorge Luis Borges, including fourteen letters they exchanged between 1945 and 1952. She died in Buenos Aires, on June 3, 1994.

Publications

Los espejos de la sombra (The mirrors of the shadow). Buenos Aires: Claridad, 1945.
El muro de mármol (The marble wall). Buenos Aires: Losada, 1945.
El retrato y la imagen (The portrait and the image). Buenos Aires: Losada, 1950.
"Sylvina Bullrich: Bodas de cristal" (Sylvina Bullrich: Crystal weddings). *Sur* 211–12 (1952): 130–33.
El hombre del crepúsculo (The dusk's man). Buenos Aires: Sudamericana, 1953.
El estanque (The reservoir). Buenos Aires: Goyanarte, 1956.
La noche y el barro (The night and the mud). Buenos Aires: Platina, 1959.
La ciudad embrujada (The bewitched city). Buenos Aires: Abril, 1960.
Isabel entre las plantas (Isabel among the plants). Buenos Aires: Falbo, 1966.
Los otros, las máscaras (The others, the masks). Buenos Aires: Losada, 1973.
La hora detenida (The frozen hour). Buenos Aires: Emecé, 1974.
El jazmín negro (The black jasmine). Buenos Aires: Emecé, 1976.
Ronda nocturna (Nocturnal ronda). Buenos Aires: Emecé, 1978.
Detrás de la medialuna (Behind the half-moon). Buenos Aires: Vergara, 1982.
Borges a contraluz (Borges against the light). Madrid: Espasa Calpe, 1990.

Secondary Sources

Fares, Gustavo. "This Text Which Is Not One." *Hispanic Journal* 12/2 (Fall 1991): 277–89.

Gibbs, Beverly Jean. "Spatial Treatment in the Contemporary Psychological Novel of Argentina." *Hispania* 45 (1962): 410–14.

Jurado, Alicia. "Estela Canto en la novela." *Ficción* 12 (1958): 83–90.

Moreiras, Alberto. "Borges y Estela Canto: La sombra de una dedicatoria." *Journal of Interdisciplinary Literary Studies* 5/1 (1993): 131–46.

Interview

1. Which authors have had the greatest influence on your work?

    It is difficult to say, because I would have to list those who have influenced my ideas and those who have influenced my style. I will mention the foreign writers, because I don't want to name the Argentines, since I wouldn't want to forget someone or leave anyone out. Bernard Shaw, Tolstoy, Proust, [and] Thomas Mann I would say are the ones who have influenced me the most—oh, and also Alexander Dumas.

2. When did you begin to write, and why?

    I began to write very young, inventing stories and repeating them. When I was ten years old I began to write them down. I did it, I would say, to free myself from my fantasies. At eighteen or nineteen I wrote a few stories, some good, others bad.

3. How does the political situation influence your choice of themes?

    The book that I'm going to give you is *La hora detenida,* which has to do with the death of Eva Perón. I don't know if you remember, but when Eva Perón died, at 8:30 P.M., there was a moment of silence everywhere. The idea of the book is about the middle class. A professor who feels the attraction of the oligarchy, and then ends up waiting in line during Evita's funeral in order to see her. So the whole story takes place around the night when Evita dies.

4. Have you ever encountered difficulties, as a woman writer, with publishers?

I have been lucky, because I entered a contest in 1945, the book was published by Losada and, after that, I have always published. Yes, they have sent a book back now and then, but I haven't had any reasons not to be a writer. I have never had to pay to get published. The wait is sometimes a year, or six months. Now the problem is more specific: there is no money.

5. What do you think of feminism?

Look, what I think of feminism in general is that women should have the same rights as men. Now, feminism as it existed forty years ago is no longer viable. Women have defects that are equal, and complementary, to those of men. So said Bernard Shaw, and it is true.

6. How would you describe Argentina's women readers?

On that question we would have to refer to an earlier time, because at this moment, due to the cost of everything, buying books isn't a high priority. But there is a curious thing: women read more than men. Men are much more involved in work or politics.

Selection from *Los otros, las máscaras*

Estela Canto's selection for this volume is the chapter "Sonia" from her novel *Los otros, las máscaras*. The text presents a conversation between Sonia and her friend, in which the former describes the pain she has suffered for being in love with a homosexual man. The explicit dialogue, characterized by coarseness, also marks Canto's later work. In this fragment the author presents intimate situations framed by the historical and political reality of the Argentina of recent decades. The political backdrop suggests the author's indirect manner of dealing with her country's situation. Human relationships presented in the context of definite historical periods is a trait that characterizes Canto's narrative, which can also be observed in her novel *La hora detenida*. The fact that politics keep emerging in the context of human relationships highlights the importance of the political climate not only for the author, but also for her Argentine readers. The suspenseful quality of the text brings to mind a detective novel. It masterfully reflects certain deep-rooted characteristics of the Argentine middle class.

By Way of an Indispensable Foreword

Some time ago I had a telephone call from Pedro Delcaze, a boy who had worked with me on a newspaper for the Organization. His call took me by surprise; we hardly even knew each other by sight.

There were rumors about Pedro, all unsubstantiated, but discouraging, nonetheless; they said he was somewhat crazy and that he had troublesome relationships with people capable of harming the Organization. But I remembered Pedro's eyes, his curiosity, something exalted and romantic about him. Pedro attracted me and, for that reason, I was happy that he wanted to see me.

The man who presented himself to me didn't even have Pedro's eyes. It was as if he had deliberately sought not to look like himself. He handed me a manuscript.

"I would like you to read it," he said.

"What is it? A novel?"

He wavered.

"Not exactly . . . it's something that happened to me. I had to write it."

He left; I was sad, thinking about the inevitable passing of the years with their transformations and upheavals. I left the manuscript in a corner, in plain sight, intending to read it. Months passed. Pedro didn't appear again and, one day, casually, when I was sorting through papers to throw out, I picked up the manuscript.

At first I thought it was a novel, written in the style of Wilkie Collins, with several characters that take up the thread of the story whenever the others abandon it at a crucial moment. But afterwards I noticed other things: there was too much homogeneity in the style; Pedro hadn't even attempted to change the tone of each character. But they were different characters. Another detail: the name of Pedro D. wasn't, as it should be expected, Pedro Delcaze, but another surname that also began with "D" and which he, I don't know if deliberately or not, confuses in his manuscript with "Ducasse," that is, Lautreamont.

In order to find out if this was a real event, as the author had said, I made inquiries. I haven't been able to discover, as of yet, at least in Buenos Aires, any sect that "worships the truth." Neither has anyone been able to tell me if in 1963 there was a mysterious, covered-up death in an apartment on the North Side. (This would have been possible to determine, since the actors of the drama seem to be, or to have been, persons pretty well known in social or artistic circles.)

I have the sensation, however, that it is a *true* story. But, in that case, why the interference of fictional characters? Why not tell everything frankly and openly in first person, or third, whichever was appropriate? Why this penchant for putting the thought, the intrigue, into characters?

I have reached a conclusion: Pedro *decided to tell the story adopting several personalities* because of a desire to vindicate or condemn a girl named Pirincha, around whom all the other characters revolve. It could be a question, therefore, of Pedro's different disguises. Pedro dresses up in the clothing and the disguises of the others in order to understand himself and to try to understand the events. This is also suggested by his insistence on talking about Shakespeare, as if he wanted to prove that we are in a theater, that we are all interpreting, according to the moment, Iago or Romeo.

In the manuscript there are also reiterations, repetitions that demonstrate his desire to prove something at any cost.

After I read the story I looked for Pedro, but no one could tell me what had become of him. I covered almost all the cigarette and stationery shops in Liniers, but I never ran into him. I think this means that I'm authorized to publish his writing. I present it just as he gave it to me, divided into three unequal parts, each one with a title. And I trust that, if Pedro finds out about the publication of this story, he won't sue me. After all, he wanted it all brought to light; if he hadn't, he wouldn't have given me the manuscript.

Sonia

Weighed down with little lamps and brilliantly colored balls that they had prepared for the Christmas season the pine tree shivers in the garden, but the decorations aren't lit now; they suggest the European winter in this resort, with its wind muffled by the sand dunes. The dark, dark night makes the stars luminous, and the clouds pass towards the south, like snowflakes, with that sadness mortified plants have.

I heard her cross the path, knock against the fence, approach the long hotel building. If God is above us, far above us, here one can comprehend that distance. In the vestibule, some landscapes of bluish seas, meticulous rocks, those little paintings that seek to recreate what can never be recreated because all places are different; and, at the end of the hall, the room that we share.

She opened the door carefully.

"Is that you?" I asked.

"Are you awake, Sonia?"

"More or less," I said, switching on the lamp on the bedside table. The room was like a stateroom, scanty, closed: all that it lacked was the noise from the machines.

"What a wind!" said Pirincha. She sat on the edge of the bed. The light from the lamp illuminated her legs. She could see me, but she didn't look at me. She covered her face with her hands and began to cry. A soundless cry, not asking for consolation, not asking for attention: someone who really is going through bad times.

I turned out the light. After a few moments the slats of the Persian blinds let the wan illumination from the garden shine through. The shadows of the acacias trembled, suddenly existing, like animals.

"What's the matter?" I asked.

"Nothing," said Pirincha reluctantly, "it's just nerves, that's all. Sometimes I think that they're following me, that people are against me . . . then I escape. And I feel like crying."

"If that's it, you can relax," I said, while the end of the cigarette she had lighted traced circles in the air; "they're following all of us."

She blew her nose. She grew calmer as she smoked.

"Today I met Pedro; I've told you about him. While I was with him I had the sensation that they were not following me . . . Narso is an imbecile," she added violently, "he tried to rape me in the dunes. Or make me believe that he's capable of raping me. An idiot, do you hear me? The only thing I'm interested in is being an actress."

I heard her sigh, but she didn't hear, didn't sense my sigh, which I swallowed with difficulty. "They're looking for someone to take refuge in, but you don't interest them, Sonia, you're nothing but an ear, you hardly exist."

"When one interprets, she understands," continued Pirincha; "one realizes what goes on in the world. Juliet never doubted, she never hesitated to enter death, she knew she would leave again. Romeo doubted."

"Don't talk nonsense," I murmured.

"Romeo didn't understand that Juliet was going to wait for him; that was what he should have known, don't you think?"

"Metaphysics," I said. The wind rounded the corner, we were isolated in the hotel, in a place near the ends of the earth. "What do you know about problems, little girl?" I asked suddenly. "Do you know what mine is? El Gordo. Do you know? It's his friends' fault. It doesn't bother me that he's homosexual, but it hurts when he insults me. When things are going badly for him, he attacks me. If he has a young man he's the best guy in the world. You can't deceive yourself around him. That's an advantage. When he has admirers he's the best."

"Mama should marry José María," continued Pirincha, without hearing me; "it's ridiculous that she doesn't. She thinks that Papa's coming back, and she's living in a dream world, even though she hates him. She believes she wants him back because she loves him, but that's not it; it's because she hates him, she wants him beside her so she can torment him."

"Why do you torture yourself? It's not your life."

"It's my life as well."

"Bah!" I said to forestall the conversation, which could take me down unforeseen paths, "since you like *Romeo and Juliet* so much, why don't we talk about the performance? You would have to put more strength into it. Juliet isn't a spoiled girl, she's a woman, sure of herself, you yourself said it."

"No one's sure here."

She put out the cigarette, extinguishing it on the marble table. I had told her once or twice that the odor of stale cigarette butts bothered me, but she never listened, she didn't pay any attention to me.

"Let's go to sleep," I said. "If someone has tried to rape you I understand that you're upset. There are things that one wants and then regrets not having followed through on. We don't know how to surrender, we're the opposite of Juliet. Zefirelli explained it to me in London. A fabulous type, skinny, but I love El Gordo and I want things to be clear."

"I'm not like you," she said with rage.

"Let's go to sleep," I repeated, wrapping myself up in the covers.

Pirincha began to undress, and I heard her get in bed and turn toward the wall. I closed my eyes, opened them again, and I heard the peace of those places in which leaves rustle; but El Gordo can't stand the silence. He needs to hear the noise, to see the dawn break in order to get into bed fearlessly, feeling finally that he's part of the grand scheme of things . . . The room was like a cell and the ghost of Pirincha's white coat was hanging on the clothes rack. From her breathing, the rhythm that one can't fake, I knew that she wasn't sleeping either: she was there knitting a web of thoughts all around me.

"Why did you say that they were following you?" I asked brusquely, lifting my arms from under the covers.

Pirincha turned over, hesitating before answering.

"The other day a friend took me to a house, and I felt surrounded . . ."

"And what's that got to do with it?"

"I just dreamed about that house."

"I thought you were awake."

"One dreams in an instant," said Pirincha; "in any case, I dreamed. But I wasn't in the house but in a round plaza, with one-story houses all around. I was happy and the sea was near . . . I think I was in Río de Janeiro one summer night and I was looking for something among the houses. I had been invited somewhere, but I couldn't find the entrance. The invitation was to the house of a friend of Luti's; I'm afraid of Luti."

"Why?"

"If I knew, I wouldn't be afraid."

"What frightens you is having seen Pedro again," I said, and I felt an uncontrollable desire to talk about myself, like a beggar who shows a scar, first so that he'll be pitied, and also out of disdain toward the others, affirming the power of his ugliness. "Your problems are nonexistent, they are will-o'-the-wisps," I said slowly, "I would like you to know about *my* problems. El Gordo is wonderful, the most intelligent, the most sensitive man I have met, but he needs men, and he has to pay for them. Last year I gave him everything we earned so that he could take a trip with Antonio Caldas, you know him, right? . . . So much the better. Pure rubbish. El Gordo was with him in London, in Norway, they wanted to go north. Antonio is a Spaniard, like El Cordobés, and he went looking for a Nordic type, but El Gordo suffered a lot and, when he returned, he refused to have anything to do with me; he said that he felt stained, contaminated when he touched me. I thought that they had cast a spell on him and so it appeared. My sweet, you won't sleep with me any more, he said. We have slept many, many nights beside each other, and he would put on more clothes, because he was cold, he said, or because he wasn't feeling well . . . He's very nervous, he rubs his hands together until he scrapes away the skin out of fear of germs . . . but, in reality, it was to make me feel that the two tee shirts, his underwear, his pajama tops and bottoms, some stockings like booties, isolated him from me, and once when I tried to touch him he withdrew, furious. I asked him if I disgusted him, and I began to cry, and he confessed that yes, he found me repugnant, and he thought that his affair with Antonio had broken up because of me, through some sort of magic in reverse, and that he couldn't touch me any longer, although he valued me. . . That's my life; I don't dare leave him, I would feel very alone, lonelier than anyone . . . I work and I want El Gordo to find another great love like Antonio, who can bring his self-confidence back, but it's difficult, because he's become suspicious . . . Did you notice that lately he's wearing glasses to read? That happens with age, but he isn't old, he's become far-sighted because he wants to see me far away, and pay for his guilt, do you understand?"

Pirincha had been left speechless. I was happy I had bothered her. "That's why I need to triumph at everything, that's why I hold auditions, I produce theater, I buy and sell properties. But I lack strength . . . something crumbles in you when they find you repugnant. He hasn't kissed me on the mouth for three years . . . I understand that he's disgusted, but I love him, and he needs me, do you see?"

"A curious situation," said Pirincha, with an icy voice, which didn't reveal any opinion.

"I chose *Romeo and Juliet* because I like to think about two people who surrender themselves without reservations. We cannot. We surrender pieces, a mouth, our sex; no one surrenders entirely. You love with a little piece of you, like El Gordo loves me, with the third corner of his left ear lobe; there he understands that I love him, and also that I am capable of carrying him forward, because without me he would sink, I swear to you, he could never even imagine those suits that he designs, I tell him how they should be . . . After working with Zefirelli I know what a theater costume should be, and that fascinates him; he understands that I know how to move in the right circles, how to treat people, earn money, everything he needs, and, believe me, sometimes I despise him. But he's disabled and he thinks he's important, do you understand?"

"Yes," said Pirincha, "but it seems to me that you also love him with a piece of your body . . . the one between your legs."

"That's not true," I affirmed, but I felt that I was turning red; somehow, what Pirincha had said provoked a sensation of triumph in me, as if she had finally discovered my soul, although God knows that wasn't the impression I wanted to leave on telling her my sad story.

Pirincha got up and loosened the Persian blind, to lower it all the way.

"Don't do that," I asked her.

"Are you afraid of the dark?"

"I don't like to wake up in a room that I don't know. I think of Juliet; waking up in the depths of a tomb and not recognizing anything, except for the odor and the darkness."

"You're morbid," said Pirincha, pulling to open the slats further. "I wasn't thinking of closing the blinds. I like this light . . ."

She got into bed again, but she remained sitting up, leaning against the headboard, hugging her knees with her arms.

"Did it bother you what I said?" I asked.

"Why would it bother me?" . . . After a silence she added, "I would have preferred you not to tell me anything. I admire you, Sonia, I don't want to stop admiring you. Why do you want me to pity you? Pity is an ugly sentiment, it makes us make mistakes . . . That's what I'm afraid of . . . And also of other things, such as those that Pedro doesn't understand, for example . . . when I met him it was incredible, my happiness was tangible, but it escaped like sand . . . he said it, and then I knew what . . ." "What?" I asked, suddenly tired. I had spoken, had bared my soul, and this idiot girl was still thinking about love stories of the kind you can read in women's magazines, stories no one believes.

"This room is a boat, we are in a boat . . ." said Pirincha.

"Acting, always acting," I murmured, and I went to sleep.

María Esther
de Miguel

María Esther de Miguel was born in the province of Entre Ríos, Argentina, in 1929. She undertook advanced studies in journalism at the University of Buenos Aires, and conducted graduate work at the College of Letters in Rome. She directed the journal *Señales* from 1958 until 1963. Between 1961 and 1962 she traveled to Europe with a scholarship from the Instituto de Cultura Italiano and studied in Rome. She was an advisor to the publishing houses Codex and Pleamar and directed the literary section of the magazines *Femirama* and *Para Ti*. Her honors include the National Arts Fund Prize and the Municipal Prize, the Argentina Writers Society Medal of Honor, the First Municipal Prize for Novel, the Second Municipal Prize for Short Story, the Pen Club Silver Feather, the Konex Prize for Short Story, and the 1996 Planeta Prize for her novel, *El general, el pintor y la dama*. She has been a member of the Board of Directors of the National Arts Fund. She currently writes literary criticism for the national newspapers *La Nación, Clarín,* and *El Cronista Comercial;* for local newspapers such as *La Gaceta* of Tucumán, *Los Andes* of Mendoza, and *La Voz del Interior* of Córdoba; and for the arts magazine *Lyra*.

Publications

La hora undécima (The eleventh hour). Buenos Aires: Emecé, 1961.

Los que comimos a Solís (Those of us who ate Solís). Buenos Aires: Losada, 1965.

Calamares en su tinta (Squids in their ink). Buenos Aires: Losada, 1968.

"La mujer en su literatura y su responsabilidad como escritora" (The woman in her literature and her responsibility as a writer). *Revista de la Universidad Nacional de Córdoba* 10/1–2 (1969): 321–37.

En el otro tablero (On the other board). Buenos Aires: Fabril, 1972.

Puebloamérica. Buenos Aires: Pleamar, 1975.

Espejos y Daguerrotipos (Mirrors and daguerreotypes). Buenos Aires: Emecé, 1978.

En el campo las espinas (In the field, the thorns). Buenos Aires: Pleamar, 1980.

Jaque a Paysandú (Checkmate to Paysandú). Buenos Aires: Bruguera, 1984.

Dos para arriba, uno para abajo (Two up, one down). Buenos Aires: Pleamar, 1986.

Norah Lange (Biography). Buenos Aires: Planeta, 1991.

La amante del Restaurador (The Restorer's lover). Buenos Aires: Planeta, 1993.

"El lazarillo electrónico" (The electronic blind's guide). *Violencia II: visiones femeninas*. Buenos Aires: Instituto Movilizador de Fondos Cooperativos, 1993.

Las batallas secretas de Belgrano (Belgrano's secret battles). Buenos Aires: Planeta, 1995.

El general, el pintor y la dama (The general, the painter, and the lady). Buenos Aires: Planeta, 1996.

Secondary Sources

Barufaldi, Rogelio. "Soledad y vocación en la última narrativa argentina." *Señales* (1962): 5–18.

Fuentes, Pedro Miguel. "Dios y la teología del incidente en 'La hora undécima'." *Estudios* 528 (1961): 610–21.

Hermann, Eliana. "María Esther de Miguel. *Norah Lange.*" *Chasqui* 22/1 (May 1993): 93.

Peltzer, Federico. "Dos nuevas novelistas argentinas." *Ficción* (1961): 169–71.

Riess, Cheryl Rae. "Narrating History: Five Argentine Novelists (Movsichoff, Demitropulos, Castillo, Mercader, de Miguel)." *Dissertation Abstracts International* (1989): 3610A.

Interview

1. Which authors have had the greatest influence on your work?

    I have always read a lot, and I mean a lot. In my early writings, *La hora undécima* and *Los que comimos a Solís,* perhaps the influences were François Mauriac and William Faulkner. Later on, I suspect, Borges and Cortázar. Now I'm looking for my own voice.

2. When did you begin to write, and why?

    Even when I was very young I knew that I was going to write "a book." When I was eleven, unbeknownst to my parents and teachers, I sent a selection to a children's magazine, *Figuritas.* The theme was "The Malvinas are Argentine." And they published it, greatly surprising everyone, including me. Thereafter, I won a school contest with an essay on the General San Martín. Since they thought it could not be my work, but that someone had done for me, they made me pass a test: just little me, closed up in a room, I had to write about "Mother." Back then I had a very tortured relationship with my mother, since I was very rebellious, but it seems that in the composition that little girl knew how to shine. When I was fourteen and in high school at Gualeguay, I won a literary contest for the student's festival. Ever since, I've had the label . . . writer. But I would only enter "the profession" many years later. I lived in the countryside, had to study away from home, and then existential reasons separated me from that road which, in truth was the one that my vocation marked for me. When I was thirty I found the path again and, ever since, more or less regularly, I've been publishing.

3. How does the political situation influence your choice of themes?

    It certainly does. *Puebloamérica* is a book in which I tried to witness the period of the seventies with its explosions of violence and repression, the military takeover, the consciousness of the priests, etcetera. In *Jaque a Paysandú* the war of the Malvinas Islands appears as an echo, the war which unfortunately we had undertaken. In all of my works—stories and novels—in one way or another one can find traces of social and political conflicts. I am, in truth, very sensitive to them. Besides, I have a militant political stance although that does not appear, directly at least, in my writing.

4. Have you ever encountered difficulties, as a woman writer, with publishers?

The truth is I've always found publishers. Even in these difficult times. After some of my stories were published by *La Nación* and *Clarín*, a publisher appeared, called Librería Fausto, for a book that was not written. I think that, in general, the problem in finding publishers is for the first book. Then that difficulty becomes somewhat relative. I was lucky when my first book was published after having won a contest, the Emecé Prize.

5. What do you think of feminism?

I have always been a sniper. Now I believe that one must continue supporting women's rights, which are encountering more subtle, underhanded, forms of obstacles than before. But I don't have any texts that are directly related to the problem.

6. How would you describe Argentina's women readers?

I think that Argentine women are very lucid and intelligent. Unfortunately they, like other elements of our society, have lost the habit of reading. Nevertheless, I believe that a large portion of the public who continues to read Argentine writers is female.

Selection from *Dos para arriba, uno para abajo*

"La guerrita en la mira" (The little war in their sights) is a short story from *Dos para arriba, uno para abajo.* This volume of short stories is divided in two parts; the first includes a series of stories about the war that Argentina fought in 1982 against Great Britain over the Malvinas (Falkland) Islands. The second part of *Dos para arriba . . .* is more intimate and depicts human conflicts with great skill and a certain sense of humor, leading the reader through many different places and emotions. "La guerrita en la mira" belongs to the first part and refers to the ups and downs of the war between Argentina and the U.K. In April of 1982 the military government of General Leopoldo Fortunato Galtieri decided that it would be a good idea, so as to rejuvenate its languishing popularity, to wave the flags for a cause considered just by the majority of Argentina's people: the reclaiming of the Malvinas Islands. Neither the moment nor the means were adequate to undertake such an endeavor, but the government, more interested in internal politics and survival than in the human cost of the war, carried forward its plans for recovering the islands. The well-known results were the untimely deaths of hundreds of soldiers and the unconditional surrender of the Argentine army, which provoked, in turn, the fall of the military regime and the democratic opening that led to the 1983 elections. The events related to the war are told in de Miguel's story from two different points of view called "Alfa" and "Omega." The first one presents a vision of the war held by an unnamed person, who represents in a way the thinking of the majority of the population. This voice recapitulates, in a third-person narrative, the events of the war, and talks about the president-general, unnamed in the story but immediately recognizable as Galtieri. This voice speaks in the name of a "we" and describes the situation from a point of view somewhat removed from the events, starting the day when the recovery of the islands was decided, and ending with the sinking by British forces of the Argentine ship "General Belgrano." The second part of the story, "Omega," is narrated in first person by one of the many young soldiers, this time from the province of Corrientes, who is drafted into the army. He has to leave his usual job, abandon his home, shoulder a rifle, and go wage war in a place he does not know, against an enemy that he has never before faced. In this second part of the story the author uses a narrative form associated with the oral tradition, as the soldier merely speaks to a listener who does not intervene in the dialogue, which becomes a monologue. The draftee's vision, that of the conquered, is far more precise in telling exactly what happened during those days at war. The story masterfully uses these disparate points of view in order to give a complete, yet tragic, picture of the "little war in their sights." In doing so, the author foregrounds the country's political and social situation. Thus, she clearly shows the political process that led to the war as well as its personal, intimate consequences.

The Little War in Their Sights

Alpha

The General woke up that morning with the urge to start a revolution, but his aide told him: no, my General, you already made a revolution; that's why you're the president now. Therefore, after meditating for a few moments, the President General resolved: then I will make a historic decision. What decision? murmured the High Command. We will recover the islands that are ours, as everyone knows, even though for nearly a hundred and fifty years they've been in the hands of pirates who, one day, without saying "boo," took to the water and didn't stop until the islands were theirs.

The High Command agreed: oh, yes, we'll take them by surprise, they'll surrender immediately. And the people, oh, those people who were in a depressed mood to begin with since everything had been going from bad to worse (there were no jobs and to top it off, the national team was doing badly), the people, I say, felt the fire burning in their breasts, where grand ideals erupt and are hidden, and said "great," and they filled the Plaza de Mayo and offered up their blood and the women, their wedding rings, the children their prayers and even Liberty, so called because of the islands, sang and handed over some precious drop earrings that the *mexicas* had given to her years before. Anyone who didn't have drop earrings gave what they did have, and everyone else did the same. Overcoming sectarian little games that had divided them, their spirits were stirred. Bound together by the lofty ideal of territorial integration, they set to the task of recovering the lost little sister. United, it's easier: the little soldiers marched, determined, rataplán-rataplán-

rataplán; the students stopped studying to pack rations for the combatants; the little old women chuc-chuc-chuc knitted scarves in the Plaza of the Republic; the rock musicians danced for hours and hours to earn money for chocolate bars and cigarettes; the politocrats, strategists and analysts blah-blah-blah spoke over the radio, on television and incessantly; the diplomats mobilized, sending dispatches, notes and cards to neighboring and distant countries to disseminate the reasons that motivated the operation (because they realized that with so many years of disorder and difficulties in the government the country didn't have the best reputation abroad and a little showing off would go over well); the women became experts at bandages and treating fainting spells and breaks, not to mention sutures and acupuncture and what else can I tell you?: everyone did what they could because this is a nation of real people who know how to take things to heart and then never look back, and, in the end, the war brought an interesting quota of vitality to that sleepy peace in which everyone was dying, some faster than others. A pinch of History never goes over badly.

Oh, the second of April! The will of the people dignified a bizarre show of patriotism: from now on nothing will be the same, we said tenderly and we said it to Latin America, we, the common people, and the unionists and the politicians who left on a patriotic tour. And we said it to Mr. Haig when he came.

Because Mr. Haig (exemplary Americanoid, typically Made in the USA), came to play peacemaker. Nice and neat, smiling and generous, he only wanted to light a candle at the wake to which he hadn't been invited, and he came and he talked and he talked and he showed his face and his profile, straight on and sketchy, and he played tennis and took holy communion in the Santísimo and we applauded his march through the streets of Buenos Aires. But when the wind changed, Mr. Haig screwed us. For reasons related to old preexisting pacts, for questions relevant to Yalta and Palta, for motives pertaining to the North and the South, for interests totally convincing to Allied Capitalism and Camouflaged Arrogance, I chose with Mrs. Thatcher and my country does too. Oh, Mrs. Thatcher, traitor, legitimizing the Traditional Power, playing the Patriarchy game, loyal to your kind rather than to your condition as a woman, said the feminists, and the masculinists used names like old witch, menopausal, vampire. But she, cold-bloodedly, sweetly, sent the Task Force with its corsairs and as many forceps as she could: Welsh, English,

Irish, Nepalese, Marines, Aviators, paratroopers, Sea Harriers, frigates, corvettes, transatlantic liners, land-to-air missiles, air-to-sand, death-to-death missiles and down to the sea in ships, and on the ships, the *gurkas* (who take a professional delight in the slaughter).

And while these were the preparations of the ex-Empire on its way to an Hysterical Colonialist Recuperation (or the Sunset of the Gods in Search of a New Dawn), I'll tell you right away what the Great Cowboy from the North did: first he winked a complicitous eye, then he signed a decree of solidarity, then another of logistical aid, afterward another one of missilistic tribute, and he dirtied the southern sky with espionage satellites which night and day counted the Navy ships on which those "Argies," dying of hunger, more or less, toiled, the Regressing Before They Started Developing Nations, adrift enough as if to kick over the boards of the International Accords (?) in a fit of the delirium tremens also known as patriotism. As if Yalta didn't exist! protested the Chancelleries and European bureaucracies, according to the best conventional style, and the Common Market, NATO, the PATA and the whore that fucked us up that day on which the General woke up with the urge to start a revolution.

Naturally, since war brings back in men the conduct of beasts and that of angels, because it draws out the best and the worst that is in them, marvelous things happened which remain to be immortalized in folk and campfire songs; and others that were shameful (phew, what an odor): a little soldier who saved his chief and a chief who took off running; a junior officer who gave the last puff of his last cigarette to a dying man, and a dying man who exhaled an ugly oath with his last breath; a general who said No More and saved thousands and another general who said even if nobody's left standing, let that nobody keep firing; a *gurka* who castrated an Argentine for pure pleasure and an Englishman who killed for mercy; a Queen of Cards who all the time was at *Caraja* and a Prime Minister Defender of the West who considered the Empire restored because they, with the help of hunger and cold, had defeated a bunch of adolescents. Oh, and an Admiral of the Royal Navy who raised the pirate emblem at our home port: skull, crossbones and, in the background, the innocent shadow of an out-of-focus frigate, with youngsters on board . . . until they shot it with their missiles.

But all of that happened over there and that doesn't matter to us so much; at least, after extracting the appropriate moral, which is: from such places nothing good comes. Better, then, let's examine how things are going at home. And how are they going? After the General woke up with the urge to make a revolution and since he couldn't because he had already made one, he decided on a recovery operation? Look: for now, a lot of idle promises; one of the stated objectives of the Restructuration of the Process of Recomposition of the Reorganization is the Reimplantation and the Concertation of the Constitution, which is repeated morning, noon and night. Nevertheless, I and others believe that the law of the henhouse still exists. You already know which one it is. Which one is that? That the hen on top shits on the one underneath. And tell me, is that why one day the General woke up with the urge to take a patriotic stand and we all said great and we sent the boys to the slaughterhouse? For that?

Omega

Of course, sir, I will try to make an objective report about what happened to me when I went to the islands and I faced genuine enemy forces who were better equipped and had more sophisticated weapons, as everyone knows, because it was in all the newspapers. In the first place I want to tell you that the day in which I was assigned to go was a great moment in my life, if not the greatest. I have a rather puny physique; I'm not much to look at, as you can see, but that day of the summons, determined to convince everyone of my manhood, I put on my grown-up face, wrinkled my brow, as I had seen the station chief do, and I even stood on tip-toe to look taller. I wanted to go, to fight against the invading forces, although I didn't want to leave Corrientes, which as you know is an incredibly beautiful place with many orange groves and a delightful sun which, I will tell you, is what I missed the most, although I also missed my family, my mom and my dad and my chums, Nata and Pedro and Juana and Lula and . . . well, since there are eight, I won't bore you. I am the son of my dad and my mom; but perhaps I am only the son of my mom, because at the time when I was born, between Juana and Lula, my dad was a prisoner, sort of a prisoner of war, for nearly two years because of Peronist politics, and when I grew up I realized that without my dad my mom couldn't have had me. Well, she could have had me, of course, but not with my father, do you understand? But my dad, who is Rolo, has always been a father to me, so I've never been orphaned like some unfortunate beings, and that's the reason that I'm telling you that it was hard to leave them, but I was happy as I left, because to serve the nation when it calls is a duty and they taught me a lot the year I was in the service, duty and valor, and I understood it well, even though I'm a little slow to learn, besides having no formal schooling, you see? First grade and out. On the other hand, look, I have a quick ear, so I can play on my concertina, by ear, anything once I've heard it. The compensations that life offers, you see? But I couldn't take the concertina with me, so I felt a bit alone; but I was relieved right away to see that there were hundreds like me, and what a pretty sight, all in our new uniforms, although they were fatigues since we were at war, see? which is much more serious than being on maneuvers; and the ankle boots, you see, the right size and brand new, and the rifles that were a pleasure to behold: each one cleaned his, caressed it, and thought, I never had such a pretty toy and thought again: it's not to send others to their death but to defend myself, see? Thoughts from the beginning. In those days, you know? I saw myself in my new guise, as a soldier, and the truth was that it seemed magnificent to me. What did it have to do with the boy who sold shad on the streets of Corrientes or with the musician playing "Flowered Nights"? What did one have to do with the other? Very little. And I would have liked Lula to see me all dressed up: he is the one who, although half brain-impaired, has a fantastic imagination, and he is the best friend among the eight brothers and sisters that, as I told you, I have in my family.

Well; now I was a soldier on my way to war and nearly a hero, which was what the nation needed. That's what the General said, what he was always talking about: sovereignty and valor and such matters. But the one who really got to me, who touched my heart, see, was the Lieutenant. A good guy, refined, a man with a good background, you'll see, like doctor Pérez Argüello, with whom I spent time as a boy. He was tall, with his hair groomed, his mustache trimmed and manners . . . I don't understand manners, but the ones that Lieutenant Osorio had, were as they should be. And when he commanded (what he had to command, that's why he was a Lieutenant, right?) you see, it seemed, and I'm not saying that he said please, but it sounded like it. He wasn't anything like a Lieutenant. And I say that, knowing what I'm talking about; about Lieutenants, I mean, because I have known a lot of them . . . and I know what I mean. I don't know if you do. Consider the following: when we were in the casemates, under hard firing from the enemy forces, who fired and fired incessantly, it was he, the Lieutenant, I mean, you should see how he talked to us.

What we had to do after the war, that's what he talked to us about. We had to find a trade, but first we should finish grammar school and, if possible, high school, he said: because now the nation needs you this way, with rifles in your hands, he said, but this will not last forever because peace will come, and then our families, and all the people, he said, will need other things: machines, and lathes, and factories, he said. And one day I asked, and what about truck drivers? because I had dreamed about becoming a truck driver. And he told me yes, truck drivers also. He told us things like that; things about feelings. Look what he told us! That had nothing to do with battle instructions, see? What did it have to do with? With life, I say. You know, sir, I know all about Lieutenants but this Lieutenant had nothing in common with them, and that's what made him better.

Shit, I am off on a tangent again. We were in the south in our new uniforms ready to go to the islands, which were our destination. And we went there. A Hercules took us to the theater of operations, or Puerto Argentino. I was thinking: Oh! when I tell Lula this! Because when we arrived, you should have seen how happy we were. And all of that, the emotion, see? was for the things that they had planted in us because, the truth is, all of it was more like a wilderness and if it reminded me a little of Corrientes (which, in reality, is the only thing I know about world geography) it was only of some open fields of the Iberá, where in the marshlands you can walk and disappear, walk and disappear until suddenly you disappear and you walk no more because you disappear once and for all. But there it went along with weather that was real weather, not like here where everything is frigid. So cold, sir, as cold as it must be at the Poles, where they say the cold spells come from around the whole world and all of them join together and never leave again. But into the cold we went as though we were getting used to it, see? Besides, with so much to do we got hot or at least warm: digging trenches, mining fields, leveling roads, building shelters. Look how I learned to do pretty useful things, me, who only knew shad at eight per pound! or how to play the concertina. I had abilities that I had only recently discovered! No way around it, I said to myself: a war teaches useful things if one pays attention. I'll tell Lula about it. And I'm telling you: more than the cold, what fucks you up is the wind. Look: I know all about the swelling of the river, but the swelling of the wind, I'm telling you now, is much, much worse. And there we were, day and night, night and day, in the foxhole, with the noise of planes and falling bombs. At least they let us have maté: not drinking maté makes you really restless, you know? Hunger, I'll tell you, we were hungry too but we could tolerate that. If the provisions were watery when they got to us because someone else had eaten the solid part first, in the evening, well, we went out collecting. And we always managed to find something . . . There were several of us, some being very cunning, and everyone knew something: I, from my days of trespassing into someone else's cornfields and the others, from doing more serious things, there in Tucumán or Avellaneda, where they were from. Besides, if the islanders robbed in broad daylight (that's quite an expression, because we never even saw the sun), but, I say, if they charged us ten or fifteen bucks for a pack of cigarettes (and I'm giving you only one example), couldn't we make up the difference? But the ones who were best at robbing were the mutants. Mutants were the ones who had deserted; I don't know why they were given that name, but that's what they were called, mutants. They were the ones who always, from the start, were mixed up in some rebellion: look at the boss who says advance instead of saying let's go, and why do they eat hot food and we cold, and things of that nature. It's true though, that at the end, they were worse off than we were. I don't know how they've ended up. Well, I know the way many of them ended up, why talk about it.

Now I'll tell you, by that time, half defeated, almost all of us had found our desire to fight diminished. To top it off, those foreigners like to fight on holidays. Because look, even if few things in life are repeated and even less often in the Malvinas, one thing was certain: every weekend the enemies attacked. At first we thought it was out of pure heresy that they did it on Sundays, which are the Lord's days, as any Christian knows and Father Vargas used to repeat. But afterwards, when our forces were in direct contact with the invaders, we learned that it was because on the weekends they earned double salary for overtime. I suppose you know that: they don't fight for their country and for things like duty and honor, but for a salary, see? Each to one's own, but to let yourself be killed for money, I say, I wouldn't even consider it. But apparently others do, see? Of course only foreigners.

But we were almost all, and I among them, feeling worse and worse, in spirit and physically also. We saw that things were getting ugly, but we all looked at those things with different eyes: the Lieutenant's eyes were the most stable; mine, the least, why should I lie. I didn't even want to be a hero any more, although we waited and waited for that day to come, fucking cold and hungry in the middle of the mire. But everything comes at its proper time, see? and the worst of the bad days did too. It was when the confusion had started on and the planes with the provisions didn't appear and communications were almost cut off and we had seen people die in mass and I won't tell you that we'd gotten used to it because you never get used to that, see? but now I didn't feel that panic with trembling as at first, when a bomb touched down near me, and I raised my head, as if asking the heavens why it was my turn or it wasn't my turn, but in reality without asking anything because I didn't have a single thought in my head; even less than Lula has in his, I'll tell you. And I add that, without even thinking, I grabbed my rifle and I ran shooting toward the other trench, the one that was farthest from the bomb, and that was the worst thing I could have done, as the Lieutenant told me later: to run under wide-open enemy fire. Next time pay attention, the Lieutenant told me, after having shouted at me, hit the dirt! private Saludueña, but I didn't pay any attention to him. Listen to me next time! the truth is that I don't like to give you orders, because it makes me feel more like an MP than a comrade and what do you expect, here, he told me (and he looked at himself, as filthy as I was) here we are all brothers. That's what he told me: as you see, words that weren't Lieutenants' words, but I already told you that Lieutenant Osorio wasn't like the other officers and that day I had been frozen with fear, what do you expect, and he really understood that. And that was another of the things that I mentally noted down to tell Lula later.

The truth is that I thought a lot during those nights that I spent watching the heavens (did I tell you that the sky is bigger there? And look, I know skies, because in Corrientes they are beautiful. But this one, I don't know . . . it is deeper, more sky, I think). And I'll tell you how my thoughts went: the heart beats faster in wartime. One moves from courage to fear, from being gung-ho to losing your gumption, from fear of religion to disbelief, from Holy Mary Mother of God to the whore who gave birth to you. The only thing that doesn't leave you is the cold. And the hunger. And finally, the hatred too. Because, as I was telling you, with such cold, with days and days of enduring eighteen degrees below zero centigrade, the only thing you want is for it all to end, even if it's in pieces, like what happened to Ramírez, who was a fellow from Goya and who never even said "Ouch" when he took a wrong turn, stepped on a mine and flew through the air in pieces that we ended up gathering. But I swear to you: I didn't recognize Ramírez from Goya in a single one of the pieces.

Now, as I was telling you, the worst of the bad days was when, by order of our commanding superior officers, my company began its march toward the southeast, which was where Mount Longton was, then under enemy control, which we were supposed to recover. The fierce fire from enemy guns was relentless but we kept advancing anyway. When we arrived to what had been our forces' forward post, what can I tell you sir! I wish I didn't have to say it or tell you what I saw with my own eyes. But I'll take heart and I tell you: there was a slaughter. The Argentine soldiers got mixed up with the others, they were all the same in death and they all made you feel pity. Was all this necessary? It's information that I'm seeking, sir, but I don't think I'll ever find an answer. I'll tell you: in one shelter we found only men from our side. One could see they had been attacked by surprise. A savage affair! It would have been better not to have found them: decapitated and their heads on their chests and other details that I don't want to repeat, but which you can imagine because they have to do with men's private parts, those that remain nameless out of respect, unless one has been drinking. Afterwards they told us that the *gurkas* had passed through there and that was the way they treated their enemies, that is, us. More like some sort of beast than men, I'll tell you. But I thought: I don't believe such baseness is a question of race; it changes from person to person. Some people react to rage that way. In Corrientes I knew, although not in person but by reputation, some fugitives who cut men's private parts off, and I said to myself: being that way is a curse that strikes some, be they from Corrientes or *gurkas* from I don't know where. Because the enemy, I'm telling you, you hate him when you don't see him, but when you see him up-close, with eyes and a face, your feelings change. I don't know how to tell you what it is, but they change. I, for example, can tell you: I was serving as an aide to our troops who were in charge of mortar-fire, when I had the occasion to see an entire Englishman. Disoriented, he had wandered too close to the enemy, us. And what do you expect, instead of being happy to have him so close, I got sad. It seemed to me that I was seeing his blue eyes like marbles, and his blond hair and his face full of those fears that one gets from seeing so much death up-close, see? what do you expect me to say, I felt pity, and I almost said Watch out, but I didn't say anything, I fulfilled my duty, that is, I pressed the trigger but, the thing is, just then I closed my eyes, because the truth is, I didn't want to know anything and especially not what had happened to the blond guy with those blue eyes. Afterwards, yes, I had to look, because I heard a shout and the call was from the Lieutenant. Yes, Lieutenant Osorio, just when we were retreating, because no way were we going to retake Mount Longton, according to the way things were going, with those almost two thousand English infantrymen who were coming in waves. And then, I mean when we were retreating, I heard a voice that seemed more like a sigh, and then I saw him, pale with all the paleness of the world and in his gut a hole and coming out of the hole the tripe (excuse me, they were the guts, of a Christian and a Lieutenant), and his eyes, which until then were like a light, all of a sudden seemed to convey an incredible oldness. I went up to him and a sergeant did also and we tried to pick him up but we saw that if we moved him he would die, because there are warnings and there are warnings and the one he was carrying was a warning of death, and he, with a thread of a voice told us, go on, tell them what happened to me, he said, and the sergeant covered him with his topcoat and took his hand and said yes, my Lieutenant, and tears fell from both men's eyes, and from mine too, why deny it. The sergeant left but not I; and when the Lieutenant realized I was still there he told me go on and I gave him excuses for not being able to get my legs to move, they got me too and I can't walk, I told him. And right there I stayed, at his side; I hadn't been shot at all, but how was I going to leave the Lieutenant alone, for him to die like a dog! Tell me. And besides, what was I going to tell Lula later. So I stayed, but not for long, because his eyes were slowly closing, as if he just couldn't stay awake, and afterwards his body jerked once and then nothing. And then I put his hand— the one I found—over his chest, and I made the sign of the cross and I said the prayer for the dead that my grandmother used to say at wakes and I began to run and run. Because suddenly I no longer valued my commanding officer and I began to love myself. And I ran and ran until everything was dark and I in all the blackness managed to ask myself how am I going to tell Lula about this? But I had no time to find an answer.

I woke up in the infirmary of the enemy forces because of my legs, which were what was in pain, as you can see now. I then told myself: luckily, the grenade didn't hit my head. Because a leg is a leg and another leg is another leg and the two legs together are worse, but one's head, that's always worse because there's no way back. And I still had my head. I also thought I still had my legs because, as I'm telling you, the bastards, what a mystery!, they kept hurting me. Until someone told me: stop fantasizing. And afterwards they told me the rest, about the amputation and everything. Then I thought, I'll tell you: good, at least besides my head, I still have my hands. Because of the concertina, see? Besides, I'll tell you, I think I resigned myself to it, with total resignation, because right away I remembered Pepe, called Shorty, because he is an abbreviated human: trunk, head and only his upper limbs. Pepe, Shorty, do you know? spent all his life selling lemons and oranges and tangerines, citrus, in Corrientes there's a lot of that, in the market near the plaza. And why couldn't I do the same, especially since mine hasn't been because of microbes from some disease or because of an accident at birth but because of a patriotic, wartime duty, because I was defending our country? Besides, poor Pepe always had to walk on his stumps and me, surely, they're going to give me a wheelchair, now that I'm a hero, as they all tell me and it was even in the newspapers. There is something I regret, I won't tell you there isn't: not being able to ever drive a tractor, which is what I most wanted to do in my life. But I think: even though I don't have legs it's not so serious, my destiny isn't so gloomy, as they say. If life brings misfortunes it also brings beauty, Look at this day, so sunny, for example! You're smiling? What do you expect? I got through the dangers of death that war brings. Now, I'm inclined to think calmly and keep a quiet heart. Oh, and play the concertina, to make others happy, because luckily, as I was telling you, I still have my hands.

Alina Diaconú

Alina Diaconú was born in Bucharest, Rumania, in 1949. In 1959 she settled with her family in Buenos Aires, acquiring Argentine citizenship. Between 1968 and 1970 she lived in Paris. Among the honors she has received are the 1979 Medal of Honor from the Argentine Writers' Society (SADE) for her novel *Buenas noches, profesor;* Honorable Mention in the 1980 Coca-Cola Prize for Journalism; Special Mention in the National Prize for Literature for her novel *Enamorada del muro;* and finalist in the *La Nacion* (Buenos Aires) short story contest for a selection of stories titled *El infierno de cada día* (unpublished). In 1988, she received a Bronze Medal from the magazine *Cultura* for her work as a columnist. She was awarded the Meridiano de Plata Prize for *El penúltimo viaje,* and in 1994 she received the American-Romanian Academy of Arts and Sciences Award, rewarding her creative labor and her work in defense of freedom. A 1985 Fulbright Fellowship allowed her to participate in the International Writing Program of the University of Iowa for four months, along with forty other honored writers from throughout the world. During her stay in the United States she was invited to lecture about Argentine literature at universities in Arizona, Illinois, and South Carolina.

Several of her stories were translated into English and appeared in journals such as *Short Story International* and *Exquisite Corpse*. Currently she works for the Fundación Antorchas, a private foundation which supports the Arts and Literature of Argentina. Besides writing fiction, she collaborates with several journalistic media, both in Argentina and internationally, including two Mexican cultural magazines directed by Octavio Paz, *Vigencia* and *Vuelta,* and the newspapers *La Nación, La Prensa, Clarín* (Buenos Aires), *La Gaceta,* (Tucumán), and the national magazines *Cultura* and *Asuntos Culturales.*

Publications

La señora (The lady). Buenos Aires: Rodolfo Alonso, 1975.
Buenas noches, profesor (Good night, professor). Buenos Aires: Corregidor, 1978.
Enamorada del muro (The ivy on the wall). Buenos Aires: Corregidor, 1981.
Cama de ángeles (Bed of angels). Buenos Aires: Emecé, 1983.
"Soliloquio ante una ausencia" (Soliloquy in absence). In *Libro del Padre* (Father's book), edited by Antonio Requeni. Buenos Aires: Torres Agüero, 1984.
"Con Ciorán, en París" (With Cioran, in Paris). Suplemento Literario *La Nación,* 17 November 1985: 1–2.
Los ojos azules (The blue eyes). Buenos Aires: Fraterna, 1986.
"Victoria Ocampo: Historia de un apasionamiento" (Victoria Ocampo: History of a passion). Suplemento Literario de *La Nación,* 22 January 1989: 6.
El penúltimo viaje (The penultimate journey). Buenos Aires: Javier Vergara, 1989.
Los devorados (The devoured ones). Buenos Aires: Atlántida, 1992.
Alberto Girri: Homenaje (Alberto Girri: Homage). Buenos Aires: Sudamericana and Fondo Nacional de las Artes, 1994.
"Autogeografía." (Autogeography) *Alba de América: Revista Literaria* 12/22–23 (July 1994): 111–15.
¿Qué nos pasa, Nicolás? (What is happening to us, Nicolás?). Buenos Aires: Atlántida, 1995.

Secondary Sources

Agosín, Margorie, ed. *Secret Weavers.* Fredonia, N.Y.: White Pine Press, 1992.
Comorosan, Sorin. *Rumania, Sociedad de Responsabilidad Limitada.* Bucarest: Cartea Romaneasca, 1995.
Fares, Gustavo. "La utopia de escribir: Entrevista con Alina Diaconú." *Alba de América: Revista Literaria* 14/26–27 (July 1996): 507–11.

———. "This Text Which Is Not One." *Hispanic Journal* 12/2 (Fall 1991): 277–89.

Fares, Gustavo, and Eliana Hermann. "Alina Diaconú: La utopía de escribir." *Alba de América* 14/26–27 (July 1996): 507–11.

———. "Exilios internos: El viaje en cinco escritoras argentinas." *Hispanic Journal* 15/1 (Spring 1994): 21–29.

Flori, Mónica. "La articulización de lo inexpresable: Metaforización del cuerpo femenino en *Los ojos azules* de Alina Diaconú." *Alba de América: Revista Literaria* 12/22–23 (July 1994): 351–60.

———. "Autoritarismo, exilio y recreación feminista en *El penúltimo viaje* de Alina Diaconú." *Alba de América: Revista Literaria* 10/18–19 (July 1992): 183–94.

———. "Entrevista con Alina Diaconú." *Alba de América: Revista Literaria* 9/16–17 (1991): 381–86.

———. "Interview with Alina Diaconú." *Letras Femeninas* 14/1–2 (Spring–Fall 1988): 97–103.

———. "Madres e hijas y creatividad femenina en *La señora* de Alina Diaconú." *Confluencia: Revista Hispánica de Cultura y Literatura* (Spring–Fall 1993): 229–35.

———. *Streams of Silver: Six Contemporary Women Writers from Argentina.* Lewisburg, Penn.: Associated University Presses, 1995.

———. "La técnica de la inversión en las novelas de Alina Diaconú." *Selecta: Journal of the Pacific Northwest Council on Foreign Languages* 11 (1990): 92–96.

Gimbernat González, Ester. *Aventuras del desacuerdo: novelistas argentinas de los 80.* Buenos Aires: Vergara, 1992.

Gimbernat González, Ester, and Cynthia Tompkins, eds. *Utopías, ojos azules y bocas suicidas. La narrativa de Alina Diaconú.* Buenos Aires: Fraterna, 1994.

Hermann, Eliana. *Viajes en la palabpa y en la imagen.* Buenos Aires: Gaglianone Ediciones de Arte, 1996.

Herrera, Francisco. *Antología del erotismo en la literatura argentina.* Buenos Aires: Fraterna, 1991.

Marban, Jorge. "Estructura y simbolismo en *El penúltimo viaje* de Alina Diaconú." *Confluencia: Revista Hispánica de Cultura y Literatura* 7/2 (Spring 1992): 131–35.

Muñoz, Elías Miguel. "La búsqueda de un sexo 'verdadero': *Cama de ángeles* de Alina Diaconú." *Chasqui: Revista de Literatura Latinoamericana* 21/1 (May 1992): 49–54.

Tompkins, Cynthia. "Los devorados de Alina Diaconú ¿Vía mística? ¿Atracción tanática? ¿Alegoría social?" *Confluencia: Revista Hispánica de Cultura y Literatura* 9/2 (Spring 1994): 88–97.

Yang Ching-Chu. *Dialogue with International Authors.* Taipei, 1987 (published in Chinese).

Interview

1. Which authors have had the greatest influence on your work?

I am a daughter of the French and Russian classics by tradition, since in my country of origin those were the authors to whom I was first exposed and who astonished me the most. Later on, in the West, I chose Kafka, Joyce, Ionesco, Borges, and Cioran as parents. But the influences change in accordance with the personal moment that one lives in, and my influences were far more numerous than the ones I mentioned, and they will go on being modified with my own future changes. Besides, literature is not the only influence. In my case, movies, the theater, paintings have also been a very strong presence in my life and, therefore, I suppose that my books reflect that.

2. When did you begin to write, and why?

I learned to read when I was four years old. And knowing how to read meant immediately a need to write my own texts. It was a very curious process because then I began to imagine and to put on paper my own stories, which I invented and which seemed to entertain me more than the ones they used to read to me. Now, if we're speaking seriously, or rather about a conscious literary intention on my part, that appeared at age ten when I began to write, like everyone else, poetry. Those poems were written, obviously, in Romanian, my native language. Also at that age I began a novel that reached ten or twelve pages. Then came exile and our arrival in Argentina. For a year or two I wrote in French, which was my second language. It was a very strange period, a transition, with a great sense of insecurity with respect to my identity and from that period I still have poems, plays, and even a novel in French. Well, the truth is, I don't know if I still have them or if they are lost in some corner. And, after that stage, when I felt that I could handle Spanish with a certain fluency, I began writing novels and stories. In 1975 I published my first novel. That is the genre with which I feel most comfortable and that's why I have six novels published, and a few others not yet in print.

3. How does the political situation influence your choice of themes?

My life, or rather the discord that was in my life, was a product of politics. Therefore, my literature cannot be exempt from that commotion, existential if you will, linked, perhaps without my realizing it entirely, to politics. I lived my childhood and my adolescence in what can be called "a dictatorship of the proletariat" and, afterwards, chance or fate caused me to settle in a country like Argentina, where I came to know military dictatorships, with very brief periods of institutional democracy. For that reason, I can say that the principal political problem that I have suffered, both in the East and in the West, has been the lack of freedom. For example, during the last military regime my book *Buenas noches, profesor* was censored. However, my literature does not allude directly to politics, but rather it attempts to present a reflection on the human condition, from my experiences, of course, but with a much broader vision and without the limitations that any dogmatism impinges upon a work.

4. Have you encountered difficulties, as a woman writer, with publishers?

The life of a writer in Argentina is different in each case. I do not like to make generalizations. There are common problems, such as the fact that many times the writers have to do other works, extra-literary and better-paid ones, that allow them to live a bit better. In the case of a woman the question is still more complicated because she lives different lives among her tasks at the office, in the house, and in the work of writing. For me life has always been like that since I was eighteen years old, when I went to study and to work and then, after getting married, everything has been a constant challenge to organize myself and my work within that diversity. In this fashion I wrote my seven novels. In general I have been very fortunate in Argentina. The novels that I wrote and that I tried to publish found an editor. With *El penúltimo viaje* the story might be considered miraculous. The first editor who read it, in this case Javier Vergara, decided to publish it. I did not even have to undergo the usual pilgrimage. But this is somewhat atypical. The only thing that I have not accomplished, and that I would like to have done, would be to publish all my books with the same publishing house. I mean, for a single publishing house to support my work and form a sort of "marriage" that I believe useful for authors, readers, and, in the long run, for the editors as well. But I know that is a lot to ask. Almost an insolence nowadays.

5. What do you think of feminism?

My struggles, ever since I was a little girl, and a sense of the justice and equity that forms part of my personal ethics, have made me a feminist without my realizing it, and they have made me agree with some of the same tenets that the feminist movement fought for with more awareness, with a concrete, defined ideology and with the necessary organization. I never belonged to that movement and, on principle, I still do not belong to any movement. But that does not invalidate taking a position that I have always taken in my articles in the press, in my public speeches, et cetera.

6. How would you describe Argentina's women readers?

It is absolutely impossible for me to answer that question. I am completely ignorant of the answer, if one exists.

Selection from *El penúltimo viaje*

Diaconú's work represents that portion of Argentine current literature that focuses its attention on the topic of utopia, as conceived in three main categories: the existential, the sexual, and the spatial. Diaconú herself has stated that her narrative "is centered in the conflicts of the human condition, in the utopia that, indeed, marks everything in as much as I consider that life itself is a great utopia, full of ideas many times impossible to render real" ("La utopía," 508). The existential utopia questions the identity of the characters and, in doing so, reveals it as a cultural construction rather than a permanent and fixed referent. As such, it is present in the majority of Diaconú's work. A second kind of utopia, this time related to the sex and gender of the novel's characters, appears in Diaconú's work as a mistake, a *méconaissance* in the Lacanian sense of the term, that is to say, as in the case of the existential utopia, as a cultural construction rather than as a biological fact. That is indeed the case in Diaconú's novels *Los ojos azules* and *Cama de ángeles*. The spatial or topological utopia appears in the relations between the space the character occupies in contrast to the one where s/he originates. This takes place in *El penúltimo viaje,* a selection of which we include in what follows, and which refers to the fantasy of a utopian return to the ancestral home. The motif of a journey presented in this work is treated in different ways by other Argentine women writers, and also appears as a common theme that often ties together diverse narratives of one author. Not only have there been many migrations from Eastern European countries to Argentina, as in Diaconú's case; in recent years there has been an exodus in Argentina too, external as well as internal, also referred as "insodus." Such movements were the result of political or economic factors and affected the ways authors (female and male) lived and perceived reality. The comparison between the country left behind and Argentina allows Diaconú to write a critique of her own, and the country's, situation and to highlight the utopian nature of her final journey. Diaconú makes reference in this story to autobiographical events, for example, the fact that she was born in Romania and emigrated with her parents to Argentina in 1959. The novel seeks to recover that part of her life from the very beginning, from the dedication which reads: "To those who were born in the East and remained there. To those who could undertake a voyage that would only be one-way. To them. And to all the exiled ones." In Diaconú's text the narrator takes a train to a town in the far North of Argentina, suggestively designated by her as the land of San La Muerte (Saint Death), with the purpose of remembering, or constructing during her trip, who she used to be. She needs to know to be able to recognize who her parents and her siblings were and, with that knowledge, construct her own past. The novel concludes with the much-desired encounter with her identity, unveiled inside a darkened train, in the middle of a police interrogation. The narrator cannot answer the questions posed to her by the detectives who followed her, but sees, or imagines that she does, the figure of her mother, who comes looking for her to guide her to her "final destination," on the "last voyage" suggested by the novel's title.

III

Period

> "But you?, but I, but we?"
> —Jaime Sabines

What was it that happened after that journey by train?

We wandered aimlessly from town to town. From country to country. Living in borrowed rooms. Knowing the sorrows of so-called philanthropy.

Nothing, we could do nothing.

Father could do nothing, there in Europe.

We weren't tourists yielding to curiosity and enjoying a leisurely adventure. With desperation, we were searching in any latitude for a stable lodging where we could invent a routine for ourselves.

On those trips, on those roads over land and water, we conversed with people, we traveled along streets.

But no one can enjoy anything if the darkness has lodged in the middle of one's chest, in the depths of one's thoughts.

Everything is the same.

Some of the dreams I have dreamt were an unassailable reality.

For the first time since I had abandoned the East, I had an almost physical sensation of poverty. And I understood what greed was.

How could we love those cities, those countries that turned their backs on us?

What that long European trek offered me was being with people Father hadn't seen in decades, and those reunions cooperated to clear up some of the doubts that were eating me up and which I had believed impossible to untangle.

Through indirect commentaries, through overhearing conversations while hidden behind a door or pretending to be asleep, I learned that the guilty one, the one responsible for all our misfortunes, the one who had betrayed Father, had been Duduia.

It seems that she had told all to the Cupula: she had informed them about Father's absence two nights a week and about that custom of placing a place setting on the table for his dead wife.

The Cupula investigated.

They found out that Father had a friend, a daughter of one of the most aristocratic landholders of the country, a woman with a noble surname who had been forced to earn her living as a laborer in a tractor factory.

She spoke seven languages, and lived in a miserable room for which she spent almost her entire salary. But, in that hovel, there were still odd pieces of silver, some byzantine icons, hand-embroidered tablecloths and beautiful crocheted runners, feather pillows, macramé curtains.

Father was summoned by the Cupula to a first meeting. Then he was forced to carry out his self-criticism in public. Long sessions of four or five hours, confessions, "mea culpas" about that "unhealthy relationship" for a man like him, excusing himself for his other ridiculous habit that in no way was to be considered as a spiritist ceremony, but simply as an absurd method, and he recognized it, for the children to reconcile themselves with the idea of their mother's death.

The "mea culpa" sessions left him a defeated man. When one arrived to them, one knew that one wouldn't leave there the same person. He would face degradation, the destitution of his caste, perhaps forced labor, perhaps confinement, or a psychiatric hospital.

Father confessed everything.

He accepted that his amorous connection hadn't been with the most reliable person, and swore he would break off with her with the greatest alacrity. He also recognized his error, upon understanding that those present there could mistake a benevolent and ingenuous intention toward his children with some esoteric belief that was totally alien to him.

He accused himself as he was supposed to, he begged pardon, he lamented his actions, he promised not to backslide, he reaffirmed his faith in the Great Objective of the Process of Liberation, his faithfulness to this, his impassioned militancy. But nothing worked. Those sessions were the inexorable humiliation before the final defeat.

Father was already a dead man.

He was expelled like a worm, like a traitor, and his encounters with the woman who was the daughter, granddaughter and niece of "enemies of the Fatherland" grew fewer and further apart, until they were no more.

What he couldn't do was desist from putting our mother's place setting on the table. He had done it and he would continue doing so, "for our own good."

That was the time in which the world tumbled down, suddenly. And one cannot rebuild on top of ruins. He would have to begin again from nothing.

But Father had been left without strength, and his wits deserted him completely.

In reality, since he had occupied a privileged position in the Cupula, he knew that all of that was just a farce. Everyone knew it. But one had to continue. For his children. So that they would know a certain degree of security, so that they would not be tormented as the rest of the people were. That hadn't been selfish on his part, that was necessary; rather: he had no choice.

Horrible deeds were reserved for those who had fallen into disgrace: concentration camps, deportation, or the most perverse of all: the asylum. That was the destination for those whose beliefs didn't coincide with those of the Cupula and who, consequently, were considered demented.

On being "invited" to attend the meetings of "self-criticism," Father feared the worst. But his acquaintance with one of the members of the Cupula—the father of the idiot with long arms—resulted in the miracle.

He was a survivor. A happy man.

All of this information cleared up my cloudy panorama. What I kept questioning as a result of all this was if I could believe Father sometimes . . . or never again. If he had been able to lie, and lie to himself so much, what credit could I give him from now on?

But the journey continued.

We took another train. And another.

One night we boarded a boat, and after fourteen days we arrived in southern South America. The cradle of "Tangolita." (Do you remember, Alisio-Dragomir, how we danced that "tango"?)

God would appear on the scene of our new existence, with uncommon vigor. What did He have prepared for us . . . ? His fist or his open arms?

Alelí and I enrolled in a religious school where they didn't charge us tuition, since we were unfortunate creatures who came from a Godless country.

Alisio, for his part, entered a religious school managed by priests.

In time, our daily lives were plagued by new set phrases that took us by surprise. In another language, though. There were also new heroes, new villains.

Father advised silence.

Where was freedom?, I asked him one day when tanks rolled down the street and an old man was evicted from the Presidential Palace.

"We exchanged freedom for prosperity," he answered.

Another catch-phrase. One more.

I was tired. Twenty-three years old and already very tired. What was this prosperity that he was talking about? The prosperity that came with his job, in a post office, selling stamps?

"Don't ever forget how things were There . . ."

"There" was the name of our native country in the new era that Father had initiated.

"There."

He was right about that. One mustn't forget. But one does forget. One gets distracted and forgets. All the time.

After disembarking, we went to a boarding house. And then another. Someone lent us, for a short while, an apartment. We shared another with other people, until Father, thirteen months after our arrival, got a job. During those thirteen months we subsisted thanks to monthly checks from one of his rich friends.

All through the years, my mother never abandoned me. She had traveled with me everywhere. She too was getting acquainted with the new world.

I finished school and began to work as a telephone receptionist for a real estate firm. My language at that time was sufficiently correct for me to be able to say "VIP Brothers," "Good morning," although my foreign accent was noticeable. At night, I took college classes.

Alelí never worked. While she was in school, she got engaged, and then immediately thereafter, she married. Her husband is a lawyer who talks only about his cases and who doesn't consider the situation of his own wife who, following her tradition, every day places on the tablecloth another place setting, for our mother who will return some day . . . My two nephews must wait for—or not—their grandmother's return. They have a luxurious house in the suburbs. I see them infrequently, as little as possible. The distances, enormous here, serve as a pretext. Although those distances have always existed between Alelí and me.

Alisio tried to enroll in the school of Philosophy. He gave up. His physical condition was worsening day by day. He understood Spanish, but refused to speak it. He had locked himself into an absolute muteness, and if someone asked him something, he responded in his native tongue, provoking thus the repeated perplexity of his possible interlocutors. He had the radio on constantly and he listened to operas. We should have resolved among us his terrible fate. Although that fate had already been determined, but not by us.

In the interim, the bad news ensued. First, our maternal grandmother died. A year later, our grandfather, from Parkinson's disease. They were followed by a widowed aunt, our weak, timid grandfather, the spinster aunt. The last one to succumb was our paternal grandmother, the one in the wheel chair.

Tragic news, foreseeable, but undesirable.

Father will retire soon, I suppose. He is still there, behind that little window, in a building that's falling down, surrounded by walls covered with cobwebs, and a dirtiness and a deterioration worthy of the public offices in his home country.

But he assures us he's fine.

He rents a one-bedroom apartment, with a bathroom and a kitchenette, near Alelí's house, and to get to work it takes him twenty minutes by train.

Always trains.

I have changed jobs several times, and the last one is never the definitive one. I like changes. I get bored in any office. But I need to earn money.

Some months ago, I started to paint again.

I don't know how long this hobby will last, this craft. I don't know if it is a resuscitated vocation, or pure nostalgia.

I was on the verge of marriage several times, but the idea of living with someone else terrifies me and, therefore, I live alone. I recognize, on the other hand, that I'm also terrified of loneliness. I don't know what I'm most afraid of, deep-down.

I'm Amapola. Doina died (no matter how long she may live on in my documents).

Even in my dreams they call me Amapola. That means that the past doesn't exist for me now. Although until now I've done nothing but refer to it. Which makes me suppose that it exists in spite of my desire to erase it.

What do I know . . .

I find myself at this moment in the most Nordic point of the southernmost country in South America. The land of San La Muerte. Sick of spending hours in the waiting room, where there's nothing to wait for, I returned to the train. Here, in this empty car where the cold freezes my soul, here, on this dead train tracks . . .

Unfinished Business

"Documents!"

A lantern fastened on her face. The light accused her; the two silhouettes in the darkness formed a monster with two heads.

"Didn't you hear me? . . . Your identification!"

She wavered for an instant.

"I don't have an identity . . ." she whispered.

"What did you say?" growled one of the two mouths of the two-headed monster.

She searched among her belongings, groping, since the light cast was insufficient. Like five blind dwarves, her fingers fumbled through shapes and objects, each one with its story and its reason for being, and for being there, until she finally came across the exact shape.

She saw a large hand, a dark fist that threw light on the not very voluminous billfold of brown leather that had once had the raw color of sheepskin.

She took out the plastic rectangle. The fist bifurcated into two fingers that trapped that plastic rectangle. Time passed by with extreme slowness and her feet were frozen.

"What are you doing here?"

"I'm writing a book . . ."

The two heads of the same monster looked at each other, as if one were consulting the other.

"Let's see . . . Where is that book?"

"In my head . . ." she mumbled.

After another moment of silence, the other head of the two-headed monster spoke:

"What are you doing here, at this hour, alone, in this car?!" This other voice shouted, as if he hadn't heard her earlier response. Or perhaps she had whispered it so softly that it had resulted truly inaudible.

"I'm waiting for the time to pass . . . for the train to leave for the capital."

"The bag! Come on!" She handed it over. The two-headed monster divided, and then there were two lanterns and two twin brothers in the shadow that rummaged and rummaged. Two lanterns shone on her, and ran over her body, up and down, and finally they ordered her to stand up. It had gotten so cold in there that her body was numb.

In the distance, she seemed to hear a shot. Without wanting to, she looked out the window, but she didn't see anything: only the claustrophobic curtain of the night.

The silhouettes whispered to each other. They didn't have faces; they were just two uniforms that moved.

And yet, she realized that she didn't care what they said, or what could happen to her.

For that reason, she curled up again in her seat, not that it was comfortable, certainly. She stretched her coat until it covered her feet, and pulled up her turtleneck until it covered her ears.

And then, there, a few steps away from the uniformed shapes that were searching through her things, she saw her. A sound, similar to wings fluttering, accompanied the apparition. That was the way it always happened.

"Doina, my dear Doina," she murmured, calling her like that for the first time.

Her face had the white light of the moon. Her violet mouth had sweetened her expression, even converting it into a smile.

"Come, it's so cold here, you'll get sick . . . Come on, come with me, don't be afraid."

She wasn't afraid; to the contrary.

The woman wrapped in veils, in clouds, in unformed mists of gauze and tulle, attracted her magnetically. She was walking backwards, receding, receding and calling her.

And she, without feeling the weight of her body, began to follow, through a barely illuminated corridor, where the light must have come from the lunar face of her mother, showing her the way.

And she remembered the first verse of an unforgettable poem: "Every death is by way of a crime."

What had that gentle and ethereal woman in that remote country done except hasten the instant?

She was following her now, wherever she might go, wherever she wanted her to, through the empty cars of the stopped train, down a very long aisle, not feeling tired in the least. She had already covered so many roads, dirt roads, and sea roads and air roads. So many cars . . .

What road was this, what new road?

It didn't matter.

The woman wrapped in veils was her guide. She couldn't possibly get lost. Any moment they would merge into a great embrace: mother-daughter. And that fusion would mean that she had reached the goal. The final destination.

Angélica Gorodischer

Angélica Gorodischer was born in Buenos Aires on July 28, 1928, and received her education in Liberal Arts in Rosario, Province of Santa Fe, where she lives. Her work has been translated into several languages, and her stories have appeared in numerous anthologies. Among her best collections of short stories are *Bajo las jubeas en flor* and *Casta luna electrónica*. She has been a visiting lecturer in Argentina, the United States, and Germany. In 1988 she received a Fulbright Fellowship for the International Writing Program of the University of Iowa. She was a 1991 Fulbright Scholar, teaching two courses at the University of Northern Colorado, Greeley. Several of her stories have been translated into English, German, Czech, and French. She is the recipient of numerous short story awards, including the Sigfrido Radaelli Prize for the best short story of 1985, the Gilgamesh Prize for the best fantastic story of 1986, and the Gilgamesh Prize for the best fantastic story published in Spain in 1990. Her other literary prizes include second prize for a short story that appeared in the magazine *Vea y Lea;* the Club del Orden Prize for her book *Cuentos con soldados;* the Más Allá Prize, Buenos Aires Center for Science Fiction and Fantasy, for *Kalpa imperial II* (1984); the Poblet Prize, Buenos Aires, for *Kalpa imperial I* (1984); and the Emecé Prize, Buenos Aires, for *Floreros de alabastro, alfombras de Bokhara.*

Gorodischer is one of the most recognized Argentine women writers. If it is true that every writer has a way of expressing him or herself, a manner that differentiates him/her from all other authors, this is particularly the case of Gorodischer's work. She recognizes her affinity to what is, or can become, monstrous, extreme, which is why she finds the genre of science fiction to be an adequate vessel for her fantasies. She is one of the few science fiction women writers in the country. But she does not use the genre to escape reality, as is usually the case. On the contrary, in Gorodischer's hands, science fiction provides insight and a means by which to criticize the everyday Argentine reality, as in the story selected for this volume.

Publications

Cuentos con soldados (Stories with soldiers). Santa Fe: Club del Orden, 1965.
Opus dos (Opus two). Buenos Aires: Minotauro, 1967.
Las pelucas (The wigs). Buenos Aires: Sudamericana, 1968.
Bajo las jubeas en flor (Under the tamarinds in bloom). Buenos Aires: De la Flor, 1976. 2nd edition, Barcelona: Ultramar, 1987.
Casta luna electrónica (Chaste electronic moon). Buenos Aires: Andrómeda, 1977.
Trafalgar. Buenos Aires: El Cid, 1979. 2nd edition, Rosario: El Peregrino, 1984. 3rd edition, Barcelona: Orbis, 1986.
Mala noche y parir hembra (Bad night and giving birth to a girl). Buenos Aires: La Campana, 1983.
Kalpa imperial I. Buenos Aires: Minotauro, 1984.
Kalpa imperial II. Buenos Aires: Minotauro, 1984.
"Las mujeres y las palabras" (Women and the words). *Hispamérica: Revista de Literatura* 13/39 (December 1984): 45–48; *Confluencia: Revista Hispánica de Cultura y Literatura* 4/2 (Spring 1989): 3–9.
Floreros de alabastro, alfombras de Bokhara (Alabaster vases, carpets from Bokhara). Buenos Aires: Emecé, 1985.
"Narrativa fantástica y narrativa de ciencia ficción" (Fantastic narrative and science fiction narrative). *Plural: Revista Cultural de Excelsior* 188 (May 1987): 48–50.
Jugo de mango (Mango juice). Buenos Aires: Emecé, 1988.
"Borges y los judíos" (Borges and the Jews). *Confluencia: Revista Hispánica de Cultura y Literatura* 8/1 (Fall 1992): 9–18.

Las Repúblicas (The republics). Buenos Aires: De La Flor, 1993.

Fábula de la Virgen y el bombero (Fable of the Virgin and the fireman). Buenos Aires: De La Flor, 1993.

Prodigios (Prodigies). Barcelona: Lumen, 1994.

Técnicas de Supervivencia (Survival techniques). Rosario: Secretaría de Cultura de la Municipalidad de Rosario, 1994.

Secondary Sources

Dellepiane, Angela B. "Contar: Mester de fantasía o la narrativa de Angélica Gorodischer." *Revista Iberoamericana* 51/132–33 (July–December 1985): 627–64.

Eberle McCarthy, Karen. "Worlds within Argentine Women." In *La escritora hispánica. Actas de la decimotercera conferencia anual de literaturas hispánicas en Indiana University of Pennsylvania,* edited by Nora Erro Orthmann and Juan Cruz Mendizabal. Miami: Universal, 1990.

Fares, Gustavo, and Eliana Hermann. "Angélica Gorodischer, escritora argentina." *Hispania* 75/5 (December 1992): 1238–39.

Goorden, B. "Quand Angélica Gorodischer écrit de la science fiction, elle écrit mieux que les hommes." *Ies et Autres* 24 (1980).

Lojo, María Rosa. "Dos versiones de la utopía: 'Sensatez del círculo,' de Angélica Gorodischer, y 'Utopía de un hombre que está cansado' de Jorge Luis Borges." In *Mujer y sociedad en América: IV Simposio Internacional,* edited by Juana Alcira Arancibia, 93–104. Instituto Literario y Cultural Hispánico, Universidad Autónoma de Baja, 1988.

López, E. "Intertextualidad en un cuento de Angélica Gorodischer." Ph.D. diss., Universidad Nacional de Rosario, Argentina, 1984.

Mathieu, Corina. "Feminismo y humor en *Floreros de alabastro, alfombras de Bokhara.*" *Letras Femeninas* 17/1–2 (Spring–Fall 1991): 113–19.

Mosier, M. Patricia. "Communicating Transcendence in Angélica Gorodischer's *Trafalgar.*" *Chasqui: Revista de Literatura Latinoamericana* 12/2–3 (February–May 1983): 63–71.

———. "Comunicando la trascendencia en *Trafalgar* por Angélica Gorodischer." *Foro Literario: Revista de Literatura y Lenguaje* 15–16 (1986): 50–56.

———. "Women in Power in Gorodischer's *Kalpa imperial.*" In *Spectrum of the Fantastic,* edited by Palumbo, 153–61. Westport: Greenwood, 1988.

Vázquez, María Esther. "Angélica Gorodischer, una escritora latinoamericana de ciencia ficción." *Revista Iberoamericana* 49/123–24 (April–September 1983): 571–76.

Interview

1. Which authors have had the greatest influence on your work?

   All of them, and I will tell you that not only authors of books, but also of other types of writing, such as comic strips, cinema, or art books. When I was little I didn't know how to read or write, but I already loved books with drawings in them, and the books with illustrations that were in my parents' house were art books. I made up stories for the paintings that I saw. The *Drunkards* by Murillo, *The Duchess of Alba,* and many more. I told the stories to myself and to whoever else was around to listen to them. In an interview, the other day, they asked me who were my literary parents, and I answered Mandrake the Magician and Francisco de Goya, the painter. Besides, we shouldn't discard the importance of the language on the street, the vegetable grocer, my seamstress, the two old folks who sat behind me on the bus, the taxi driver. You should hear what they say! When I was nineteen my favorite author was Aldous Huxley but, if I had to name more than one, I would say Balzac, Borges, of course, the North American black novelist Boris Vian, Hemingway, also Chandler.

2. When did you began to write, and why?

   I began to write, as I told you, without knowing how to write. I used to tell stories to myself because I was alone and had no one to play with. I didn't write them, but I imagined them well, and I was capable of repeating them over and over. When I was twelve, I said one day: "Kafka is my colleague." Look what I said! I did not say "I'm going to write like Kafka," or "I am a colleague of . . . ," no, "Kafka is my colleague!" Why did I write? Why then? I don't know; now, because it is my life.

3. How does the political situation influence your choice of themes?

   Of course it does. Unless one is totally crazy or autistic, it influences you. Here, in Argentina, politics infiltrates everything because the situation is so unstable, so tragic that politics infiltrate everything. Look, I wrote *Kalpa imperial* I convinced that I was writing traditional stories in the fashion of

A Thousand and One Nights. I was convinced of that and I treated the text as such, and when it was published I realized that I had written about the Process [Proceso de Reorganización Nacional].

4. Have you encountered difficulties, as a woman writer, with publishers?

Now nothing is being printed. I have never had difficulties before. I never felt discriminated against, but there is discrimination, indeed there is. And if not, look at Sosa de Newton's book, there are like a hundred and ten women writers mentioned, and if you take out the thirty or so who are best known, there are still eighty plus that no one's ever heard of. We know that they wrote, but have they earned anything with the publication and sale of their books? No one knows. They never discriminated against me, but that doesn't mean anything. Another example: ask any Argentine author, "In Argentina today, who are the writers?" and that author will answer: "Fulano, Mengano, Fulano, Zutano . . . ," but he won't name a single woman. And someone will say, "But, what about Griselda Gambaro?" "Oh, but of course, of course!" Yes, of course, they love us, but they forget us. Do you know when they remember? When one dies, and if it's a suicide, so much the better.

5. What do you think of feminism?

What do you want me to say, I am a feminist and I am active. I believe that there should be equal opportunity for all.

6. How would you describe Argentina's women readers?

At this time no one is reading. But I believe, of course, that they are good readers.

Selection from *Trafalgar*

The theme of the journey is presented in this work by Gorodischer through fiction and humor. Our selection belongs to the science fiction genre, which often introduces fantastic elements while, at the same time, rendering them believable, infiltrating as if were, everyday reality. In Gorodischer's text the everyday setting is the Burgundy Bar, with its tables, its waiter, its tranquility, where the characters chat about inter-planetary adventures. The story we have chosen, "By the Light of the Chaste Electronic Moon," appeared for the first time in the collection *Casta luna electrónica* in 1977. Here one can already find some of the elements present in Gorodischer's book *Trafalgar* (1979), including the protagonist, Trafalgar Medrano. In this story, Trafalgar arrives at the Burgundy after an unexplained absence and, answering the questions of his curious friend, a prosperous lawyer who assumes the narrative voice, he begins to morosely retell the reasons for his disappearance. The conversation becomes more and more strange, making references to unfamiliar galaxies, planets and peoples, all the while interspersing allusions to the characters' surroundings, the tables, the waiter, the drinks, the cigarettes. This keeps the story on the level of the believable, in spite of the strangeness of the events narrated. With lively humor and narrative rhythm, Gorodischer delivers another adventure of her character Trafalgar, whom, she wants us to believe, we could meet at any moment, around a street corner of her town of Rosario, or perhaps in Buenos Aires itself.

From this very moment, dear reader, before you begin to read this book, I have to ask you a favor: don't start at the table of contents, looking for the shortest story or the one that has the most appealing title. Since you're going to read them, something I am grateful for, read them in order. Not because they follow one another chronologically, although there is something of that, but because in that way you and I will understand each other more easily. Thank you. A.G.

By the Light of the Chaste Electronic Moon

Yesterday I was with Trafalgar Medrano. It's not easy to run into him. He's always in a hurry from here to there for that import-export business of his. But from time to time he runs from there to here and he likes to sit and drink coffee and chat with a friend. I was at the Burgundy and when I saw him enter I almost didn't recognize him: he had shaved off his mustache.

The Burgundy is one of those bars of which only a few remain, if any. No formica or fluorescent lights or even Coca-Cola. A slightly worn gray rug, tables and chairs of real wood, some mirrors along the paneling, small windows, a door with a single window pane and a facade that doesn't say much. Thanks to all of that, inside it's fairly quiet and anyone can sit and read the newspaper or converse with someone else or do nothing at a table covered with a tablecloth, a white porcelain and glass china, as they should be, an actual sugar bowl, and no one, especially Marcos, coming over to bother you.

I'm not telling you where it is because maybe you have teenage sons, or worse, teenage daughters who'll find out, and goodbye tranquility. I'll give you just one bit of information: it's downtown, between a store and a gallery, and no doubt you pass it every day when you go to the bank and you don't see it.

But Trafalgar Medrano came to my table right away. He certainly recognized me because I still have that fleshy, tweedy and Yardley aspect of a prosperous lawyer, which is exactly what I am. We greeted each other as if we had seen each other a couple of days ago but I calculated that it had been about six months. He made a sign to Marcos that meant where's my double coffee, and I continued with my sherry.

"I haven't seen you in a while," I told him.

"Well, yes," he answered. "Business trips."

Marcos brought him his double coffee and a glass with fresh water on a little silver tray. That's what I like about the Burgundy.

"Besides, I got in a little trouble."

"One of these days you're going to end up in jail," I told him, "and don't call me to bail you out. I don't take those cases."

He tasted the coffee and lit a dark cigarette. He smokes regulars, no filter. He has his quirks, like everyone.

"Trouble with a woman," he clarified without looking at me. "I think it was a woman."

"Traf," I said, getting very serious, "I hope you haven't acquired an exquisite inclination towards fragile young boys, with smooth skin and light colored eyes."

"She was like a woman when we were in bed."

"And what were you doing with her or with him in the bed?" I asked him, to prod him a little.

"What do you think one does with a woman in bed, sing a duet by Schumann?"

"Okay, okay, but explain: what did she have between her legs? Something that stuck out or a hole?"

"A hole. Rather two, each one in its appropriate place."

"And you took advantage of both of them."

"Well, why not?"

"It was a woman," I resolved.

"Hummm," he said. "I thought so."

And he returned to his black coffee and filterless cigarette. You can't hurry Trafalgar. If you meet him sometime, at the Burgundy or at the Jockey or any place else, and he begins to tell you what happened to him on one of his trips, by God and the whole celestial choir, don't hurry him; watch that he stretches things out in his lazy and cunning way. So I ordered another sherry and some pretzels and Marcos approached and said something about the weather and Trafalgar decided that changes in climate are like boys, if one pays attention to them, one is lost. Marcos agreed and returned to the bar.

"It was on Veroboar," he continued. "That was the second time I was there, but the first one doesn't count because I was just there passing through and I didn't even land. It's on the edge of the galaxy."

I've never known for sure whether or not Trafalgar really travels to the stars but I don't have any reason not to believe him. Many stranger things happen. What I do know is that he's fabulously rich. And it doesn't seem to matter to him a whit.

"I'd been selling reading materials in the Seskundrea system, seven clean and brilliant little worlds in which sight reading is a luxury. However, one that I imposed. There, people listen to their texts or they read them with their fingers. The common people continue as they were but I have sold books and magazines to everyone who thinks they are anybody. I had to land on Veroboar, which isn't far, so they could repair an induction screen, and I took advantage to sell the rest." He lit another cigarette. "They were comic books. Don't make that face; if it weren't for those comic books I wouldn't have had to shave my mustache."

Marcos brought him another double coffee before he asked for it. This Marcos is incredible; if you only drink dry sherry, well iced, as I do, or fresh-squeezed orange juice with gin, like Salustiano, the youngest of the Carreras, or seven double coffees at a sitting, like Trafalgar Medrano, you can be sure that Marcos will be there to remember it even if it's been ten years since you've been to the Burgundy.

"This time I didn't go to Seskundrea; I wouldn't want the luxury to become a habit because then I'd have to start thinking about something else. I was taking Baya Aspirin to Belanius III where Baya Aspirin has hallucinogenic effects. It must be a question of climate or metabolism."

"Didn't I tell you you'll end up in jail?"

"Doubtful. I convinced the chief of police on Belanius III to try Coffee Aspirin. Imagine."

I tried but I couldn't. The Belanius III Police chief punishing himself with Coffee Aspirin goes beyond the limits of my modest imagination. And the truth is I didn't try very hard because I was intrigued by the trouble and by the woman who perhaps wasn't one.

"Belanius III isn't too close to Veroboar, but since I was there I decided to try with a few more magazines and some books, just a few so as not to frighten them. Of course I was going to wait a while and not offer them to the first lackey that appeared, for him to sell them and abscond with my profit. I parked my jalopy, put my clothes and merchandise in a valise and took a bus that was going to Verov, the capital."

"And customs?"

He looked at me, disdainful:

"In civilized worlds there's no such thing as customs, old man. They're more advanced than we are."

He finished his second coffee and looked toward the bar but Marcos was waiting on another table.

"I had decided to talk with someone strategically situated who could tell me where and how to organize the sale. For a commission, of course."

"So in civilized worlds there's no customs, but there are bribes."

"Well, more or less civilized. Don't be so picky. They all have their short-comings. There, for example, I had a tremendous surprise: Veroboar is an aristomatriarchy."

"A what?"

"That is, there are a thousand women, I suppose that they are women; young, I suppose that they are young; divine."

"You suppose they're divine."

"No, they are. You can see that a mile away. Rich. You can see that a mile away, too. They have all of Veroboar in their hands. And with what a grip! You can't even sneeze without their permission. I'd been in the hotel for two min-utes when I received a note with seals and a letterhead in which I was sum-moned to the office of the Governor. At 31 hours, 75 minutes on the dot. Which meant I had half an hour to bathe, shave, and dress."

Marcos arrived with the third double coffee.

"And unfortunately," said Trafalgar, "except in the houses of The One Thousand, although I didn't have time to see them, on Veroboar there are no sophisticated dressers as on Sechus or on Vexvise or on Forendo Lhda. Did I ever tell you that on Drenekuta V they travel in ox-carts but they have three-dimensional television and cubicles of compressed air that shave you, rub you down, massage you, and make you up because on Drenekuta men wear make-up and roll their hair and paint their nails, and they dress you in seven seconds?"

"No, I don't think so. One day you told me about some mute people who dance instead of talking, or something like that."

"Please, Anandaha-A. What a useless world. I could never sell them any-thing."

"And did you arrive on time?"

"Where?"

He drank half a cup of coffee.

"At the Governor's office, where else?"

"And what a governor! Blonde, green eyes, very tall, with legs that, if you see them, will give you a coronary."

Tell me about splendid women. I married one 37 years ago. I don't know if Trafalgar Medrano is married or not. I add that my wife's name is Leticia and I continue.

"And two firm little apples that could be seen through her blouse, and round hips," he paused. "She was a viper. She didn't waste saliva on ceremony. She planted herself in front of me and said, 'We were wondering when you would return to Veroboar, Mr. Medrano.' I thought we were off to a good start and I couldn't have been more wrong. I told her I was very flattered that they remembered me and she looked at me as if I were a pile of cow dung that the street sweeper forgot to take away and she said, do you know what she said to me?"

"No idea."

"'We haven't watched with approval your clandestine activities at the port of Verov.' What do you think?"

I didn't say anything.

"Why repeat the dialogue? Besides I don't remember. Those witches had shot the poor fellow who was selling my magazines," he took a little more coffee, "and they had confiscated the materials and decided that I was a criminal."

"And you took her to bed and convinced her not to shoot you too."

"I didn't take her to bed," he explained very patiently.

"But you said . . ."

"Not with her. After that she told me that I had to address her by her title, which was Illustrious Lady in Charge of Governing Verovsian."

"Don't tell me you had to say that each time you spoke to her."

"That's exactly what I'm telling you. After she told me that, she told me that I couldn't leave my hotel without her authorization and of course not to try to sell anything and that they would let me know when I could come again. If I ever could. And the following day I would have to appear before one of the members of the Central Government. And to leave."

"Good Lord!"

"I went to the hotel and smoked three packs of cigarettes. I wasn't enjoying this at all. I ordered room service. Disgusting, the hotel food, and that was the best there was in Verov, and to top it off the bed was too soft and the window didn't close all the way."

Surely the rest of his coffee was already cold but he drank it anyway. Marcos was going over the daily racing section of the paper; he knows all there is to know about horses and a little more. He has a son who's a brand new colleague of mine and a married daughter who lives in Córdoba. There were only two other occupied tables, so the Burgundy was more peaceful than Veroboar. Trafalgar smoked a while without speaking and I looked at my empty glass asking myself if this was a special occasion; only on special occasions did I drink more than two glasses of sherry.

"The next day I received another note, on letterhead but without seals, wherein they told me that the interview would be with the Illustrious and Chaste Madam Guinevere Lapislazuli."

"What did you say?" I jumped. "That was her name?"

"No, of course not."

Marcos had put down the racing form, collected from one of the other tables and now was bringing the fourth double coffee. He didn't bring me anything because this gave no hint of being a special occasion.

"Her name was," said Trafalgar, who never puts sugar in his coffee, "something that sounded like that. In any case what they told me was that the interview had been postponed until the following day because the Illustrious, Chaste and the rest, who was a member of the Central Government, had begun her annual formalities before the Division of Integral Relations of the Secretary of Private Communication. There the year lasts almost twice as long as it does here and the days are longer and the hours too."

Frankly, I couldn't care less about the chronosophy of Veroboar.

"And all of that, what did it mean?" I asked him.

"How was I to know?"

He was silent, watching the three characters who entered and sat at the table to the rear. I'm not sure but I think one of them was Basilio Bender, the one who has a construction business, you must know him.

"I found out later, little by little," said Trafalgar with his coffee in his hand, "and I don't know if I understood it totally. And the next day it was the same story because the Illustrious one continued with her duties and the next also. The fifth day I was very tired of blonde matriarchs and their secretaries, of being locked in the hotel room, of the hog slop that there was to eat, of the bed and the window and everything and of walking around twenty square meters thinking that they would keep me hostage there in Veroboar for an indefinite time. Or that they would shoot me."

He was flustered for a while, angry retroactively, while he drank his fourth coffee.

"So I bribed the waiter who brought my food. It wasn't difficult and I had already figured that out because he was skinny with a hungry face, decayed teeth and threadbare clothes. Everything is miserable and sad in Veroboar. Everything except for the One Thousand. I will never return to that worthless world," he thought out loud. "That is, I don't know."

I was getting impatient.

"You bribed him. And?"

"The guy was scared out of his wits but he got me a telephone book and he let me know that to interview a member of the Central Government one has to go in evening dress, damn it."

"Traf, I don't understand anything," I almost shouted. "Marcos, another sherry."

Marcos looked at me strangely, but he took out the bottle.

"Ah, it's because I didn't tell you that the last of those notes informed me that since the Illustrious one had finished her formalities she was going to spend between five and ten days locked in her house. And since they weren't calling me into the office, I wanted the address of her house to go see her there."

"But they had forbidden you to leave the hotel."

"Yeah."

Marcos arrived with the sherry: special occasion.

"I had to do something. Five to ten days more were too many. Therefore, that night, since I didn't know what evening dress was on Veroboar, and neither did the skinny waiter, how was he to know, I dressed as if I were to be a godfather at Church: tuxedo, white dress shirt with pearl buttons, cummerbund, patent leather shoes, top hat and cape. And cane and gloves."

"Really!"

"You can't imagine what I carry in my luggage. Remind me to tell you what ceremonial dress is on Foulikdan. And what you have to put on if you want to sell something on Mesdabaulli IV," he laughed. "So, dressed, I waited for the signal from the skinny waiter and when he called me on the phone to tell me no one was downstairs, I left the hotel and took a taxi, which was waiting for me, and which took me five blocks, not much faster than I could have walked.

We arrived. My God, what a house. Of course, you don't know what houses are like in Veroboar. Hardly better than those in a slum. But Guinevere Lapislazuli was one of the Thousand and a member of the Central Government. Man, what a palace. All marble and crystal half a meter thick, set in a garden full of flowers and fountains and statues. The night was dark. Veroboar has a feeble moon that doesn't illuminate anything, but there were yellow spotlights among the plants in the garden. I crossed the garden with a fast pace, as if I knew the place. The driver was watching me without believing his eyes. I arrived at the door and looked for a bell or a doorknocker. There wasn't any. Neither was there a door knob. I couldn't stand there waiting for a miracle. I pushed the door, and it opened."

"Did you go in?"

"Of course I went in. I was sure they were going to shoot me. If not that night, then the next day. But I went in."

"And?"

"They didn't shoot me."

"I had already figured that out."

"There wasn't anyone inside. I coughed, I clapped my hands, I called. No one. I started walking around. The floors were marble. There were enormous round spotlights hanging from the ceiling with chains encrusted with jewels. The furniture was of finely carved gilded wood."

"What do I care about the decor of the house of Lapislazuli? Please tell me what happened."

As you can see, I preach but I don't practice. Sometimes Trafalgar alters my way of thinking.

"For a while nothing happened. Until I pushed open a door and found her."

The sherry was very cold and the fellow I thought was Bender got up and went to the restroom.

"Blonde, also?" I asked.

"Yes. Excuse me, but I have to talk about the decor of that room."

"If there's no other choice."

"There isn't. It was monstrous. Marble everywhere with several shades of pink on the walls and black on the ceiling. Artificial plants and flowers sprang out from the walls. Made of plastic. Of every color. Corner cupboards for incense burners. Above, a fluorescent moon was shining, hanging like a tortilla from transparent threads which swung when I opened the door. Next to one wall there was a machine the size of a bureau that was humming and had little lights that flashed off and on. And against another wall an interminable golden bed, and on the bed she was naked and watching me."

I thought seriously about having a fourth sherry.

"I had prepared a magnificent speech that consisted in not lying or in lying as little as possible, but the picture had left me breathless. I took off my top hat, bowed, opened my mouth, and nothing came out. I tried again and I began to stutter. She kept looking at me and when I was about to stammer that bit about Illustrious and Chaste etcetera, she raised a hand and motioned me to approach."

I hadn't noticed, but he had finished his fourth coffee because Marcos brought him another cup.

"I approached, of course. I stopped beside the bed and the machine that was humming was at my right. I was nervous, you can imagine, and I stretched my hand and began to gauge whether I could turn it off while still looking at her. It was worth it."

"She was just a woman, no need to make a fuss."

"I told you that I think so. What I'm sure of is that she was incredibly hot. At that point, so was I. With my right hand I found a lever and I lowered it and the machine turned off. Without the humming I began to feel better, and I bent over and kissed her on the lips, which apparently was the most appropriate thing to do under the circumstances because she grabbed me around the neck and began to pull me down. I took off my cape and I used my two free hands for the two little apples, this time without a blouse or anything."

"Lovely night."

"More or less, as you'll see. I undressed in record time, I threw myself on her and I said something like baby you're the most beautiful thing I've seen in my life, and I assure you that I wasn't lying because she was beautiful and warm and it seemed to me that I was a troubadour and king of the world all in one, and do you know what she told me?"

"But how would I know. What did she say to you?"

"She said 'Mandrake, my love, don't call me baby, say Narda.'"

"Traf, stop with the jokes."

"They're not jokes. I, who was not for subtleties, rushed forth with everything I had, although I had the sensation of having made love to an already unsteady vessel."

"Was she chaste?"

"Like she would be. Perhaps illustrious but certainly not chaste. She knew everything. And between the moans and the pirouettes she kept calling me Mandrake."

"And you called her Narda."

"What did it matter to me? She was beautiful, I tell you, and she was tireless and tempting. As soon as I tired a bit and dozed off holding her, she would run her fingers and her tongue over my body and she would laugh, nuzzling my neck and she would nibble me and I would return to action and we would roll around like a knot all over the golden bed. Until after one of our somersaults she realized that the machine was off. She sat up in the bed and began to scream and I thought, what a pain. It's as if you were to begin to howl because the hot water heater was turned off."

"But that wasn't a hot water heater, I suppose, was it?"

"No, it wasn't. I wanted to continue with the revelry and I tried to pull her back to me but she shouted even louder, asking what I was doing there. I said, but what a bad memory you have, my darling, and she kept shouting who was I and what was I doing in her room and to leave immediately and she tried to cover herself with something."

"Certainly unbalanced," I commented.

"Ah, that's what I thought, but it happens that she was somewhat sane, and right."

He was quiet for a moment and afterwards he remembered that I was there:

"Did I tell you I undressed in record time? Well, I dressed even quicker still, I don't know how, because although I didn't understand what was happening, I had the impression that the situation was becoming more dangerous than I had supposed. And while I was putting on my shirt and forcing my pants on and putting the sash in my pocket all at the same time, I thought that really it would have served me well to be Mandrake so I could wave a magic wand and appear totally dressed. And then I knew I *was* Mandrake."

"But, hold on!"

"Don't you realize?" he asked me, a little irritated, as if anyone could understand anything in all this hodgepodge. "I was dressed like Mandrake and I have, I had, a mustache, and lightly slicked, black hair. And The Thousand had confiscated my comic books."

"And Ms. Lapislazuli had read them and had fallen in love with Mandrake,

I understand that. But why was she shouting if she thought you were Man-drake?"

"Wait, wait!"

"Because, what else could she want, with the evening that she was having?"

"Wait, I said, no one can tell you anything."

The ashtray was full of dark, filterless butts. I stopped smoking eighteen years ago and at that moment I regretted it.

"I finished dressing and I backed out with the cape and the top hat in my hand and without the cane or the gloves, while the blonde was wrapping her-self in a silk sheet, golden silk although you won't believe it, and she was threatening me with torture and death by quartering. I don't know how I didn't get lost in all the marble. I could hear her screams all the way to the door. On the street, not a taxi to be seen. I ran two or three blocks, in the darkness, through a silent neighborhood where surely five or six of The Thousand lived because each house occupied at least a block. After an avenue that was wider than the others, at the edge of the slum, I found a taxi. The driver was a yellowish old man who wanted to chat. I didn't. Perhaps I had become yellowish too, I don't say I hadn't, but I did not want to chat. I climbed the steps three at a time, there was no elevator in that filthy hotel, I entered the room, took off the tux, shaved my mustache off, put on a blond wig, I told you that I carry everything in my luggage on my trips, and glasses and a cap and a checkered coat and brown pants, and I began to put things in my suitcase. And then the skinny waiter arrived, he had taken a special inter-est in me, not because of my irresistible personality but because of the possi-bilities of my wallet, and he found me flinging underwears."

"Tell me, Traf, why were you escaping from a handful of women who were stupendous and eager besides, from the way I see it, or rather from the way I hear it?"

He was in the middle of his sixth cup of coffee and we were alone in the Burgundy. It was getting late but I didn't even look at my watch because I had no intention of leaving until I had heard the end. Leticia knows that at times, at times, I arrive whenever and it doesn't mind, as long as it's only at times.

"You weren't on Veroboar," said Trafalgar, "nor did the Governor scream at you, nor did you know that hungry, skinny, frightened waiter or the guy they shot for a few dozen magazines, an asthmatic mechanic who had purulent conjunctivitis and who was missing two fingers from his left hand and who wanted to earn a few extra bucks so he could spend two days off at the port.

Nor did you see Ms. Lapislazuli's house. Misery, grime and mud, and the smell of sickness and rot on all sides. That is Veroboar. That and a thousand shockingly rich and powerful women who do what they want with the rest of the world."

"You can't trust women," I said.

I have four daughters; if one of them hears me, she'll strangle me. Especially the third who is also a lawyer, God save us. But Trafalgar cut me off:

"From what I've seen, men either."

I had to agree and I haven't even traveled like Trafalgar Medrano. Mexico, the United States, Europe and places like those, and I spend the summers at Punta del Este, by the sea. But I've never been to Seskundrea or to Anandaha-A.

"It could be that you think I was, shall we say, too prudent, but you're going to see that I was right. I realized that if the blonde from the Central Government caught me, she would quarter me for sure."

He finished the coffee and opened another packet of filterless dark cigarettes.

"The skinny waiter gave me some details as soon as I told him I was in trouble, although I didn't tell him what kind of trouble. The position of The Thousand isn't hereditary; they're not from notable families. They come from the countryside. Any girl who's pretty, I mean very pretty, and manages, which is certainly not easy, to get together a certain sum before she begins to wrinkle, can aspire to be one of The Thousand. If she makes it, she repudiates her family, her past, and her social class. The others educate her, polish her, and afterwards they turn her loose. And the only thing she has to do from then on is have a good time, keep getting richer because everybody works for her, and govern Veroboar. They don't have children. It is supposed that they are virgins and immortal. The people suspect nonetheless that they are not immortal. I know they're not virgins."

"Yours wasn't."

"The others aren't either, I'll bet my soul. They don't have children, but they make love."

"With whom? The Thousand Men?"

"There aren't any Thousand Men. I suppose they do it secretly with each other. But officially, once a year, at the Secretariat of Private Communication. They apply and while they wait for an answer, the rest congratulate them and send them little presents and give parties for them. The Secretariat always answers yes, of course and then they go to their houses, dismiss the servants, arrange everything, turn on the machines and go to bed. With the machines. Like the one I turned off. The machines give them two things: first, visual, auditory and tactile hallucinations, all kinds, that respond to the model they chose, which is now programmed into the machine. The model can exist or not, it can be the doorman at the Ministry or a monster imagined by them or, in my case, a character from the damned comic books that I myself sold to the mechanic. And second, all the sensations of orgasm. So Ms. Lapislazuli was in seventh heaven with what she thought were the effects of the machine and she thought, I imagine, that the illusion of going to bed with Mandrake was perfect. How was it not going to be perfect, poor kitten, since I arrived just in time. The electronic romance lasts a few days, the waiter didn't know how many, and afterwards they return, with bells on, to govern and act like kings. Like queens."

"The waiter told you all this?"

"Yes. Not as I'm telling you but full of mythological details and fabulous explanations. While I was packing my suitcase. He even helped me. I closed it and left running because I already knew that the pots were boiling over and why, and the waiter was right behind me. Such courage caught my attention. But while we ran down the three flights of stairs he started to tell me, stammering, that he had a daughter more beautiful and blonder than Ver. That's what he said."

"Ver?"

"The sun. And that he was saving up so that she could be one of The Thousand. I stopped cold at the second floor and told him he was crazy, that if he loved her he would let her marry the fried pie vendor or the cobbler and sit down to wait for grandchildren. But he was crazy, and didn't listen to me, and if he did, he paid no attention: he asked if I was rich. When I tell you that you can't trust men either . . ."

"You bribed him."

"I kept on running down the stairs and he got me a taxi."

"You bribed him."

"Let's not talk about it. I got in the taxi and told the driver, I don't know if he was old or yellowish or both or neither, that I would pay him double if he took me to the space-port post in haste. He flew and I paid him double. I was looking behind me all the time to see if Ms. Lapislazuli had sent the dogs after me."

"She hadn't sent anything after you."

"Don't be foolish. I got away by a hair. I turned on the engines but I was still on the ground when they arrived with sirens and searchlights and machine guns. They began to shoot and I took off. They must have shot everyone else for letting me escape. Or perhaps they quartered them instead of me."

"What an escape."

He drank his coffee and patted his wallet.

"Wait," I told him, "my treat. To celebrate your return."

"I was not for celebrations," he doubted before putting away his wallet. "I detoured a little and went to Naijale II. There you can sell anything. And buy for peanuts a plant that the chemists from Oen use to make a perfume that can't be compared with any other. But while I was there I never took out my merchandise, and I didn't buy anything. I went to a good hotel and I spent a week eating well and sleeping as I could. Aside from that the only thing I did was go to the beach and watch television. I didn't drink, I didn't look at women, and I didn't read comic books. And I assure you that on Naijale II all three are first quality. Afterwards I returned. I had a nightmarish trip, sleeping in snatches, erring in my navigation all the time, making calculations that perhaps aren't worth anything because I don't know how long the pregnancy period lasts on Veroboar. I didn't ask the waiter and if I had asked him he would have told me about his wife's pregnancy and she must be an old wrinkled woman and more squalid than him, and how should I know if The Thousand have the same physiology as common women? How do I know if they're not changed somehow? How do I know if they can even get pregnant? And if they can, how do I know if Ms. Lapislazuli got pregnant that night? By Mandrake? How do I know if The Thousand aren't machines themselves or if they have shot or done something worse to the skinny waiter's daughter just like all of those who aspired to be like them, so they can keep the money and continue making love with other machines?"

"You were in bed with her, Traf. Was she a woman?"

"Yes. I think so."

"Pity," I told him. "If they were machines you wouldn't have any reason to return to Veroboar."

I paid, and we got up and left. When we walked out, it had stopped raining.

Alicia Jurado

Alicia Jurado was born in Buenos Aires in 1922. She pursued a doctorate in natural sciences at the University of Buenos Aires but later dedicated her life to writing. In 1961 she took courses in English literature at the University of London. From 1966 to 1967 she was a John Simon Guggenheim Memorial Foundation Fellow, working on a biography of W. H. Hudson, which was published in 1971. She has been a member of the Board of Directors of the Argentine National Arts Fund; she is an elected member of the Argentine Academy of Letters and an honorary member of the Chilean Academy of Language. She has lectured in the United States, Scotland, and Spain. In 1986 she was invited to give the Jorge Luis Borges Lecture at the annual meeting of the Anglo-Argentine Society, in London. In 1990 she was the Argentine delegate to the Anglo-Argentine Conference in England, sponsored by the Argentine Council for International Relations. She is a highly respected author in

Argentina and abroad. She is a contributor to the magazine *Sur,* directed by Victoria Ocampo, and to the newspapers *La Prensa* and *La Nación.* She has received, among other honors, the Municipal Prize for Novels, the Municipal First Prize for Essays, the National Literature Prize, the Alberdi-Sarmiento Interamerican Prize, and the First National Prize for her critical works and essays written between 1977 and 1980. She avoids the limelight and thinks of her writing as something she does for pleasure. Her personal library is lined with rows and rows of books in English, French, Italian, and Spanish, evidence of her broad background and education, and of her interest in culture. Her fiction usually takes place in refined and educated atmospheres and social milieus, and her characters usually talk about literature, music, painting, and of their travels in Europe. Peace and tranquility are necessary for her writing; she finds both in her country home, where she works.

Publications

La cárcel y los hierros (The jail and the irons). Buenos Aires: Goyanarte, 1961.

Genio y figura de Jorge Luis Borges (Genius and figure of Jorge Luis Borges). Buenos Aires: EUdeBA, 1964.

Leguas de polvo y sueño (Miles of dust and dreams). Buenos Aires: Losada, 1965.

Los rostros del engaño (The faces of deceit). Buenos Aires: Losada, 1968.

Vida y Obra de W. H. Hudson (W. H. Hudson's life and work). Buenos Aires: Emecé, 1971.

El cuarto mandamiento (The fourth commandment). Buenos Aires: Emecé, 1971.

En soledad vivía (In loneliness she lived). Buenos Aires: Goncourt, 1972.

El escocés errante: R. B. Cunninghame Graham (The wandering Scot: R. B. Cunninghame Graham). Buenos Aires: Emecé, 1978.

Los hechiceros de la tribu (The sorcerers of the tribe). Buenos Aires: Emecé, 1980.

"Victoria Ocampo y la condición de la mujer" (Victoria Ocampo and the woman's condition). *Sur* 348 (1981): 137–42.

"Victoria Ocampo, mi predecesora" (Victoria Ocampo, my predecessor). *Boletín de la Academia Argentina de Letras* 46/179–82 (January 1981): 81–95.

Páginas de Jorge Luis Borges (Jorge Luis Borges' pages). Buenos Aires: Celtia, 1982. (In collaboration with Jorge Luis Borges).

"La literatura y sus protagonistas: Homenaje a Jorge Luis Borges" (Literature and its protagonists: homage to Jorge Luis Borges) *La Nación,* 24 August 1986: 1.

Descubrimiento del mundo: Memorias (Discovery of the world: Memoirs). Buenos Aires: Emecé, 1989.

"La amistad entre Gabriela Mistral y Victoria Ocampo" (The friendship between Gabriela Mistral and Victoria Ocampo). *Boletín de la Academia Argentina de Letras* 54/213–14 (July–December 1989): 523–61.

El mundo de la palabra (Memorias) (The world of the word: Memoirs). Buenos Aires: Emecé, 1990.

Las despedidas (The farewells). Buenos Aires: Emecé, 1992.

"Autobiografía" (Autobiography). *Alba de América: Revista Literaria* 11/20–21 (July 1993): 87–98.

Secondary Sources

Borges, Jorge Luis. "Alicia Jurado." *Boletín de la Academia Argentina de Letras* 46/179–82 (January 1981): 75–79.

———. "Darío, Enrique Banchs, 'Homenaje a Góngora,' Alicia Jurado." *Hispamérica: Revista de Literatura* 17/50 (August 1988): 63–72.

Flori, Mónica Roy. *Streams of Silver: Six Contemporary Women Writers from Argentina.* Lewisburg, Penn.: Associated University Presses, 1995.

Pucciarelli, Elsa. "Alicia Jurado, hechicera de la tribu." *Sur* 348 (1981): 41–48.

Interview

1. Which authors have had the greatest influence on your work?

   So many, that it is hard for me to choose among them; I would have to say that I am influenced by all the literature I have read since my childhood, and especially by English literature. One of my favorite authors has been Aldous Huxley, but his influence is more in terms of ideas than of style. I would hope that my thirty-plus years of friendship with Jorge Luis Borges and my having worked with him on many occasions have given me some of his clarity and concision, since the rest isn't transmissible.

2. When did you begin to write, and why?

   I have always written for fun, since I was very young. I began my career as a scientist and I never thought of publishing anything until I was over thirty. I write because I like to and I cannot conceive of any other reason to do so. In Argentina you can't make money with it, and the vanities of success do not interest me.

3. Does the political situation influence your choice of themes?

   I have never used a political theme as a plot, but it is natural that, in novels that take place in Buenos Aires, there are passing references to some governments under which we have suffered.

4. Have you encountered difficulties with publishing houses?

   All writers, regardless of sex, have great difficulties these days trying to publish their books. In better times, I never noticed any discrimination against women.

5. What do you think of feminism?

   I am a feminist in the strict acceptance of the term, that is, I believe that intelligence has no sex and that women and men should enjoy equal rights and opportunities. I don't understand, on the other hand, the so-called feminists who say they hate men, because that is anti-biological. I know that the male is not too rational, but he does have great charm. Besides, I am alarmed by the claiming of our rights in the hands of women who pursue them with disgusting violence or make a show of sexual anomalies, because it is worrisome to see a just cause defended by bad attorneys.

6. How would you describe Argentina's women readers?

I don't have any way of keeping statistics, but I believe Argentine women tend to read more than the men, at least more fiction. Of course, one would have to see more data to be sure about what the majority of them read.

Selection from *Los hechiceros de la tribu*

In *Los hechiceros de la tribu* Jurado traces a realistic, faithful representation of Argentine intellectual life from the point of view of those who cultivate it most assiduously: the writers. The characters of her novel are not drawn with the intention of reflecting anyone in particular, according to her disclaimer in the "Notice to the Reader" that opens the collection. They are, rather, archetypes one could find, according to the character Horace, in any intellectual milieu, in Buenos Aires, Paris, New York, or London. The story selected not only describes the activity of writing and its practitioners, but also reflects on that process and on its purpose. In the story, Horace decides to author a book about the literary profession and about the writers he knows, changing their names, mixing their characteristics and identities, making the characters into generic types, very much as Jurado herself does in writing the novel. In the chapter we chose, Lilita throws a party at her house to celebrate her discovery of a young, homosexual poet. The characters that parade through the pages, with their egos, pretensions, and secret histories, capture the cultural and "refined" Argentine literary milieu perfectly.

Notice to the Reader

Any similarities between these fictional characters and actual writers, living or dead, are strictly coincidental. I do not like novels in code and my intent was only to create generic character types, as varied and picturesque in this curious business as in any other. The only thing I took from reality (besides, of course, the abundance of personal experience that is a novelist's prime material) are the texts submitted to a literary contest that I have included, with slight variations, in the first chapter; documents that my limited imagination would not have allowed me to invent.

A. J.

Chapter VI

The party at Lilita's house brought together, as one could imagine, a good number of writers, supplemented by other people involved in the bookselling industry and still others having to do with the administration of what—for lack of a better word—one would have to call culture. One could also find a few businessmen, Lilita's husband's friends, and the usual visual artists, academics, diplomats and military officers. To this representative multitude one would have to add Lilita's own personal friends, who weren't artists of any sort, and photographers from two widely read magazines, sent by their editors after they had been pestered repeatedly by the hostess.

The poet guest of honor, as Horacio commented to his wife, wasn't merely homosexual; he was a caricature of a homosexual in a vaudeville sketch done in very poor taste. He moved languidly through the rooms like a gazelle and, rather than sit, he draped himself on a couch or an armchair as if he were made of gauze. After much pleading from Lilita, he condescended to read three or four poems from his book, and the crowd applauded politely although no one had understood a word and it wouldn't have made any difference, in terms of the poems' intelligibility, if he had read them from right to left like an Arabic manuscript. Lilita, dressed in a sea-green tunic overlaid with color-coordinated embroidered beads, revealed mallow-colored harem-style pants under the hem. "It's the latest fashion in Paris," she said, swaying her hips and shaking an armful of bracelets. Her golden sandals allowed her scarlet-painted toenails to peep through which, in the proximity of those harem-style trousers, made Graciela close her eyes in pain. Poor Lilita! She had never had the slightest idea as to how to combine colors. On the other hand, she did know how to entertain her guests, and her cocktail parties were famous for abounding in dishes that didn't usually appear in Buenos Aires any longer; the caviar, smoked salmon, prawns, all kinds of cheeses and hot sandwiches offered a gastronomic compensation for Carlitos' poetry.

Horacio, being quite a gourmet but having his diet very restricted at home by his wife's vigilance (she watched his waistline), saw that Graciela was conversing with Rubén Pietrabianca and slid toward the dining room where, on the table, two magnificent turkeys and a glazed ham had just been deposited, already carved so that the guests could make their own sandwiches with the little rolls from a neighboring platter. Turning towards him, trying to smile with her mouth full, was the beautiful face of Cecilia Velarde.

"Hello! It's been ages! What's happening in your life?"

"The same as always: writing."

"How lucky, to be able to spend all your time writing! I wish I could say the same! But there's no doubt that this is a man's world: men always have a woman beside them who takes care of buying the groceries and running the household, and, if there are children, getting them out from underfoot when Daddy is working and keeping them quiet when Daddy is inspired. So like that, it is easy isn't it? Daddy's peace and quiet is sacred, but Mommy's, well, we know what happens."

"You could leave home."

"Don't think the idea doesn't tempt me. There I am, pulling my hair out trying to write a dialogue, and every five minutes: Mom! How much is seven times nine? Ma'am, we've run out of detergent. Mom! Can I go to the movies this afternoon? Ma'am, they're on the phone to ask you for a contribution for homeless dogs. Mom! What does polyfaceted mean? And so on, all day long. And at night, when I finally get a little peace, Juan José gets home and he wants to spend time with me or else we have to go out somewhere. They may call me a feminist, but I assure you that there are times when I feel like taking to the streets with a poster declaring *A woman deserves a life! Freedom from domestic-slavery! Down with children!*

Cecilia laughed, with her intelligent eyes fixed on the turkey, as if the bird, rapidly being plucked by dozens of avid hands, could offer a solution to her complicated life. Besides being a very good friend of his, she was Horacio's favorite writer: not an improvised one, like so many others, but an educated woman, capable of reading Shakespeare and Dante in the original and of comprehending perfectly why they were geniuses. A refined writer, temperate, with a delicate sense of humor and an instinctive poetry; her stories had a special grace, almost ungraspable, whose subtlety Horacio envied at times.

"What do you think of Lilita's new discovery?"

Arching her eyebrows in a overly expressive gesture, Cecilia served herself some turkey.

"More or less like all the rest, but this one's a bit more flirtatious. Look how he is looking at Serafín."

In effect, the young poet was conversing animatedly with an old poet, known for his preferences in that arena. From that conversation and from others that no doubt would follow, they might develop some pact of mutual assistance in which the mature poet, already deified and with influential ties, would open some doors for the neophyte, while the latter would offer— "What could he offer?"—Horacio asked Cecilia. "His youth? His admiration? His slim adolescent figure, to be displayed like a boutonniere throughout of Buenos Aires salons?"

"Not much more," murmured Cecilia, with that neutral voice that she always reserved for saying something particularly biting. "The boy seems better prepared to receive than to give."

Making her way through the compact cordon that defended the table, Georgina Balcarce approached to say hello. Worse than mediocre as a poet, she was nevertheless a good person, always inclined to do favors and to organize dinners to salute colleagues who were leaving on vacation or who had received one prize or another.

"I didn't see you at the book store. Didn't you go?"

Simultaneously, Cecilia and Horacio mumbled vague excuses.

"What a pity! It was lovely: there were tons of people. Lots of copies were sold."

"You spoke, right?" asked Horacio. "What did you think of the book?"

"Wonderful. You must buy it. There is a great repressed passion!"

"It will soon be liberated," said Cecilia, with a slight nod, intended only for Horacio, in the direction of Carlitos. The former, who had the courage to stand by his opinions, replied that he had just heard some of the poems and, as he hadn't understood a single line, wasn't in any position to offer his judgment.

"Poetry isn't meant to be understood, but to be felt!" exclaimed Georgina, scandalized. "You, fiction writers, don't know what it's like to come close to that mystery. You don't have a cosmic perception."

"That's it; we aren't very cosmic," said Cecilia, very seriously.

"And not too telluric, either," added Horacio. "We lack direct knowledge of the soothsayer and the fortune-teller. We have to move forward painstakingly, like Ponce de León in the Florida swamps, step by step, by way of syllogisms, in order to understand the universe even halfway."

"How informative to find you!" shouted a jovial voice behind Horacio. "I was just trying to call you on the phone, but no one answered, or perhaps the lines were down; we know how they work about half the time. We've organized a cycle of lectures for this spring at the International Writers' Union— I'm the secretary now, did you know?—and we would like very much for you to give one. We've arranged a beautiful room, lent to us by the chain The Silver Thimble; the general manager is a friend of our vice president."

"Well, hello, Alfredo! How are you?" murmured Horacio, hiding his panic. "A lecture about what?"

"About anything; that's the least important thing. We need about six speakers and we would like you to be one of them."

"But, why do you organize these things that don't make anyone happy?" Horacio dared to ask. "It takes a tremendous amount of work to convince people to speak and it's no less arduous to drag the members to the talks; and all of that, what's it for? To make everyone waste time they didn't have or could have spent much more happily doing something that they liked."

Alfredo Martínez, the brand-new secretary of the International Writers' Union, was perplexed, as if suddenly he'd been shown a heretofore unseen truth.

"What strange thoughts you have, man!" he defended himself weakly. "We must do something besides have dinners, because if not, the Union is reproached for not doing anything for the culture, for having a Board of Directors that is useless, or because no one does anything . . . in short, it's a way for the Union to appear in the newspapers, to get a little publicity . . . And you, Cecilia? Won't you give a lecture for us about the short story in Argentina, for example?"

"Me? It can be about the short story, though some time later on, provided that the maid returns; she went to visit her sick aunt in Santiago del Estero two weeks ago. But not about the short story in Argentina. Don't put those limitations on me. I don't want anything that contains the word "Argentina," or "national," or "domestic," or "vernacular." You can believe that I adore my country; my great-grandparents and my great-great-grandparents were born here and this land is ingrained in my very bone marrow. But I don't need to be declaring it all day long, with those anxieties of the nouveau riche or the recent immigrant, who has to spend his life reminding himself where he is so that he wouldn't forget and believe himself still to be in his country of origin."

"We could find another topic . . ."

"The same thing happens to me with symbols and heroes," continued Cecilia, interrupting him. "I believe one should use them in their proper place and time, with the respect they're due, because they are not things to be misused by the general population. It made me ill to see people, the day of the World Cup championship, take to the streets with the flag worn like a scarf or a poncho, or dragging it through the streets, tied to the hoods of automobiles."

"Last year I was in a northern province, which I will not name," Horacio chimed in, "and I saw the flag painted even on water towers. They had also used it to ruin the view in a park that before had been rather pretty, with old trees and turn-of-the-century statues."

"It's the same with General San Martín," continued Cecilia, emboldened. "Is it right for an honorable and meritorious man, through no fault of his own, to be made insufferable to his own compatriots because he's forced upon them at all times? Can you imagine anything more unjust?"

"Okay, Cecilia, how about the short story in general?" said Alfredo, returning to his duty. "Would the last half of September suit you?"

Taken by surprise, the poor thing had no choice but to agree. Horacio dug in his heels even further.

"I'm writing a novel" he argued. "I can't write novels and prepare lectures at the same time."

"And what about an old lecture, one you might have given in some other city? Anything!" implored Alfredo. "Something from a few years ago, that people would have forgotten."

Horacio sighed.

"All right. I'm just putting my papers in order these days; I'll see what I can find. Could you call me in a few days?"

"You can count on it," and the afflicted secretary, calmer, began to cast his vision towards the four cardinal points, like a cat in search of its next prey. "Excuse me. There's Serafín Díaz Collado, who will suit me to a tee. See you later!"

"What I can't stand about Lucio Tilatti," said Rubén Pietrabianca to Graciela, "is his vanity. I know he has talent, but he must not feel too secure if he has to have everybody verifying it for him continuously."

"Vanity is very much a part of his profession, it seems to me," interrupted a man who had been introduced a while earlier, although neither of them remembered his name.

"They're not all like that," Graciela hastened to respond. "My husband, for example, is the least conceited man in the world. On the contrary, he hates publicity and I've never heard him admit that anything he's written has turned out well."

"I'm not vain, either," said Pietrabianca. "Even though I won the Municipal First Prize for Poetry, and the Second National, and the Laurel from the Writers' Association, and the Goose Quill from the International Union. But Tilatti is insufferable: if they're not talking about him all the time he gets depressed and leaves."

"At least he's a good writer; others are just as vain with only a fraction of his intelligence."

"The one who just came in, for example."

At that moment a woman made her way across the room, tall, about fifty years old, robust and stout with a forbidding face; she wasn't ugly, perhaps, but there was in her penetrating look an obstinate resolution that didn't foretell anything good for the rest of humanity.

"That one," continued Rubén, implacably, "would be capable of selling her fourteen-year-old daughter to get something published on the first page of some big newspaper's literary supplement. The best she's ever managed is page four, as far as I know. She won't even look at me, because my poems are always on the front page, and highlighted."

"What's her name?" asked the man, who knew nothing about literature.

"Adelaida Carranza. But that's not her real name, it's a pseudonym. I think she has a last name that's Russian, or Polish," explained Rubén. "She's a celebrated author of novels that are more or less pornographic, which sell like hotcakes, naturally. Items of quality have no market." His face became somber, remembering the piles of his nine books of poems, self-financed, that crowded the warehouses of the publishing house that had loaned him its name.

"I don't like her at all," Graciela offered. "Luckily they have never let her become a member of the Union; Horacio told me that they blackballed her three times."

"It's not for lack of trying. She's been intimate with all the governments, from the first presidency of the Unnamable One up through the latest military government, without exception. Look how she went straight for the brigadier general, and how enthusiastically she's talking to him. What do you bet she thinks she can get in through that route!"

"In spite of the three blackballs, she keeps looking for a way to become a member, and pestering half the world so that they'll let her join."

"I should tell her that they don't blackball others who have better moral credentials, but who, as writers, are much worse. There's the case of Jovita Castro de Villanueva, whose literary vocation awoke at sixty-some years: she got someone to publish half a dozen articles about "El Tigre" [a resort North of Buenos Aires] from her youth and then she never wrote another line. However, she was a friend of several members of the board of directors, who waited until others (more upright) were absent and they voted her in without even looking at her *vita*, which surely never existed. Didn't Jovita come today? I haven't seen her."

The unknown man, who was taking small sips from his glass of champagne, arrived at the conclusion that Rubén Pietrabianca was unbearable and that he ought to save that very nice woman from him. He pointed out to her that she hadn't eaten anything and he offered to accompany her to the dining room; although Rubén, also hungry, followed closely behind them, Alfredo Martínez cut him off at the pass to ask him if he wouldn't like, in the month of November, to give a lecture about contemporary poetry for the cultural cycle of the International Writers' Union. Graciela, moving toward the carcass of the ham, because there wasn't a shred of the turkey left, saw her husband gobbling a hot appetizer while he was conversing with his old friend Rafael O'Connor.

The centerpiece, made of pink and white carnations, was the only thing that was still untouched in the midst of the devastation; Graciela observed its curly petals and the soft gray-green tone of its stems and leaves, a fragment of beauty that had remained there arbitrarily, in the heavy silver bowl on the damask tablecloth that had been spotless at the beginning. But now they were coming to take away the carcasses and replace them with fruit and meringue pies, little caramel custards and chocolate bonbons. The waiters, skillfully circulating their huge trays, offered ice cream. Horacio, who hadn't seen Graciela, served himself of everything, as carefree as a child; she, maternally, turned her back so he wouldn't feel spied on if he happened to see her.

"Dante Gabriel Rossetti," said O'Connor. "No one takes any notice of him, or else they think he is a Pre-Raphaelite painter. But his poems! He's capable of saying so much with so few words! Perhaps that's the most difficult virtue: economy. Anyone can write five pages describing how a woman is falling in love with her brother-in-law, until both of them realize it, and boom! a catastrophe. But one needs the other Dante, Alighieri, to suggest it all in a single line, when Francesca and Paolo together read the book of chivalry:

Quel giorno più non vi leggemmo avante

"That is a marvel. Seven words," he counted them on his fingers, "to say what Adelaida Carranza would have described in an entire chapter of minute obscenities. Those are the things that tear a person's heart out," he added, accepting some ice cream. "It makes you want to throw everything out the window and dedicate yourself to business, which, furthermore pays the bills."

"But you dedicate yourself to business, anyway."

"Yes, I know; if not, how could I feed my children? But to go back to Rossetti, do you remember a short little poem called 'The Woodspurge?' It's a plant. The poet, desperate in the middle of a forest, stares, with his heart in pieces, at the shape of a flower; some time later, the only memory that remains out of all that affliction is that the woodspurge has three little flowers on each stem. Once, I recognized the plant in a forest in Hampshire County and the emotion almost gave me a coronary."

"That's because literature is miraculous in two ways. First, because creating beauty with words—those who can do it, mind you—is already a miracle. And second, because what one becomes acquainted with through this medium is somehow annointed and resplendent. I'm not saying that daffodils aren't pretty in themselves, but Wordsworth—that "host of golden daffodils"—has added to their beauty another, which moves us as not even the most splendid unsung tropical flowers from some African country can. The same thing happens with landscapes. One could write a treatise about the emotive value of literary or historical associations; surely someone has already done it. I remember once I was traveling through Greece in the middle of a stony, unplowed field, capable of saddening even the most optimistic person, and the guide pointed out to us that precisely there, in those mountains, was the steep mountain pass of the Thermopylae. Then, the landscape was transfigured, the light changed, the stones revived and that landscape stopped being a wasteland and became sacred ground."

"But literary associations are somewhat stranger still," replied O'Connor. "History, after all, is more concrete. One goes to Bonn, is shown the piano where Beethoven played, and feels the urge to kneel right there on the floor, even at the risk of leaving openmouthed the hordes of tourists present, who are listening to explanations in three languages without hearing any of them, because the only thing they ask is when lunchtime is. But Beethoven was made of flesh and blood, after all; on the other hand, what did Shakespeare do to the flowers that Ophelia names with sadness or Perdita with joy, so that they will never be the same as they were before? For you or for me, of course; I suppose that for the young man that Lilita introduced tonight, they won't have changed in the slightest."

"What did you think of him?"

Rafael answered briefly and precisely, without sparing any vulgarity.

"Yes, I know. But I'm referring to the way he writes."

"His writings? He writes something? He does what so many others do: he puts words together that are more or less euphoric, and from time to time he shocks you with one that is entirely *apoetic,* such as "real state" or "economic conduction," and with that he believes he has made a poem. But you'll see that he'll be showing up all over the place now, because he knows where his bread is buttered. First he pursues and seduces Lilita, God knows how."

"Reading everything she's written and commenting on it flawlessly and thoroughly. She told me herself."

"Oh, good! If he did that, it's clear that the boy has guts. And afterwards, there are her comrades; they are a tightly-knit group of eight who make the Masons seem like an open society."

At that moment, Graciela discreetly approached. Horacio swallowed the last bonbon and resigned himself to drinking a little cup of coffee.

"What's that you were saying, Rafael? It's been a long time. How's the new novel coming along?"

"It's coming, little by little. But it's making me suffer."

O'Connor was what is usually called a Catholic writer; that is, a writer for whom his religion was a preponderant theme in his work. Like those of Graham Greene, whom he admired greatly, his novels revolved around irresolvable conflicts: those set forth by people who believe in the obligatory nature of an established conduct before the days of psychoanalysis, contraceptives and sexual liberation. Neither in his work nor in his life was he helped by his Irish blood, which made him prone to fanaticism and to passionate love affairs. He had a patient wife and a patient confessor, who found reflected in his novels what the confessor knew and the wife suspected; but, in spite of the irresistible infidelities that dragged him periodically into the gullet of hell, his domestic life was peaceful and his five children adored him. He was, besides, an excellent prose writer and an acute psychologist; the reader who shared his beliefs, or who was inclined to accept those beliefs in his characters, could be profoundly moved. He began to relate, at Graciela's request, the plot of the book he was writing, but when the sin was just beginning to threaten the protagonist he interrupted himself suddenly, looking with horror towards the door as if Lucifer himself had come in.

"My guardian angel!" he shouted. "We're lost!"

A short, fat woman, resplendent in sequins and topped off with an enormous turban, was entering with a majestic stride.

"What's happened, man? Have you seen a ghost?"

"Much worse. I've seen Eleonora de las Nieves."

"Is that her name?" asked Graciela.

"Only the devil knows what her name is. Whoever finds out what it is will be struck by lightning, surely; but she insists on being called Eleonora de las Nieves everywhere she goes."

"I've never seen her before," said Horacio. "Why does she make you so nervous?"

"She's completely nuts and she has the incomprehensible gift of making connections with everyone. Besides, she is the high priestess of a literary circle that meets in a café on Mayo Avenue, and for a long time she's been trying to drag me there, to fraternize with a bunch of horrid poets of both sexes, who read their creations all through the night, until dawn. From time to time they find a victim and they take him or her to the *sabbath,* to speak to them about something. I've already told her till I'm blue in the face that I'm not a poet, but it doesn't seem to matter; she asked me to talk to them about the existential anguish that can be seen, according to her, in my novels."

"And she writes, too?"

"Poems. It's better that we not mention them. A third-grader would be ashamed to show them to her classmates. Do you think she's seen me?"

"No one can make you go, if you don't want to. Give her some pretext."

"I told her last time that I was leaving on a spiritual retreat with the Trappist monks; afterwards I had to go to confession, because it was a lie."

"Can't you just tell her no, frankly and openly?"

"I can see you've never tried to say no to Eleonora. Have you heard about those sea creatures called remoras that attach themselves to a boat and then can't be pried loose? Well, they're fickle and weak-willed compared to her. I've got to run away, while I still have time."

And Rafael bid farewell to his friends and took refuge in the kitchen, from where, since he knew the house well, he could return to the entrance hall through passageways that Eleonora de las Nieves didn't even suspect existed.

Horacio looked at his watch.

"What do you think if we leave too? You must be tired."

"Whatever you like. No, I'm not tired, but I don't have any particular interest in staying, either, although I do enjoy observing this world."

"Tomorrow I can take you to the zoo, which is more entertaining."

"Who's to say? I imagine that you're going to have a good time, with your novel, describing all of this."

"Do you think I could do it?"

"You've done things that are more difficult."

"Don't believe it. Tragedy is easier than comedy. Besides, tragedy and comedy are two sides of the same coin: it's just a question of changing the point of view. Lilita, for example: everyone thinks she's a comic character, but how much sadness there is at the heart of her failure as a writer, although she may be very successful with what now could be called public relations! She married Benavidez for money, and although she manages well enough, she's not happy; I believe she lost a child, also, a long time ago. And Eleonora, what an abyss of solitude must have led her to form her circle of calamitous poets, every bit as bad as she is, playing at culture the way that Marie Antoinette played at milkmaid in Versailles! But Marie Antoinette's game was the whim of a bored queen, and Eleonora's game is an atrocious farce; sometimes she must be aware that she is ignorant, ridiculous and gaudy, and that serious people bolt as soon as they see her, like Rafael did. And then there's Rafael himself, who is a very good writer and an intelligent sort, but he has his extramarital affairs, which he can't even enjoy because his remorse won't let him. He writes tragedies about his problems; someone else could write hysterically funny comedies."

Once in the car on the way home, Graciela observed: "The bad thing is that you're going to upset all these people. Many will see themselves in your book and they won't like it."

"No. It would never occur to me to copy any of them. On the contrary, I'm going to shuffle them like a deck of cards: I'll disguise the essayist as a poet, the man as a woman, the married woman as single, and on and on. And then I'll shuffle them again, to swap their characteristics: I'll attribute the stinginess of the elderly novelist to the young critic, and the dramatist's political opinions to the girl who's just begun publishing her first short stories. It will be like those cardboard figures that we used to play with as kids, divided into three parts, and you could switch the heads, the trunks or the legs."

"And that hodgepodge, could it be convincing?"

"Why not? Human beings are complex and contradictory. Anyway, I'm not interested in portraying or caricaturing anyone; the characters will be archetypes. You will find them in any big city, Buenos Aires, Paris, New York or London. Lilita, just to name one, is identical to a writer I met in Rome, at the International Union Congress; the only difference was the face."

"And how will you disguise yourself, I would like to know? As an aspiring fat man who escapes from his wife at parties to camp beside the table, eating like a glutton?"

"That wouldn't be a disguise, sweet heart; it would be the sad reality. But I don't know if I could disguise myself, except on the surface, such as my physical appearance or my family. The most important thing, which is the writing profession, I'll have to relate from my own experience. Besides, don't forget that I have to answer Otto's challenge: write a novel about a happy marriage."

They entered the apartment and Horacio, who was feeling particularly affectionate after his third glass of champagne, put his arm around Graciela's shoulders.

"In the novel I'll be an excellent writer," he murmured, "and that's disguise enough."

"You're always talking nonsense!"

"And I'll write a revolutionary novel, without bedroom scenes, about a modest, calm character, the very enemy of adventure, who returns from a party at midnight with the unspeakable purpose of making love to his wife."

"Not even the parish priest will read it," answered Graciela sweetly. "You're going to bankrupt your editor."

■ María Rosa Lojo

María Rosa Lojo was born in Buenos Aires in 1954, the daughter of Spaniards who emigrated after the Civil War. She studied in the College of Liberal Arts at the National University of Buenos Aires. In 1988 she was chosen by the Executive Committee of Buenos Aires' Feria del Libro to serve as a representative of the new writers of the 1980s in the roundtable "Encounter of Young Spanish and Argentine Novelists." Her many awards include Honorable Mention in the Emecé Narrative Contest; the 1982 Coca-Cola First Prize for Literary Criticism; First Prize for poetry in the Exposición Feria Internacional del Libro for the biennium 1984–85; the 1986 National Arts Fund Prize for Novel; the 1985 Short Story Prize from the National Arts Fund; the 1991 Fundación Antorchas Prize for literature; and the Alfredo Roggiano 1991 First Prize for Poetry. Lojo also obtained a scholarship from the Fondo Nacional de las Artes for "¿Qué ciudad es ésa . . . ?" and was named a finalist for the 1994 Planeta Prize for best unpublished novel. She is a researcher for the CONICET (Council of Scientific and Technical Investigations) in the Argentine Institute of Literature. She has published numerous studies about Argentine and Spanish literature in diverse Argentine and foreign media. She collaborates on a permanent basis as a critic for the Literary Supplement of *La Nación* and also periodically publishes essays, fiction, and poetry in *Clarín*. Her assiduous labor in criticism, essays, poetry, and fiction has resulted in more than one hundred fifty publications to date.

Publications

"La mujer simbólica en la narrativa de Leopoldo Marechal" (The symbolic woman in Leopoldo Marechal's narrative). In *Ensayos de crítica literaria*. Buenos Aires: Editorial de Belgrano, 1983.

Visiones (Visions). Buenos Aires: Exposición Feria Internacional El Libro, 1984.

La poética neorromántica de Ernesto Sábato (Ernesto Sábato's neo-romantic poetics). Buenos Aires: García Cambeiro, 1985.

Marginales (Marginal). Buenos Aires: Epsilon Editora, 1986.

Canción perdida en Buenos Aires al Oeste (Lost song in western Buenos Aires). Buenos Aires: Torres Agüero, 1987.

La hermenéutica de Paul Ricoeur y la constitución simbólica del texto literario (Paul Ricoeur's hermeneutics and the symbolic constitution of the literary text). Buenos Aires: García Cambeiro, 1986.

"Funciones de la imaginación elemental en *El Grimorio*, de Enrique Anderson Imbert" (Roles of the elementary imagination in Enrique Anderson Imbert's *El Grimorio*). *Foro Literario: Revista de Literatura y Lenguaje* 10/10–17 (1987): 31–37.

"Alfonsina Storni: Desde diversos ángulos" (Alfonsina Storni: From different angles). Suplemento Literario de *La Nación,* 23 October 1988: 1–2.

"Dos versiones de la utopía: 'Sensatez del círculo,' de Angélica Gorodischer, y 'Utopía de un hombre que está cansado' de Jorge Luis Borges" (Two versions of utopia: Angelica Gorodischer's "Circle's Wisdom" and Jorge Luis Borges' "Utopia of a Tired Man"). In *Mujer y sociedad en América: IV Simposio Internacional,* edited by Juana Alcira Arancibia, 93–104. California: Instituto Literario y Cultural Hispánico, Universidad Autónoma de Baja, 1988.

"La mujer y su 'Oscuro objeto del deseo' en la literatura de Cervantes a Latinoamérica" (The woman and her "Obscure Object of Desire" in literature from Cervantes to Latin America). In *Mujer y sociedad en América: IV Simposio Internacional,* edited by Juana Alcira Arancibia, 25–31. California: Instituto Literario y Cultural Hispánico,Universidad Autónoma de Baja, 1988.

"*Facundo:* La 'barbarie' como poesía de lo original/originario" (*Facundo:* "Barbarism" as poetics of the original/originary). *Letras* 23–24 (1990–91): 59–84.

"'El matadero' de Esteban Echeverría: La sangre derramada y la estética de la 'mezcla'"

(Esteban Echeverria's "The Slaughterhouse": The spilled blood and the aesthetics of the mixture). *Alba de América: Revista Literaria* 9/16–17 (1991): 41–63.

Forma Oculta del Mundo (Hidden form of the world). Buenos Aires: Ultimo Reino, 1991.

"La seducción estética de la barbarie en el *Facundo.*" (The aesthetic seduction of barbarism in *Facundo*). *Estudios Filológicos* 27 (1992): 141–48.

"A quinientos años, desde el país del monte" (Five hundred years after, from the northern country). *Alba de América: Revista Literaria* 10/18–19 (July 1992): 77–92.

"La mujer simbólica en *Abaddon, el exterminador*" (The symbolic woman in *Abaddon, el exterminador*). *Revista Iberoamericana* 58/158 (January–March 1992): 183–92.

"Mirar desde espacios imaginarios" (To look from imaginary spaces). *Alba de América: Revista Literaria* 11/20–21 (July 1993): 41–52.

"La elaboración ficcional de lo autobiográfico en la narrativa Sabatiana" (Fictional elaboration of autobiography in Sábato's narrative). In *Literatura como intertextualidad: IX Simposio International de Literatura,* edited by Juana Alcira Arancibia, 137–49. Buenos Aires: Instituto Literario y Cultural Hispánico, 1993.

La barbarie en la narrativa argentina (siglo XIX) (Barbarism in the Argentine narrative [nineteenth century]). Buenos Aires: Corregidor, 1994.

La pasión de los nómades (Nomads' passion). Buenos Aires: Atlántida, 1994.

"Culminación del héroe, culminación de la escritura" (Culmination of the hero, culmination of writing). Suplemento Literario de *La Nación,* 11 September 1994: 4.

Ernesto Sábato: En busca del original perdido (Ernesto Sábato: Searching for the lost original). In press.

Secondary Sources

Aliberti, Antonio. "Lectura de la inmigración." *Clarín,* 21 July 1988.

Averbach, Margara. "Los rostros de una escritura admirable." *La Razón,* 4 January 1987.

Barros, Fernando. "*Marginales* por María Rosa Lojo." *Guía de Libros. Revista Cultura de la Argentina Contemporánea* 17 (October–November 1986).

Bepre, Julio. "*Visiones,* por María Rosa Lojo." *La Capital,* 13 January 1985.

Didier de Iungman, Nora. "El desencuentro en la novela de María Rosa Lojo." *Gaceta Literaria de Santa Fe* 64 (June 1989).

Diez, Ricardo O. "Canción perdida en Buenos Aires al Oeste." *El Tiempo,* 19 March 1989.

Fares, Gustavo, and Eliana Hermann. "Exilios internos: El viaje en cinco escritoras argentinas." *Hispanic Journal* 15/1 (Spring 1994): 21–29.

———. "Y ahora? Reflexiones acerca de la literatura femenina argentina actual. Forma oculta del mundo de María Rosa Lojo, Metáforas y reflejos de Jorgelina Loubet, y Victoria Ocampo de María Esther Vázquez." *Letras Femeninas* 19/1–2 (Spring–Fall 1993): 121–34.

Fisher, María Raquel. "Intelección filosófica de una novela." *Letras, Universidad Católica Argentina* 19–20 (1988–89): 121–24.

Flannagan, Eduardo. "Ficción que es realidad." *El Tiempo,* 7 May 1988.

Furla, Luis R. "Visiones por María Rosa Lojo." *El Tiempo,* 29 July 1994.

Gayoso, Daniel. "Una exploración del espacio interior: Visiones, de María Rosa Lojo." *Tiempo Argentino,* 30 December 1984.

Gorodischer, Angélica. "María Rosa Lojo, Marginales." *Letras Femeninas* 14/1–2 (1988): 114–16.

Gudiño Kieffer, Eduardo. "Siete personajes encuentran autor." *La Nación,* 2 April 1984.

Hermann, Eliana. "María Rosa Lojo. Forma oculta del mundo." *Chasqui: Revista de Literatura Latinoamericana* 21/2 (November 1992): 82–83.

———. "María Rosa Lojo. La pasión de los nómades." *Hispanic Journal* 16/2 (Fall 1995).

Jorgí, Sebastián Antonio. "Excelente novela de M. R. Lojo." *La Capital,* 27 November 1988.

Liggera, Rubén. "Ficha bibliográfica: Canción perdida en Buenos Aires al Oeste." *La Verdad,* 17 July 1988.

———. "La recreación de dos mitos fundantes en un cuento de María Rosa Lojo." *Explicación de Textos Literarios* 20/1 (1991–92): 47–60.

Muntada, Silvia A. "Los discursos de la novela Canción perdida en Buenos Aires al oeste de María Rosa Lojo." *Alba de América: Revista Literaria* 8/14–15 (July 1990): 115–25.

Nesta, Marta. "María Rosa Lojo: Canción perdida en Buenos Aires al Oeste." *Alba de América: Revista Literaria* 6/10–11 (July 1988): 343–46.

Ortin, Graciela. "Canción perdida en Buenos Aires al Oeste. María Rosa Lojo." *Babel: Revista de Libros* 5 (November 1988).

Pellarolo, Silvia. "María Rosa Lojo: Visiones." *Alba de América: Revista Literaria* 8/9 (July 1987).

Redondo, Víctor. "Lojo, María Rosa: Visiones." *Megafón* 14 (July–December 1984).

Rodríguez Francia, Ana María. "La búsqueda del ser por el lenguaje en la poesía de María Rosa Lojo." *Alba de América: Revista Literaria* 11/221 (July 1993): 333–40.

Roteta, Isabel. "La intertextualidad en Marginales, cuentos de María Rosa Lojo." In *Literatura como intertextualidad: IX Simposio International de Literatura,* edited by Juana Alcira Arancibia, 346–56. Buenos Aires: Instituto Literario y Cultural Hispánico, 1993.

Sabor de Cortázar, Celina. "María Rosa Lojo: Visiones." *Letras de Buenos Aires* 12 (October 1984).

Smerling, Jorge. "Poesía auténtica y brillante." *El diario del Neuquén,* 14 December 1986.

Sosa de Newton, Lily. "María Rosa Lojo: Marginales." *Lucanor* 3 (April 1987).

Terron de Bellomo, Herminia. "La poesía es una canción." *Pregón* 1 March 1992.

Vaianella, Patricia. "Entrevista con María Rosa Lojo." *Alba de América: Revista Literaria* 10/18–19 (July 1992): 419–31.

————. "Visiones por María Rosa Lojo. Prosa poética y musical." *El Tiempo,* 17 March 1985.

Zenborain, Cayetano. "Joven poesía argentina." *Suplemento Cultural Asociación de Abogados de Buenos Aires* 1 (December 1986).

Zuleta, Ignacio. "Visiones." *La Capital,* 2 March 1985.

Interview

1. Which authors have had the greatest influence on your work?

From European literature I have read especially Spanish, Irish, and English authors; to a lesser degree, French, Italian, German, and Russian writers. Among the Latin American ones, Carpentier, García Márquez, Arguedas, Vallejo, Borges, Marechal, Cortázar, Sábato, Olga Orozco, and Murena. Here I'll run the risk of favoritism and insistence, because I specialize as an essayist in Argentine literature. However, I will add a few names, more recent than those, since I consider them very important, like Gorodischer, Gallardo, Laura del Castillo, Abel Posse, Rodolfo Rabanal. To this agglomeration of readings—minimal, to be certain—I would have to add that classical Greek and Latin culture, both in philosophy and in literature, were an essential part of my formation.

I would like, in spite of all this, to raise an objection to the concept of "influences." I never use this word in my work as a critic because it seems a bit mechanical, little suited to characterize the complex process of writing. Writing is an intertextual process, there's no doubt of that, but one which presupposes a profound transfiguration or transformation of the earlier material and makes it a legitimate part of that other structure, which is the new work. I prefer, instead, the word "affinities," which refers to certain coincidences or resonances that are capable of engendering "families" of writers that go beyond any spatial or temporal distances.

2. When did you begin to write, and why?

I was very young; before I was twelve I already knew that I wanted to be a writer, although I also liked painting. My first presentable works emerged, I think, when I was around fourteen. As to why . . . ? I suppose that the fundamental motive, in those adolescent days, was to find my identity, to understand my situation in this world, to give some meaning to the strange life that I felt growing and unfolding within and all around me. These needs continue to be valid, perhaps because the mystery of what is real continues growing in a denser and more complex form for as long as our lives advance.

3. How does the political situation influence your themes?

I think that the political situation always has a bearing in one way or another, because it determines the concrete context wherein we move and live; it isn't possible to escape from it, it is always there, to be affirmed or denied, to be described or to be evaded by a silence which is also charged with meaning. The context is filtered, although it oscillates between the extremes of violent presence and omission, and it is not less significant if treated by omission, because vacuums also have their readers. It was an Argentine professor, living in the United States, the attorney Marta Nesta, who pointed out in a study that my book *Marginales*—the imaginary recreation of historical, literary, or mythical characters who trace the parabola of their lives in a monologue—deliberately juggles the immediate historical context [those stories were written between 1974 and 1980, although they were published in 1986]. Marta Nesta says: "María Rosa Lojo belongs to that generation of Argentines who had to choose between exile or justification, contemporization or denial of the state of affairs. The majority of her compatriots wore themselves out in a game of distorted mirrors, where language was used as a mask to hide the desperation and the pain for those who were not present, dead, or disappeared. She rescued herself from that marginality by searching for the past. Among the classics, the close ancestors of our culture, and in her grandfather, an Andalusian idealist who died in the Spanish Civil War, she searched for the understanding of deeper meanings which would give her a reason to live through the irrationality of her present."

As for my book *Canción perdida en Buenos Aires al Oeste* the political situation is openly displayed, interwoven with the most intimate conflicts of the characters. It's about the family of Juan Manuel Neira, an exile from the Spanish Civil War, and Carmen Albarracín, his wife, whose father and relatives had fought at Franco's side. The children of this marriage live their youth during the years of the Military Process, and the youngest, Luis, dies in the War of the Malvinas Islands.

4. Have you encountered difficulties, as a woman writer, with publishers?

In this moment of total economic crisis I think that all Argentine writers, men and women, have problems with publishers. At any rate, before 1989 it wasn't easy to publish either, unless the author was inclined to pay the costs. In my personal case I could overcome obstacles thanks to my three books being published with prizes: *Visiones,* a poetry book, was published by the Buenos Aires Book Fair, whose prize it won; *Marginales,* a volume of stories, and *Canción perdida en Buenos Aires al Oeste,* a novel, came to light through funding from the National Arts Fund, which usually makes an important purchase of volumes from the publisher for distribution to libraries throughout the country.

5. What do you think of feminism?

If feminism is the fight for equal rights and duties for women and for men, I believe that men should be the first feminists. This feminism would allow them to free themselves from the ambiguous situation of the woman, subservient to masculine authority but for that reason dependent on the man, not an authentic partner but rather a "burden," a situation which often is aggravated by resentment. I am not a feminist of the sort that is "machismo in reverse" operating, in the end, with the same prejudices and distortions.

6. How would you describe Argentina's women readers?

I believe that Argentine women in general are very good readers who lead lives that are culturally, extremely active. In workshops, classes, lectures, the attendance and participation of women is now undeniably greater than that of men, and I think it would be very simplistic to say that this is because women have more time. The intellectual woman here works a great deal, perhaps too much, and demands a great deal of herself to do everything, the best that she is capable of. It seems to me that, at the present time, there is a displacement of interests, and that women tend to be the true protagonists of our culture.

Selection from *Canción perdida en Buenos Aires al Oeste*

In *Canción perdida en Buenos Aires al Oeste* María Rosa Lojo addresses the theme of the journey, already noted in the works of Diaconú and Gorodischer, present also in Mercader's and Orphée's texts. But Lojo treats the topic from an intimate viewpoint. She narrates a journey through the eyes of people who emigrated and who couldn't, wouldn't, or just didn't know how to return to their homelands. She also narrates the journey from the perspective of the sons and daughters who followed those who left and who are now, through a pile of exchanged letters, diary entries, and transcriptions of tape recordings, trying to find their identities and to write for one another the things they were not able to say in person.

The selection presents a frontier space wherein the narrators seek to find answers regarding their identity and that of their ancestors. The characters want to understand those who came before them with the evident purpose of knowing themselves better. The only record the reader has access to is the jumble of written voices in the letters, diaries, and tape transcriptions, so that what those voices say, or do not say, forms the mystery to be uncovered, this time by the reader. The fragment chosen constitutes the second chapter of the novel. It is a letter signed by Alberto and addressed to his brother-in-law Miguel, the same Miguel who appears in the title of the first chapter. The letter, written in a familiar tone, relates the feelings of Alberto, a rural doctor who "emigrated" from the big city to the towns of interior Argentina, for his brother-in-law, the one who stayed in Buenos Aires. The letter also recounts an unusual event that took place during one of Alberto's visits to the country and the way in which he came to feel well "established" in life. In this story, framed by the expedient of the letter, Lojo expresses masterfully the situation of those who, for one reason or another, had to leave, migrating within the same country or to other ones, becoming alienated, losing themselves, always with the hope of finding themselves again, perhaps through their children. It is possible to see in this compilation of messages in the multiple media that form the text, a critical presentation of the situations that forced the narrators to migrate. The ways in which Lojo uses oral tradition could justify Reina Roffé's insistence about the oral character of feminine literature.

Alberto

Cerro Azul, February 13, 1984

Dear Miguel:

I don't know how to begin this letter. But I do have to write you—a very happy birthday, by the way—because Irene's not going to. Irene put me in charge of doing it on her behalf, and she says that she's only going to add a few lines at the end so that you'll know that indeed she does remember you, even though we only hear from you every six months, and you haven't sent us your latest address, which we obtained—obviously—through other means. Well, but that's just the way she is. Women complain about everything and she complains especially about me, since I abandon her to wander through "those horrible places" where all you can catch is hunger and malaria. Of course, if truth be told, all this about complaints is a little exaggerated. Your sister is stubborn, strong and proud, like a Galician, and she really has had to bite her tongue a lot, because when she married me, as she says, "she knew what she was getting into." So we almost never argue. Almost never. When there are exceptions, of course, we have to rearrange the foundations of the house and then, without looking at each other, patiently pick up the instruments scattered all around by the hurricane, and put back the heavy volumes by Cervantes, Sábato, Hegel or Ricoeur on their shelves, where the ants had already begun to loaf about.

And so, brother, how are you? I don't know for certain, but I can suppose, by omission. What a habit you have of hiding yourself, of talking about things that are finally remote, trivialities. After your last letter I almost decided to stop buying newspapers, since I had such an attentive correspondent in Buenos Aires ... It seemed like a newspaper account: the rising oil prices, the popular reaction to the upcoming elections, the folks are getting along, I'm making enough to feed myself in my new enterprise, greetings, endearments and compliments. You wretch, how you hate it when they uncover your heart; always running from everything, burying your head in the sand like an os- trich, until whenever. I know why you're offended: it was that letter in which I wrote you about Laura and Luis, about your future, wanting you to settle down somewhere and get married, have children of your own, all those vul- gar things, if you like, "the common life," yes, with all that goes with it, that life that inspires in you a deep fear, and which nevertheless is perhaps the only thing that we are capable of and which, in the end, is the only thing that be- longs to us. Miguel, if you could, you would cry, but you're not able to, and you don't want anyone else to help you cry. I know you; we know each other.

Lately I've been thinking a lot about you and, more than anything, about your father, although he has refused to see me, even in a photograph, ever since I got engaged to Irene. With the years, my anger passed and good heav- ens, I even understand him; I understand him somewhat. It's not that difficult to put myself in his place, now that I have two children of my own. I leave Argentina—let's suppose—because I'm being persecuted, or because I don't have enough to eat, or because I feel like an imbecile, a poor wretch. I emi- grate to Australia, I find a job and I save for twenty years thinking: some day I'll return and stay forever, when things are better, when John Doe's no longer in the government, etc. I'll go back with my whole family, and my children will also feel Argentine, and my grandchildren will be Argentines. But sud- denly the son of an Irish or Polish immigrant appears and wants to marry my daughter. She leaves home, taking with her my leg, an arm, half my brain and I think: this is only the beginning, then the others will follow, one by one, and I'll return dispossessed, without any ties, alone, as alone as if I were dead. If your parents had built a good marriage, of course, things would have been different. Because there is a great difference between the two situations. I would return with Irene, to our old world, to our childhood, to a death that would perhaps be clearer, sweeter and predictable. Your folks couldn't do it because they were divided inside and definitively, because they didn't possess a common refuge where they could rest. But of that they were the only guilty ones, or the only victims. We shouldn't have had to pay for it, regardless of what the archaic Biblical pronouncement says, that sins pass from generation to generation, that curses are implacable and collective.

But back to the point: how are you? How are you *really*, Miguel? I can see your face as you read this question, the face that says, and who does he think he is, an inquisitor? And in your household, how are you getting along? Yes, the objection is just. Sometimes I am greatly tempted to answer the question myself, totally fucked up, the only way an honorable man can answer it, as my father-in-law said. To do him justice, I think that he really has been an honorable man, although he almost never seemed to understand anything that was happening around him, or at least he pretended not to. But also, how hard he was, Miguel, how needlessly hard for so many things. I worry more and more about my folks, I even obsess a little, perhaps because I'm afraid to see in them the mirror of what I, unable to escape, am going to be; what we're all going to become. Error breeds error . . . That unfortunate concatenation seems to have shaped Juan Manuel Neira's life, that man so haughty, so righteous, so foolish, so miserable, who perhaps could have been the father that I never had, and the man I nearly managed to love as if he were. I keep remembering those afternoons when he was dying from that undiagnosible viral illness, when we were watching him in silence, waiting for something terrible to happen, as defenseless as if someone had stripped the soul from our bodies. And in that voiceless vacuum the inaudible forbidden words were spoken. I can swear to you that never did I receive any revelations; never was the absence of speech more expressive. I ended up knowing so many things: about the relationship of a spirit to its body, about the magic of love and of will, about the itinerary of the soul that seeks to return to the land of its origin, intrepidly snatching emanations from the body, profound breaths of material life, dense loves of which your father was later dispossessed, because they were already somewhere else for eternity.

But I'm cheating you. I'm not confiding anything about myself, Miguel. And perhaps because I have too much to tell you, I don't dare to begin. As you might imagine, I travel a lot—sometimes in vain—to attend to someone who has already died by the time I get there, or, with luck, someone who is agonizing. And on those trips, going and coming back, I think a lot, about things that are unique or ordinarily strange that I have seen and I lived: images, vague fears, a nostalgia that I can't shake; and I think, above all, about the word "mistake." I think that no one manages, ever, to avoid the suspicion that his life is a mistake, that, among the few possible roads to take (yes, there are far fewer than one believes), he has chosen precisely the wrong one. Some nights when I'm returning especially late, the steering wheel pulls my head down in what they call "the white sleep"; I stop the car for an hour or half an hour, and before falling, in one fell swoop, into that invulnerable region of vacuum, I suddenly think (no, think isn't the right word, it happens to me as if it were a shout of alarm) where am I and what am I doing here and who is the man who is traveling once again these roads of childhood in search of something unknown. Of course, the next day, wide awake as I look at some infected tonsils in my office, all of it seems the ridiculous dream of an insecure driver. I know perfectly well who I am. I'm Doctor Alberto Krieger, I'm thirty-one years old, I have a strong will and a firm character. I have been, almost since infancy, an admirer of Albert Schweitzer, my namesake, whose portrait looks back at me with paternal solicitude from the front wall and certainly—I attest with absolute and honest satisfaction—he never calls me "schwein," as he calls Dr. Cureta in that ridiculous comic book, *Humor*. No, I behave myself as a dedicated pupil, I give him no reason to fault me. I have come, with my wife—a philosophy professor who generously transmits her knowledge to the middle-school pupils in our town—I have come, I repeat, to do my patriotic duty, philanthropy, live a tranquil life (or something similar) and be an ecologist. I have founded a little clinic in a place where there didn't used to be one, I have no competitors (unless it's the poor dentist, a very little woman whom I've had to help every now and then to extract teeth). The sick people from the colonies and from the doctorless neighboring hamlets come to see me. I am respected and loved and also (on few occasions, it's true) openly or surreptitiously cursed because, like everybody else and in spite of my best efforts, I make mistakes. But, in general, they love me. So much so, in fact, that at times I have problems with some female patients. This, which could delight others, makes me rather uncomfortable; in the first place, because I was born to be faithful and I'm still in love with Irene; in the second place because if your sister were to suspect anything, she would—very coldly—use everything in her temperamental and estimable power to kill me. And thus—as always, bah—she would again prove the legendary impotence of physicians when it comes to curing themselves. But in the end, Miguel, I can consider myself essentially happy. In addition to spiritual satisfactions, we have plenty to eat, we are making a comfortable home at the best location in town, and my ambition hasn't ever been an obstacle to my schweitzerian desire to help those less fortunate; we have two beautiful children and in spite of the hard work, we still have time to enjoy a good maté and to watch plenty of sunsets. I would be an ingrate, Miguel, if I complained. Except for the fact that I'm never going to transcend my modest sphere of a rural doctor and of knowing that the latest scientific advancements will take twenty years to reach this place; advancements that, on the other hand, aren't available either in the impoverished hospitals of Buenos Aires. But often I think about Irene and I wonder if it seems fair to her to spend her life locked in a little missionary town making sporadic visits to Posadas and, much more infrequently, to Buenos Aires. I'm not convinced at all that she is happy, but I don't think she's unhappy; most of the time, I think that Irene laughs at me a bit and at everyone else, filling her great notebooks; she has more than half a dozen, with secret notes. Who's to say, Miguel, that from that private laboratory she won't produce a knowledgeable work that will clarify human destiny in an original light; although if she only manages to clarify our anonymous, personal itineraries, that in itself would be very valuable.

But I tell you again, brother: the white sleep in the middle of a nocturnal route can disconcert anyone, to such a point that for days I can't shake its fulminating, disintegrating power. Things that I can't or don't want to understand come back to me in those moments of collapse like the brusque undertow of a flood. Faces, words, old stories, bodies. Above all, bodies. I have seen so many in the years of my practice. And even so, I think that it doesn't happen to me as it does to doctors in densely populated areas. Bodies have never become for me just *things*. I end up knowing the people too well for them to turn into mere objects in their incarnations. Sometimes it happens at home. I wake up early, a little before Irene, when the first glimmers of the sun are beginning to enter through the venetian-blinds, and I turn to that light with my eyes full of images that I had thought forgotten. The body of Dalmira Reyes, thirty-two, on some burlap sacks on the dirt floor, bleeding to death giving birth to her eighth child; the face of Teodoro Kuhn, the only time I went to the hospital in Buenos Aires, with his leg, always ulcerated, slowly rotting off. Teodoro Kuhn, who told me, with bitterness, naturally, that in five years only three persons had gone to visit him. He knew by heart the wall's defects, the stains of humidity (where he always saw the same scene: a man trapped in a trap to hunt animals). Teodoro Kuhn, yes, who later returned to the wilds, where he lived like a wounded boar, and whose ragged corpse was found in a ditch one summer afternoon, by some urchins who were playing war during the wretched weather. It's not only human faces that I see. One of my most frequent visitors is the tide of dead vipers swept away by the Paraná river in the last flood. We might find those animals revolting, but they were there in the beginning of everything and they will be there in the end, brought here and taken away by the great unstoppable waters with no destination.

All of this, of course, is nothing extraordinary for a doctor, since sickness, death, and catastrophes are our natural parameters of action. If I live to be an old man, I will have at least another thirty years of abundant practice, the extension of a life, the life I have lived until now. I wonder what images I will see then, before or after the sleep, or if none will come to me and I will have as compensation, finally, the fresh darkness, the silence; something closer to a feeling of germination and expectancy, under the peace of the earth, than to the way the violent tremor of life makes us see death.

Once you asked me, I remember, if the most painful part of my profession was seeing a child die. I don't know if it is the most painful, or if it is the kind of death that makes us feel our powerlessness with the greatest intensity. Because at times, Miguel, the end is even merciful and desirable in comparison with the life that they would have to face and which we haven't managed to improve or change. Although it may seem strange to you, I think more about the obvious deaths: the deaths of the old people. I have watched many old people die: little old Polish women who caressed in one hand their rosary beads, Germans and children of Germans, Russians in their nineties who came as children and never learned Spanish very well, and who always preferred samovar to maté. I was even admitted into some Japanese households. I remember one, poor but impeccably clean. They called me afterwards, only to fill out the death certificate, because, as the grandmother told me, "don't be offended, doctor, but it's more dignified to die among ourselves." And very few times have I seen a more dignified death, more exemplary than that of Teitaro Hikito, white on white, regulated mourning in accordance with the rite that made of death the final spectacle of a cosmic accord, a cautious submission to an impersonal and perfect justice.

Yes, as I was telling you, Miguel, it is the deaths of the old ones that bother me. Because the young ones die looking at distant horizons, thinking about everything they could have lived, about all that they could have known. The old man, no. The old man already knows, for better or for worse, what the youth is looking for, and perhaps the only thing, the fundamental thing that remains to be asked, is whether it was worth the effort to get there. Each year I feel the complexity and the difficulty of life increasing. If it's this way at thirty, how will it be at eighty? Knowing that there is necessarily very little time left before the great confrontation, that birth into the vacuum that is death. Do you remember when grandfather was alive? I was little and he was around seventy-eight, and I couldn't understand his tranquillity, knowing as he knew that at his age he could die at any moment. A short time before I turned fifteen I did my last job with him. We planted a lemon tree out back, and the old man asked me, smiling with his little eyes: did you know that Germany is the land where the lemon tree flowers? And with his voice still strong he sang a bit of that *lied,* and he put me in charge of caring for that tree, because he wouldn't live to see it matured. The last message was for me: that I shouldn't work as much as he had worked, because very few things are worth the effort. In the end, here I am, running from here to there; I follow his advice to the letter . . . Of what scant worth is someone else's experience.

Of course, at other times I think that almost surely I'll never live to be old and that I will die young, saving myself the existential problem of "the third age." Cancer, a heart attack, or an accident, like Mamá. Mamá. Oh, Miguel, that's another life whose meaning I don't understand. Of course, she raised us, she stayed with grandfather, she taught us at great personal sacrifice so that we would be honest, hard-working, pious, and have all the other humane, Christian values. But what about her? One doesn't only live for others, for everyone else. I find myself speechless when I try to answer my own question about what kind of personal happiness, absolutely personal, Mamá had. I am stunned by the little I actually knew about her in the twenty-four years we lived together. That large woman with the sad smile who almost never looked in a mirror and who went to church every Sunday, who spent her nights fighting with Martina so that she would finish her homework, and her mornings and afternoons in the grocery store. Poor Mamá, capable of spending an entire day crying because her youngest child, with his luminous adolescent pedantry, had the idea to declare that Jesus Christ had been a mere earth-bound revolutionary who was no more divine than Che Guevara. She barely managed to see me take the Hippocratic oath that she had anticipated almost more than I had. Even my "unbearable sister," as you called her, graduated and opened a day care center in that house where she was no more. The other day, Miguel, I thought about writing my sister what I'm writing you now, but I hesitated, because we never really understood each other, although we loved each other, and because, really, I don't know if I have the right to disturb her memories, now crystallized and appeased. But I can tell you freely what no one else knows, not even Irene yet. In itself it's nothing extraordinary, but for me it had an extraordinary meaning that perhaps only I gave to it. Perhaps I saw that face wrong, those documents, or I heard wrong that story, and with shreds of trivial, unrelated things, I constructed a fiction that I need. Or not. Or not, Miguel, and then I should confront it all, tell Irene, introduce into my life a fundamental change that, however, cannot alter it essentially.

It was also on a night of "white sleep," not long ago, when I was returning from Candelaria where an old patient of mine, Gertrudis Haufer, had just died. Her agony was long and we stayed with her almost until dawn. I didn't think I could keep driving and I stopped the car, almost right beside the police station, but I slept too long. When I woke up it was already morning. The first thing I saw was the face of a man who was staring at me without a smile.

"Don't be afraid, doctor," he said, anticipating my movement, "I wanted to take you to eat something and to warm up a little, nothing more. You were all curled up in the cold and you must be hungry."

He was a gringo who spoke with a pretty strong German accent, although his Spanish was correct; fairly tall, thin, and white-haired, but one could tell that his beard had been dark, almost black, as mine is now, and his hair blond. I almost laughed because it isn't easy to find two people (aside from Karadagián) with the same explosive combination that adorns me and which has cost me infinite troubles ever since adolescence.

I locked the car and followed him. We arrived at a wooden house that smelled of dampness and dark tobacco, but was comfortable. The man had lighted the wood stove. He put on maté and offered me rum. Within fifteen minutes I was feeling better and wanted to talk, but the old man (I figured him to be about sixty or sixty-five) hadn't uttered a single word. He kept watching me, though, with his small eyes, clear and sad, of a blue curiously marked with strings of yellow. Finally he opened his mouth.

"I also know what it's like to be on the road at dawn, cold and with an empty stomach."

"Were you a doctor, a truck driver . . . ?"

"No. A pastor, the pastor of a church."

"Gracious!"

"What? It surprises you, right? I don't look much like a pastor."

"No, it's not that. The truth is that it hadn't occurred to me. You've retired, I suppose."

The man shook his head slowly and then spoke, enunciating each syllable painfully.

"No. I didn't retire. They threw me out."

He was playing with the rum in his glass, as yellow as the ribbons in his eyes.

"They threw me out for being a drunk (if that bothers you I'll say alcoholic, or dipsomaniac). I was not a good influence on the faithful. You can imagine. I uttered absurdities during my sermons and I read the epistles backwards."

He smiled, looking at me sideways, while he reached for a cigarette.

"Alcoholism isn't a vice."

"Nor is it a great virtue, right? Yes, I know, doctor, I know. It's an 'illness' as you all say. But to be cured one has to want to be cured. I liked being sick. I had plenty of help, don't think I didn't. They even sent two ministers from Buenos Aires to talk to me and rehabilitate me. They were good people, honest, serious, smelling of soap and after-shave lotion. People who paid taxes, gave to charity and prayed every day. And yes, they helped me as much as that kind of people could help. They called me brother, suffered my insults, offered me peace and Christ's love, blessed me and forgave me five hundred times. And I treated them the only way I can treat that kind of people."

He cleared his throat and spit beside his sandal.

"One morning I woke up, determined, and I sent them meticulously to hell, quietly, while my wife was crying at the kitchen table. Afterwards I grabbed my rifle, I aimed it at them and I accompanied them calmly to the door that led to the mud of the open road. The poor devils left, horrified, almost speechless. They scarcely managed to mutter under their breath something about an asylum until, breathless, they got into their station wagon and left. I stayed a while beside the gate, breathing deeply in the icy morning air. I felt like I was dying and I wanted my heart to burst then and there. But it didn't, and here I still am, who's to know why in the hell or for what purpose. That was also the last time I saw my wife. When I returned to the dining room I found her dressed in her tailored Sunday suit with two suitcases by her side. The little girl looked at me, frightened, and the little boy was laughing in his mother's arms. He was still a baby. She had stopped crying and she spoke coldly. Yes, it was the right thing."

The old man stopped, as if to catch his breath. He studied the bottom of his empty glass.

"She told me that she had already tolerated enough and that she couldn't stand any more, that I didn't even try and that it was all infinitely cruel, for her and for the children. She also told me—I should remember this—that she considered herself married for her whole life and that if I returned, determined to be a good father and a good husband, then I would find a woman 'worthy of me.'"

He smiled again, with that cutting, oblique smile, worse than a scream.

"Poor, poor Clara. She was so wrong about everything, even about that. Even in not realizing that she had been and was always going to be infinitely more worthy than I. She was a good woman, loyal, capable of having waited for me all that time, of still waiting for me now. I never felt sorrier for her than on that morning, big and heavy as she was, crying in the kitchen just like an abandoned child.

"Yes, sir," he said, and he looked at me face to face. "Her only sin was marrying a man who didn't love her and who would never love her."

"And why did you get married?"

"Out of loneliness, I suppose. Clara was my second wife. I had been widowed for over a year, I had lost the only love I ever had. And I threw myself into that second marriage as into a well, partly out of desperation, partly because of my friends' advice, I don't know. But that's not justification, young man. Nothing can justify what I did."

"And you never looked for them?"

"Does it seem to you that someone like me deserves a family, is in any condition to have a family? Clara had enough money of her own to have a house, a business; she could take care of herself. I had to quit the church; I refused when they wanted to send me back to Germany, and I ended up on the street. Since then I've never had a steady job: I chopped wood, I drove trucks, I taught music classes, I translated. Between one job and another job I covered nearly the whole country."

"But you never, never went to see them?"

The man hesitated before answering.

"I went once, some fifteen years ago. I knew where they were. Clara always took the trouble, somehow, to let me know where they were. Yes, I went, but in the end I never went into the house. It was at night and I was watching her from the yard, through the venetian blinds. They were all eating: Clara, my father-in-law, the kids and one more boy who was, I suppose, a friend of my son's."

"And why didn't you go in?"

"What for? I didn't have any right to be there, none. I was a stranger. With my return I would have destroyed the bit of order in that life that Clara had worked so hard to build in their lives. At that point in time no one was expecting me. The children had their myths about me, and in that myth I was the man always away, the same as dead."

"And Clara?"

The old man looked in my eyes again, without vacillating.

"You can't go back to someone that you have hurt so deeply. No one is capable of forgiveness to that extent."

"Seventy times seven you can, or should be able to."

The old man shook his head.

"That's for God, not for humans."

His lack of faith, or what I believed to be his lack of faith, startled me.

"When did you stop believing?" I dared to ask him.

He leaned backwards and stared into space, from the wicker chair.

"Who told you that I stopped believing? I'm a sinner, not a non-believer. What's worse, a sinner who doesn't want to or can't save himself. Who can't because he doesn't want to or who doesn't want to because he can't. I still haven't decided exactly. Now go away, my friend," he was irritated. "You have been made comfortable and I feel like getting drunk. When I drink I don't like to be bothered."

He irritated me.

"Don't worry, I don't have any interest in witnessing your binge."

He looked at me with unforeseen sweetness and raised to my cheek, almost in a caress, the hand stained by dark tobacco.

"It's better that way, my son, better that way. You're a good boy, a good man, but still very tender."

I was entranced, disconcerted, on the threshold, still feeling the brush of his fingers on my beard. I dared, I don't know how, to ask him a final, terrible question.

"With whom have I had the pleasure of speaking?"

"My name is Albert Krieger. Come back whenever you like."

I could have hugged him at that moment, or I could have insulted him, shaken him, perhaps with the hope of wrenching from him a useless or impossible cry. But I didn't do anything, except breathe and look at him, wordless. I didn't tell him my name and he didn't ask. I waved, I turned around and walked out into the middle of the street, until I knew, from the peace at my back, from the growing tranquillity of my heart, that he wasn't in that space any more, that the door had been, finally, closed.

How hard it is to explain to you, Miguel, what I was feeling inside at that moment. I went back to my station wagon, put my forehead on the steering wheel and clenched my fists, boiling over with abandonment, sadness, mute screams. After fifteen minutes, more or less, I started the motor. I was lucky that the road was clear and dry that morning, without the fateful and sweet mud of the great spring rains. It was like driving on mist, on a white desert, attentive only to the interior scene, where images of vertigo were flashing. I saw so many things in such little time. My aunts in Oberá in their great cool parlor, who embroidered and were mysteriously quiet whenever I began to speak of my father. My father, who had traveled to Magdeburgo, in East Germany, for serious family matters, and who had never returned. Had he been detained, killed, imprisoned by mistake? No one knew for certain, and the embassies had no response. And the aunts had no words, too pious to lie. And we, in our nightly prayers, asking routinely to God for his return, until, in adolescence, that request, now mute, became just a sad, clear memory of childhood. I was already accustomed, more than accustomed, to the idea that my father was only the sacred absent one, the respectable and beloved dead. The old man was right in his brutal sincerity, or in his cynicism. When one has so deeply wounded, there is no forgiveness. And why the confession, if he had recognized me. No. I couldn't erase those words. That he doesn't want to because he can't or he can't because he doesn't want to. *He can't because he doesn't want to.* So, let him live with the rubble of his deeds. I wasn't going to be moved by an honesty that was enough for him only to recognize and accuse himself, but not to be intimately transformed. Or perhaps I was playing his game and my inevitable rejection was just the final punishment that his guilt demanded, the feared and desired atonement. How much I desired then for him to have left for good, saving me now the immense perturbation that his presence introduced in my life, depriving me even of my identity, of my history. When I arrived home I was trembling, as if I had a fever. Irene made me go to bed and she sent the patients home. We were alone and I had to put up with at least half an hour of her sweet interrogation: reproaches for not taking the double-lined jacket and for forgetting my maté utensils, indignant references to the Haufer family for letting me leave in that cold weather and without eating, incessant curses at Albert Schweitzer for having existed and served as my model, etc. Until she placed her stubborn red head on the pillow and fell asleep, because she had waited up for me until very late. I couldn't sleep but I appreciated her warmth beside me. I was deeply grateful that a woman, my wife, had waited for me all night to reprimand and shelter me.

I didn't want to say anything to Irene. During the two months that followed I thought I saw the old man wandering around the town. They were very fleeting encounters, always at night or in the evening, when only the shadows can be seen. I thought I recognized him by his walk, by a reflection of his look. I would have sworn that he was looking for me, I could feel it almost clearly. But I didn't want him to look for me, I didn't want to forgive him and I wasn't even sure that he was looking for forgiveness, to begin with.

One day I was passing nearby and I stopped as if I had heard him call me from Cerro Corá. I walked slowly to his hut. It was the middle of the day and no one was in the streets. When I pushed the half-opened door I saw Albert Krieger seated in the wicker chair next to the rear window. I called him two times by his name without any response. The third time I called him—as if I still didn't believe it—"Papá." But he continued silent and on touching him I realized he was dead. I embraced him with rage and almost with relief, because he couldn't answer me any more and in his silence everything was easier, much easier.

I don't know for how long I was like that, with my head on his breast. On getting up I looked carefully around the almost empty room. He had so few possessions: a German Bible, very old and well annotated, a *Kempis, Der Steppenwolf* by Hesse, and *Das Stundenbuch* by Rilke; there were also a few detective novels. His clothing was minimal: two or three sweaters, a few shirts and pants, an old valise. The rest didn't belong to him because, as I found out later, he was renting the cabin with its poor furniture. Finally I found what I was looking for: a thin packet, carefully wrapped in a silk handkerchief and sewn into the lining of a jacket. There was hardly anything, and yet so much: three letters signed by Katharina Eberhard, a yellowed photograph: the slender face of a extremely beautiful woman; another photo, somewhat more recent, where a baby and a toddler of two or three years old were smiling. I thought I recognized the faces, Martina's dress, the little shoes worn for another portrait. I only took that, along with the Bible. Then I went to the police station, to report the death. The sheriff studied the dead man's documents. "How strange," he said to me, "he has the same name as you, right? Are you related?" "I don't think so," I answered. "Krieger is a relatively common surname in Germany."

Albert Krieger was buried in the nearest cemetery. Whenever I pass through that area I take a little detour and go visit his grave. I continue a dialogue that never began, because there wasn't time. Neither of us took the time, and the fifteen years that Papá spent in Misiones were wasted, traveling from town to town, perhaps hoping, perhaps knowing that one day I would return to my homeland and that inevitably we would meet.

When I returned home it was already late. Slowly I went up the hill, and I saw the lighted windows. There was a fresh breeze, clean, smelling of a new spring, and the orange blossoms constricted my heart, harmlessly. I thought that Irene and the kids were inside, that dinner was waiting for me and that I had a place, my own place in this world. And I felt deeply, more than ever, the passion of being alive, the great gamble, the risk. I felt that I was inaugurating the life of the man with my life, for better and for worse, in happiness and in sorrow, that the dead were at peace and that the pain, the anger, and even the fear had finally been consummated.

Goodbye, Miguel. Don't forget to write or to come visit. We'll always be waiting for you. A big hug from

——————Alberto

Jorgelina Loubet

Jorgelina Loubet was born in Buenos Aires in 1918. She studied in Bahía Blanca and in Buenos Aires, obtaining a doctoral degree in mathematics, and later teaching at the University of Buenos Aires. While in Bahía Blanca, she worked as a Samaritan nurse in local hospitals. She was an active professor for several years, until she decided to "retire" and devote all her time to writing. She has traveled through South America, Europe, Israel, and the United States. She founded the Argentine Chapter of the PEN Club International. Among the many honors she has received are: the Second Municipal Prize for Novel; the Medal of Honor from the Argentine Writers Society (SADE); Honorable Mention from the Writers' Congress; Honorable Mention in a contest sponsored by the Municipality of Buenos Aires, National Fund for the Arts and Argentores; the PEN Club First Municipal Prize; the María de Hostos Prize from the magazine *Sin Nombre* in San Juan; and the Plaza y Janes First Prize for the Argentine Novel. *El biombo,* she rewrote as an award-winning play; it was performed in the National Theater Contest of Pelotas, Brazil. A widely recognized and esteemed writer, she has published numerous stories in *La Nación, Clarín,* and *La Gaceta.* Currently she is the Secretary General of the Argentine Academy of Letters.

Publications

La breve curva (Brief turn). Buenos Aires: Losada, 1962.

El biombo (The folding screen). Buenos Aires: Losada, 1963.

La complicidad (The complicity). Buenos Aires: Losada, 1969.

Penélope aguarda (Penelope waits). Buenos Aires: Carro de Tespis, 1970. In collaboration with Rodolfo Modern.

La victoria (Victory). Buenos Aires: PEN Club International, 1974.

Mi barrio, mi país, el mundo (My neighborhood, my country, the world). Buenos Aires: Ediciones Corregidor, 1978.

Los Caminos (The paths). Barcelona: Plaza y Janes Editores, 1981.

"Tres miradas en trascendencia" (Three looks at transcendence). *Boletín de la Academia Argentina de Letras* 51/201–2 (July–December 1986): 358.

"El centenario de Ricardo Güiraldes" (Ricardo Güiraldes' centennial). Suplemento Literario de *La Nación,* 7 September 1986: 2. In collaboration with others.

"*Don Segundo Sombra* y la busca espiritual de Ricardo Güiraldes" (*Don Segundo Sombra* and Ricardo Güiraldes' spiritual search). *Boletín de la Academia Argentina de Letras* 51/201–2 (July–December 1986): 303–11.

"Notas sobre la novela" (Notes on the novel). *Boletín de la Academia Argentina de Letras* 52/205–6 (July–December 1987): 283–99.

"María Luisa Bombal y el realismo mágico" (María Luisa Bombal and magical realism). *Boletín de la Academia Argentina de Letras* 53/207–8 (January–June 1988): 125–34.

"Aproximación a la poesía de Horacio Armani" (Approximation to Horacio Armani's poetry). *Boletín de la Academia Argentina de Letras* 53/209–10 (July–December 1988): 347–56.

"Introducción a la obra de Rodolfo Modern" (Introduction to Rodolfo Modern's works). *Boletín de la Academia Argentina de Letras* 54/213–14 (July–December 1989): 403–12.

"Charles de Gaulle visto por André Malraux" (Charles de Gaulle as seen by André Malraux). *Boletín de la Academia Argentina de Letras* 55/217–18 (July–December 1990): 321–42.

Metáforas y Reflejos (Metaphors and reflections). Buenos Aires: Grupo Editor Latinoamericano, 1991.

"Las olas rompían en la playa" (The waves broke at the beach). Suplemento Literario de *La Nación,* 20 October 1991: 6.

Coordenadas Literarias I. Buenos Aires: El Franco Tirador Ediciones, 1996.

Secondary Sources

Fares, Gustavo, and Eliana Hermann. "Y ahora? Reflexiones acerca de la literatura femenina argentina actual. *Forma oculta del mundo* de María Rosa Lojo, *Metáforas y reflejos* de Jorgelina Loubet, y *Victoria Ocampo* de María Esther Vázquez." *Letras Femeninas* 19/1–2 (Spring–Fall 1993): 121–34.

Gómez Paz, Julieta. "La obra narrativa de Jorgelina Loubet." *Insula: Revista de Letras y Ciencias Humanas* 37/430 (September 1982): 15.

Interview

1. Which authors have had the greatest influence on your work?

   I am interested in humankind and in its problems, which I find most generally to be a European theme. French existentialism fascinates me as well, although I also find myself attracted by the style achieved by Virginia Woolf.

2. When did you begin to write, and why?

   I began to write regularly from the moment when French existentialism began to spread through Buenos Aires, and I did it to fulfill a responsibility to myself.

3. How does the political situation influence your choice of themes?

   The political situation, locally as well as internationally, is one of the human coordinates. It is unavoidable, even when one isn't addressing it explicitly.

4. Have you encountered difficulties, as a woman writer, with publishers?

   I am pleased to remember the courtesy of don Gonzalo Losada, my first editor. I was always treated cordially by my editors.

5. What do you think of feminism?

   The injustices committed against women and men should be corrected without resorting to "ghettoization." I think that literary contests shouldn't deprive women writers of measuring themselves against men writers.

6. How would you describe Argentina's women readers?

   It is difficult to establish what the average is in order to answer that question. There are conformists, or curious women readers, or intelligent women readers. Just like men.

Selection from *Mi barrio, mi país, el mundo*

In her book *Mi barrio, mi país, el mundo* Jorgelina Loubet explores the three universes expressed in the title. The volume is divided in three parts, each of them dedicated to a distinct space that, from smaller to bigger, accounts for the author's obsessions. In those spaces Loubet establishes sites and characters that cross through diverse spatial and temporal boundaries, from our present century to the distant future. The various times and places allow the author to present an array of topics that always refer to human nature and to its characteristics. The first story of her book takes place in a neighborhood, in a childhood home, and relates the story of a family, a saintly uncle and his distrustful and skeptical nephews and nieces. The last story of the collection is located in a future century, in a galactic dimension, in the universe, also called "the world." The text Loubet chose for this anthology, "Borel and I," belongs to the second part of the book, "my country." The country is, of course, Argentina, and its temporal frame is the decade of Juan Domingo Perón's first two terms as president, between 1945 and 1955. Without other allusions to the period or the country, other than a minimal mention following the title, the author manages to establish the story's political climate, allowing the reader to relate the atmosphere of persecution and denunciation presented in the text to the one that characterized Perón's regime. Georgie's story could have been that of any politician, or of any opponent of the government during those years; the activity of the narrator could have been that of any paid informer; and the lives portrayed in the story can be thought of as no more than two sides of the same coin, in a pattern reminiscent of Borges's inversions of traitors and heroes. The name "Georgie" itself could be an allusion to the Argentine master, and to the difficulties Borges personally endured under Perón's government when he was "promoted" from employee of a suburban library in Buenos Aires to poultry inspector.

Borel and I

Argentina 1945–1955

You knew, Georgie, how some dictatorships begin and so you proclaimed: the tick digs in, claiming to be friendly and protective—you said—I'm the one who really loves you (first); you're the one who needs me now (afterwards).

And as if you were thinking that the people shouldn't be treated in the same way as many a man treats his woman, you were in the opposition from the very beginning: they never managed to fool you, either with their facile smiles or their flattering greetings.

When the smile and the greetings also proved to be, to us as well, official, your indignation, Georgie, tried to vent itself above all through your political party (let us recognize that the party was not inclined to find extenuating circumstances for that upstart who had just come to power in his first election with only half of the votes of our whole electorate). Then, some of us, your friends, began to listen to you around the table of the coffee-shop where, without skipping a single one, you commented on the minute maneuvers of our dictator in diapers. You called him Pérez—we all ended up calling him Pérez—perhaps because it amused you to reduce him to a species of common denominator. I admired the inconsistency between your innocent eyes and your roguish mouth, your persistence in trying to frighten us.

"But, hey, Georgie, aren't you exaggerating?"

You would shake your head: whatever you had just said was supported by a short article you had cut from the English newspaper. Rummaging through your wallet, you would take out a minuscule clipping and read in a vaguely British jargon (Mrs. Hilton would have flunked you one more time; your nickname always seemed like a joke). One of us would translate. You half closed your eyes, quietly, as if you were mentally controlling the translation; finally you would shrug your shoulders and raise the palms of your hands, convincingly: you see?

I remember when they discovered the first conspiracy to overthrow the facile smile and the flattering greeting. We celebrated it as our own triumph; somehow it was ours: hadn't you been announcing it? That this could not continue, this would not continue like this? We looked at you with renewed interest. We tried to get information from you: Did you know anything about it, Georgie? Were you involved? Smiling, we feigned complicity to make you yield: I have a friend with a boat, in San Isidro, who can take you to Carmelo, dodging the Prefecture: he knows all the smugglers of the Delta; one of them can guide him.

Perhaps you liked it when we would fight with each other over who would protect you. You reassured us: for now you didn't need anything, but you would keep in mind our offers for any eventuality. We understood: that "keeping in mind," that "eventuality" corroborated a suspicion that was, until that moment, perhaps, not too firm, and which acted as a pedestal for the image that we began to create of you, Georgie. An unsteady halo was appearing and disappearing over your head, according to the way the events would harm you to a greater or lesser degree. Surely you would have preferred a more stable halo. They say that one can know someone by his capacity to admire. We, those of your circle, behaved like a pendulum, and we moved from admiration to distrust: you weren't going to outshine us.

From time to time the front pages of the newspapers would be full of the news of intents at rebellion announced by the government itself. You, Georgie, catalogued them: they're just rumors; or, this time it's really happening. Your voice trembled and your alarm was the same, in either case. We should have understood that you were at risk either way.

We were getting accustomed, followers and opponents, to our fix of that drug, and we needed, more and more frequently, the irate and pathetic warnings, followed by the scrutinizing search for the conspirators, real or supposed. For a week, and sometimes longer, you would disappear from the table in the coffee-shop. When you returned, our worry and curiosity would be tinged with light sarcasm: They haven't arrested you, Georgie. You're lucky, man; half the world's in prison.

Perhaps you felt the reticence of our congratulations because one day you confided in us—and through your exaltation I imagined you felt liberated— that no doubt they would arrest you this time, finally: your party had designated you to speak at a street demonstration; you would precede the main speaker. Of course, you didn't have authorization from the police.

Once again our speculations ran wild. I was the most skeptical—at least that's what the circle said—because I attended the demonstration. You saw me as you climbed onto the bench; you rested your trusting eyes on mine at length; only afterwards your voice swelled to an indignant register to denounce the regime. Your right arm shook violently, and your hand lifted your arguments to the sky. I didn't know that sharp metal tone of your voice. Perhaps I simply didn't know you, Georgie. And now I think with sadness: neither did you, Georgie, know me.

You were still speaking when the police appeared. I knew they had just arrived by the uneasy rumor that fluttered above the heads crowded on the corner. That rumor also warned you. Along with the police came those charged with sabotaging the meeting. They fell on you. Everyone shouted; there were "long lives" and "down withs," insults, clubbings, shots into the air and great rushes. I imagine, Georgie, that you flew to the subway stop, the most direct means of transportation to your house. When I arrived at the station you had already left. Then—I think—repentant, you went directly to your apartment. I followed you there. I didn't recognize your voice in the suffocated "who is it?" behind the door that answered my insistent ringing. You opened the door still panting. I told you, before even saying hello, that the police had detained the main speaker (who hadn't even managed to speak). You sighed, glancing at the chair where a razor, comb and toothbrush were piled on a meticulously folded blanket. I told you that you had done the right thing in running. You looked at me again, for a long moment, as you had on the street corner at the demonstration. You smiled uncomfortably, and shrugged your shoulders: They'll find me anyway.

I took the initiative to serve us a whiskey, and another, and another. I opened cans, I found crackers, you made coffee. It didn't take us long to start talking about women and laughing out loud among the cigarettes and the beers. You had an arrangement, you explained, with the girl who cleaned your apartment. You described her with such humor that I supposed her to be fat and cross-eyed only so that we could shriek with laughter until four in the morning, waiting in vain for the police. At that time I left: I wasn't too sharp that morning in the office.

When you reappeared at the tertulia again, a sort of shamed modesty veiled your excessive good fortune. You had trusted in me for your defense. I offered you, like the rest, a certain malicious incredulity: say good-bye to per-secutions and electric shock therapy: an invisible armor protected you from all suspicion, you were Achilles, invulnerable even in your heel.

At that doubtful homage and with your halo tilting more and more, you made your ultimate revelation: at night, and around the gardens that bor-dered our city, you were driving the car where two different military branches were trying to unify their rebel forces. Poor Georgie: you never should have revealed that secret. I wasn't so much moved by your audacity as a liaison as by your need to pour out the secret of your courage. They said May God hear you, with more conviction than they uttered the May the Blessed God protect you, with which we bid farewell.

Your telephone remained unanswered, when the clandestine radios cor-roborated the latest news: several garrisons, distant from the capital, were challenging the regime. You were driving across the city then, at the steering wheel of a truck loaded with weapons and explosives. The redoubt from where you worked seemed then to be detected by a security service: everyone was ordered to disperse, and you retired to your apartment with orders not to move from there, and to wait for new instructions.

I evoke you, Georgie, on the way from your house, observing finally the soul of the city, your city, which until that moment had only been a checker-board over which you marked an itinerary. Now, on the other hand, like a faithful lover, you would listen to its obscure silences, you would perceive the air that smelled like a collective storm, of that retreat before it all broke out, and where mysterious lines of force are concentrated before overflowing. We all adore our port city, pulled apart by opposing forces; but you, Georgie, knew the history of each one of its neighborhoods and your steps knew its sidewalks and its streets from the place of its first founding to the riverbed of the deep stream and the old gully. Perhaps, Georgie, you told yourself, with-out too much sadness, that this journey down the road to your house, which revealed to you the soul of the city through its obscure new silences, was the last trip you would take.

Perhaps you were still thinking about that great tired animal lying in am-bush when the warm shower and the ample towel returned you to your for-gotten body. You were listening to the captive radio when you heard fists pounding on your apartment door; fists, boots, bootheels. You must have looked ridiculous, in your underwear, yielding in the doorway to the four plain-clothes investigators, who insulted you and then immediately rushed you along: get dressed now, Jorge Borel, follow us, you have a long list of ac-counts to settle, you son of a bitch. One at your bedroom door, another by the bathroom, another watching the living room, the other at the entrance, his solid legs spread wide open, the four aces of that sinister poker game were fi-nally corralling you as against your destiny.

I entered last, Georgie. And you only understood when the four subordi-nates stood at attention when I walked in. In my own way, I was also prepar-ing for my final walk. Like you, Georgie, I was searching for the dead end of my destiny, because the portable radio had already informed me what you lis-tened to in the stupefied silence of everyone, which I unwillingly imposed: the regime had just capitulated.

Martha Mercader

Martha Mercader was born in La Plata, Argentina, on February 27, 1926. She attended the College of Humanities of the National University of La Plata and the Institute of Education of the University of London between 1949 and 1950, thanks to a fellowship from the British Council.

Her professional activities include teaching posts at public and private high schools between 1948 and 1959. She also worked often as a journalist for newspapers, magazines, radio and television programs. She was co-writer for the very successful television series *Cosa Juzgada* (Judged matter), from 1969 to 1971. She has participated in various conferences and meetings about literary and sociopolitical themes, particularly as they affect women, in Buenos Aires and other Argentine cities, as well as in Madrid, Barcelona, Valencia, Seville, Paris, Strasbourg, Bonn, Eichstad, Warsaw, Athens, New York, New Haven, Washington, D.C., and New Orleans, among others. From 1963 to 1966 she served as the Cultural Director for the Government of the Province of Buenos Aires. Between 1984 and 1989 she was the Director of the Nuestra Señora de

Luján School in Madrid, which is associated with the Argentine Ministry of Education. In October of 1993 she was elected member of the Argentine Congress as a representative of the Partido Radical.

Among her prizes and distinctions are the following: Municipal Third Prize "Ricardo Rojas" for *Octubre en el espejo;* the Municipal Literature Prize for *Solamente ella;* the Club XIII Prize for *Juanamanuela, mucha mujer;* the First Municipal Prize for Literature in 1983 for that same work; and, in 1985, she received the Snow Star, awarded by the Association for Business and Professional Women in Bariloche for "her valuable contribution to the situation of women and for better Argentine letters." In 1994 she was invited as a guest lecturer to the Midland Conference at Creighton University in Omaha, Nebraska. She then gave lectures at the University of Lincoln and at Dana College in Nebraska, and later was a guest lecturer at Sweet Briar College and at Lynchburg College, both in Virginia.

Publications

Octubre en el espejo (October in the mirror). Buenos Aires: Sudamericana, 1966.

Los que viven por sus manos (Those who live by their hands). Buenos Aires: Sudamericana, 1976.

Solamente ella (Only she). Buenos Aires: Plus Ultra, 1977.

Juanamanuela, mucha mujer (Juanamanuela, a great woman). Buenos Aires: Sudamericana, 1980. 16th edition, 1988.

De mil amores (With all my love). Buenos Aires: Sudamericana, 1982.

La chuña de los huevos de oro (The bird of the golden eggs). Buenos Aires: Legasa, 1982.

Decir que no (To say no). Buenos Aires: Bruguera, 1983.

Belisario en son de guerra (Belisario in war mood). Buenos Aires: Sudamericana, 1984.

"Leopoldo Lugones y Ricardo Rojas: El nacimiento de los nacionalismos autoritario y democrático en la Argentina" (Leopoldo Lugones and Ricardo Rojas: The birth of authoritarian and democratic nationalisms in Argentina). *Río de la Plata: Culturas* 4/6 (1987): 473–80.

"El difícil matrimonio de la literatura y la política" (The difficult marriage of literature and politics). *Cuadernos Americanos* 2/4 (1988): 169–79.

El hambre de mi corazón (My heart's hunger). Buenos Aires: Sudamericana, 1989.

Para ser una mujer (To be a woman). Buenos Aires: Planeta, 1992.

Literature for Children

Conejitos con hijitos (Bunnies with children). Buenos Aires: Plus Ultra, 1976.

Un cuento de pilas y pilas de cuentos (A story of batteries and batteries of stories). Buenos Aires: Sudamericana, 1982.

Cuentos de un dormilón (Tales from a sleepy head). Buenos Aires: Sudamericana, 1983.

Una abuela y ciento veinte millones de nietos (One grandmother and one hundred and twenty million grandchildren). Buenos Aires: Sudamericana, 1984.

Fuga (Escape). Buenos Aires: De La Flor, 1984.

Theater

Una corona para Sansón (A crown for Samson). Theater for children, performed in the "Casacuberta" Hall of the "General San Martín" Municipal Theater of Buenos Aires, 1967.

Amor de cualquier humor (Love in any mood). Divertimento performed at the "Patio de los Naranjos" at the "Enrique Larreta" Museum, Buenos Aires, 1982.

Secondary Sources

Battaglia, Diana, and Diana Beatriz Salem. "La escritura como espejo de otra escritura en: *Juanamanuela, mucha mujer* de Martha Mercader." In *Literatura como intertextualidad: IX Simposio International de Literatura,* edited by Juana Alcira Arancibia, 137–49. Buenos Aires: Instituto Literario y Cultural Hispánico, 1993.

Fares, Gustavo, and Eliana Hermann. "Exilios internos: El viaje en cinco escritoras argentinas." *Hispanic Journal* 15/1 (Spring 1994): 21–29.

Hermann, Eliana. "Martha Mercader. *Para ser una mujer." Chasqui: Revista de Literatura Latinoamericana* 23/1 (May 1994): 126–27.

Gil Montero, Martha, and María Gowland de Gallo. "Beyond the Metaphors of Life: Interviews with Martha Mercader and Olga Orozco." *Américas* 42/5 (September–October 1990): 42–47.

Matamoro, Blas. "Martha Mercader: *El hambre de mi corazón." Cuadernos Hispanoamericanos* 484 (October 1990).

———. "Martha Mercader: *Juanamanuela, mucha mujer." Cuadernos Hispanoamericanos* 370 (April 1981).

Riess, Cheryl Rae. "Narrating History: Five Argentine Novelists (Movsichoff, Demitropulos, Castillo, Mercader, de Miguel)." *Dissertation Abstracts International* (1989): 3610A–3611A.

Salem, Diana Beatriz, and Diana Battaglia. "Martha Mercader: Mujeres, escritura y lectura en el siglo XIX." *Alba de América: Revista Literaria* 11/20–21 (July 1993): 273–80.

Zanetti, Susana. *Encuesta a la Literatura Argentina Contemporánea.* Buenos Aires: Centro Editor de América Latina, 1982.

Interview

1. Which authors have had the greatest influence on your work?

   I couldn't say exactly which authors have influenced me the most. I have read a little of everything, and not too much of anything. During my childhood, my masters were Victor Hugo, Dickens, and Anatole France. Later, I fell in love with Antonio Machado; then, with Virginia Woolf.

2. When did you begin to write, and why?

   I have always liked to write. In elementary school I felt real satisfaction writing "compositions." In the fifties, I wrote a number of stories for children, but the publisher to whom I took them disillusioned me when he said: "If your style is set in stone, don't bring anything else to me." Much earlier, in my youth, something similar had happened when I showed some verses to a boyfriend of mine who presumed to be a poet. I postponed my vocation (I hesitate to use such a high-sounding word) until 1966 when, inspired by the efficiency of my own performance at an important public task, I decided to collect some stories in a volume that was accepted instantaneously by the reader of Editorial Sudamericana, Paco Porrúa, the same person who discovered Julio Cortázar.

3. How does the political situation influence your choice of themes?

   When I was very young I became conscious of the political nature of life, and that is necessarily reflected in my pages.

4. Have you encountered difficulties, as a woman writer, with publishers?

   They've never rejected anything of mine in Argentina, except for those little stories, but they did in Spain, where they wouldn't publish *El hambre de mi corazón* because it wasn't "strong" [sic] from an erotic point of view.

5. What do you think of feminism?

   Feminism is the response to the discrimination suffered by women for millennia. Within that term many attitudes are housed. I think women and men are different (I like the difference) but that doesn't force us to limit our potentialities to traditional roles. Although in theory, almost all political and civil rights for women have been legalized, in practice they are not always respected. I support everything that seems to improve the conditions of women's lives and gives them greater participation in public decision making.

6. How would you describe Argentina's women readers?

I think that there is a vast female readership, diminished in the current economic recession.

Selection from *El hambre de mi corazón*

Martha Mercader's story, "Los astros decían que justo en La Habana" (The stars said it would be in Havana), is from her collection *El hambre de mi corazón*. The title of the book cites a phrase from a poem in English by Jorge Luis Borges with which Mercader renders homage to the Argentine writer. In her texts she portrays the life, travels, feelings, and desires of a particularly conflict-riddled sector of Argentine society, the middle class. The story selected portrays two middle-aged couples from Buenos Aires who meet during the flight that takes them to Cuba. The narrative voice belongs to one of the two husbands, who explains that they are taking the trip partly to celebrate the birthday of his wife, Carlota, and partly to take a vacation—and also to discover something "new," this much based on what an astrologer had predicted for them before leaving. The theme of the journey encountered previously in Diaconú's and Lojo's works reappears in this story, as if to suggest that identities are more easily discovered, or more profoundly developed or changed, when faced with a non-routine circumstance, such as that of a trip. That is exactly what happens in this story, in which Carlota, a plump, shy woman, whom her own husband appears not to know very well, discovers her desires and lives them openly, for the first time, with another woman. As in Reina Roffé's *Monte de Venus* or in some of Silvina Bullrich's novels, the narrative of Carlota's experiences challenges certain stereotypes associated with being a woman in Argentina, for example the idea that a woman's identity is ever only that of mother and wife.

The Stars Said It Would Be in Havana

Everyone was drinking rum and coke or *mojitos,* which is rum mixed with tonic water, crushed sweet basil and lime juice; you had to go to a cafe with tables on the sidewalk, where you had to order the drinks at the bar and take them to your seat. We were lucky to find a very well situated table, that is, in a manner of speaking, because it was right in the midst of all the bustle; but it was a holiday night, there wasn't even room in the plaza to breathe and everybody, even the fastidious Guitarte, and Carlota, who is restraint personified, and I myself, not to mention Dora, were inclined to shoot the works; what can I say, it's contagious. I can't tolerate that sort of thing in Buenos Aires, even if I am out of my mind, but as you see, in Havana everything seemed lovely.

The party had begun at nine, with cannon blasts. It seems that in the colonial period in Havana they put a chain across the port to keep the pirate ships out and every night at nine o'clock they shot off the cannons, and now Fidel Castro does too. Although for us the party began earlier most days, with the theater performances. Sometimes the play itself wasn't worth much but it was entertaining all the same, because of the people; Dora knew two or three members of the casts and besides, there everyone's your friend.

From the beginning we had gotten along fabulously with the Guitartes. We hit it off well on the plane and afterwards it was as if we had decided to do everything together.

Every now and then Dora would bring up her experience in vocational theater; it annoyed Guitarte to hear her talk about those days when he didn't know her, but Carlota, normally so reserved, had to ask her this, that and the other. I was surprised at her attitude, but it so happened that Carlota had also been involved with the theater in Luján, and once she even went on tour through the province; that night was the first time I'd heard about it. But I can't pretend to know everything my wife did as a young person. I met her as an adult and we got married six months later.

Dora can't contain her artistic fickleness, although she would never pass at being an extra; she wanted to let everyone know that she knew everyone. And now these two were always together, birds of a feather; you would have had to hear them talk about the time when they had performed "Mother Courage" and "Who's Afraid of Virginia Woolf?" and so on and on.

It must be the heat, it must be the heat that loosens the tongue; that must be why the Cubans are so friendly. The heat, how curious; in Buenos Aires it suffocates you, but in Cuba it makes you want to dance.

Truth be told, the music gets into your pores. Blues, jazz, ballads, salsa, rock, and I can't even begin to tell you what it was like when Silvio Rodríguez and Pablo Milanés had the microphone.

After the cannon blasts the fireworks began, and then came the Folklore ballet, an excess of, well, songs, dances, drums. Dora explained that it would be like a *macumba* with music, if we were in Brazil, but being in Cuba they were *yombos* rites with music.

From the stage, the dancers invited the public to join in. Dora jumped out of her chair as if she had been sitting on a spring and grabbed Guitarte and he didn't resist, but even if he tried, one can see that dancing isn't his forte. I also got Carlota to dance, poor fat girl, tapping away with her feet at her chair; since we got married, and it's almost two years now, we don't do those things any longer. To think that our courtship began at a dance in the disco Mau-Mau, a publicity send-off for a councilwoman who had invited half the world and we got invitations through some fluke, separately, of course.

I'm not comfortable on a dance floor, either, but in Havana it's different, you know? it's as if you had permission to do whatever you want, no problem. And after that, well, anything goes.

"I'm thirsty," Dora said every now and then, and then Guitarte or I would go find more *mojitos* and enter in battle with the people crowded around the bar. The truth is that the heat made it necessary.

We had begun by having drinks before the performance, a work by a Polish writer, don't ask me his name or what it was about, I don't understand a thing about modern theater, begging pardon of Dora and even Carlota, who began praising the staging and the acting, as if she had been able to understand what they said. Carlota is reserved, you can't get a word out of her, unless you shake her or something; I liked seeing her so animated.

It was the inauguration of the International Theater Institute. There were famous actors all over the place, not only Latin Americans, but also Yankees; and there were Hindus, Africans, all dressed in regional costumes; the Nobel Laureate Wole Soyinka was there; I learned the black man's name well because he was announced everywhere; also Gabriel García Márquez, Inda Ledesma, Sosa, Alfredo Alcón, and Sergio Renán were there and many more.

For Dora, García Márquez was a disappointment. She managed to catch him at the theater entrance, wearing his white tropical shirt, and she pounced on him and said, "what a pleasure for me to be able to meet you personally, you don't know what a pleasure it is." And he answered her, "it shows on your face," and paid no more attention to her.

That's all right. Dora is pretty forward, but it seems to me that the Nobel had gone to his head. She would have liked to have had an interesting dialogue with him, I imagine, in order that she could show off afterwards in Buenos Aires, but she wasn't going to miss this opportunity and she repeated just that anecdote to anyone who would listen all night long, but now, only to criticize him.

"Dora, dear, you already told her the story" said Guitarte, when she was going to tell her story again to an Italian woman that she had met at the hotel. Luckily, the Italian left almost in a hurry; to carry on a serious conversation in this atmosphere? no thank you. The show was almost over, it was quite late and one could breathe much better now.

And the party had just started. Because as most people left, a more compact, friendlier group remained, and then everyone began to dance with everyone else and by themselves, with many people dancing alone, or changing partners, Guitarte with Carlota, Dora with a red-bearded Cuban dramatist who attached himself to us as often as he could; even me with Dora, once, the "salsa," you'd have to have seen it to believe it.

The red-bearded man, his dramas still unperformed, as he explained to us, spoke slowly, and he felt very proud announcing the names of the musical groups half a minute before the presenter did.

"You'll see how good this one is," he said every time. He was also proud because he was responsible for I don't know what part of the organization of the festival.

"Do you think *everything* is good?" Dora asked him suddenly. With that woman you never know.

"I'm not prejudiced against any type," the Cuban answered sweetly.

"Neither am I," said Dora, and laughed to herself.

The curious thing is that Guitarte was watching his wife dancing with such pleasure, so freely, with the red-beard, without worrying at all. I don't know if Guitarte is the jealous type, you can't know that, we met on the airplane, as I said; but it's clear that he's old-fashioned. You see him and you know right away that he's a lawyer; he probably doesn't even take off his tie to go to bed.

But a vacation in Cuba can take the floor right out from under you. Of course, Guitarte was also wearing sports clothes, but it was an elegant sport, never touristy tee shirts. And the hotels! The beaches! We were staying at a first-class hotel built by the yankees, and for a trifle; it was all included in the tour and it was there, or in the bus, where we made strange friendships: Dora with the bearded one, Guitarte with the widow of a famous poet. The poet was an Englishman who had fought in the Spanish Civil War, but shortly before dying, the old man married this chick, his third or fourth wife, and now she spent her time traveling around the world with the title of distinguished widow, and with the inheritance she received.

I enjoyed myself more watching all those people than with anything else; if Carlota is reserved, well, I am even worse. Luckily my work doesn't require a lot of words. I work for an insurance company. Like Carlota. The same union, different companies. Perhaps that's what brought us together.

It had been my wife's idea to go to Cuba. Here's the story. Carlota consulted a Romanian astrologer; there are many in Buenos Aires, astrologers, I mean, and this one was fashionable. Carlota consulted her because she was a bit depressed and a friend from work recommended her. She told her that knowing oneself is the way to get better and since a horoscope costs a lot less than a therapy . . . Well. The thing is that the astrologer recommended that she spend her birthday in Havana, because, according to her star chart, the best thing for her to do was to begin a new year with I don't know which planet hovering over her head.

"And wouldn't Río de Janeiro do the same thing?" I had asked.

And no, it wasn't the same. The stars said that it would be in Havana, her birthday, Saturn . . . yes, I think it was Saturn that favored her. "Yes, it would cost us the same as a trip to Mar del Plata," Carlota insisted. And she took out the brochures.

She had been visiting agencies and looking for prices, and when she gets something in her head, well. Finally I saw that the idea wasn't totally lame, there's nothing wrong with combining tropical beaches with a famous theater festival, although names of authors and books aren't tripping over my tongue, as with Dora and Guitarte. All things considered, yes, it was all going to cost about the same thing as a trip to Mar del Plata and you can't even compare the two. And besides, what the heck; if it would make her feel better.

"The astrologer announced a change for me," Carlota explained, "but nothing happens automatically. The planets are there, they direct the flow of things, but one can choose not to go along."

Well, she convinced me. I don't believe in those things, but I don't disbelieve either, just in case. And dragging along behind her, I was also making my changes. Only you see them less in me.

And the night was advancing warmly there in the Cathedral plaza. Havana is a city full of enchantment. But watch out that you don't get yourself all wound-up.

As Guitarte said to Dora, "Don't drink any more, your head will hurt later."

As a reply, Dora took off her shoes. The stones of the street were round paving stones, big, warm. I know they were warm because Carlota said so, because I don't take off my shoes in public, not even drunk; but Carlota had hardly seen Dora do it when she took off her own shoes and said:

"How lovely to feel the warmth of the cobblestones on my feet," and they began to dance.

They began to dance alone, but soon after the red-bearded guy mingled with them: always leaning more towards Dora, so I didn't get upset. And also there was a Hindu, one of those who wears a turban. Then Guitarte got up and went right over to dance with the English poet's widow, who had been sitting for a while with some Catalonians at the next table and who had been watching him with the face of a Sphinx. Dora saw her husband's maneuver and waved her hand as though saying bye, have a good time; I don't know if the Guitartes were really married but they passed as a married couple, although it was evident that both had been married before, to other people, you understand.

And afterwards I didn't see anything else because I went to the bar and I also ordered another *mojito;* what the hell, suddenly I had begun to feel as alone as a dog and like crying.

A little while later, the red-beard grabbed on to me, slapping me on the back and saying: "Brother, she is a rose, she is *the* rose."

He must have been talking, I think, about Dora, who was wearing a sheer rose-colored dress and when she turned on the dance floor it became a whirlpool. My fat wife had on a white sundress that, tanned as she was, really went well with her hair. I say fat from pure affection; the truth is that she was very well shaped, much better than Dora. Dora may have great big eyes and an enormous uncombed reddish mane like they're wearing it nowadays, but she is skinny and her neckline looks like a clothes hanger, and to top it off she has broiled in the sun. I don't know what some people see in her; she hasn't been careful and tanned slowly, with a lot of sunscreen, like Carlota. Besides, I don't like women without tits.

Several times I left the bar with the intention of returning to the table, but when I saw them whirling, possessed by the music, I felt bad and turned around, back to the bar, but once there I didn't want to order any more drinks, since I didn't want to get loaded.

That night something had to happen.

The red-beard got tiresome; he was determined to buy me another *mojito* and everyone knows those people get offended if you refuse; finally we tore ourselves away from the bar, and when the girls got tired of dancing, the bearded one started trying to convince us to go to the beach. There's nothing like watching the sun come up over the sea, he kept repeating. I don't know how it happened, but when the crowd at the plaza was beginning to break up, the bearded one dragged us to an old car parked one or two blocks from the cathedral, the two women in front walking with their shoes in their hands, humming a catchy song by Stevie Wonder that I don't dare sing, since I'm tone-deaf, and we all got into his *carro*, as he called his car. And before I noticed, besides Guitarte and Dora and Carlota and I, I see that in the car were of course the bearded one, the Englishman's widow and a swarthy boy who spoke Spanish correctly but with a guttural "r," who said that his name was Youssef, that he was from Damascus, and about whom no one could explain to me where he came from.

We got out at a solitary beach and the bearded one made us walk to a restaurant that belonged to a friend of his, and he pounded at the door, which was already locked, but still had a light shining inside. The owner, a lustrous fat man, greeted him with open arms and immediately brought a bottle of rum, but Dora said that she wanted beer, which cuts down on the drunkenness.

We sat outside. The night was spectacular, with all those stars in the sky and the full moon.

When the fat man put the bottles on the table Dora smacked her forehead with her hand and exclaimed: "But I forgot! Hey, sir! Bring a bottle of champagne!"

The man brought it and popped the cork, which passed between Carlota and the Syrian.

"Almost, almost!" said Dora to Carlota, smiling into her eyes. And she stood up and with her glass raised she said: "A toast to Carlota. Happy Birthday!"

I realized that Dora had beaten me to it, and I got up and kissed my wife on the mouth while the others sang a frightfully bad version of "Happy Birthday."

"I don't know how I forgot," I excused myself. "We made this trip especially to celebrate her birthday here."

"Yes," said Carlota.

"Of course," I said. "An astrologer told her that she should begin the year here, in Cuba. Tell her," I said.

"They already know," said Carlota.

"I don't know," said the Englishman's widow. "Tell me." She spoke Spanish as a Catalonian would, mumbling the words.

"It's nothing," said Carlota. "Just that an astrologer advised me to do this."

"An astrologer told her that she had to travel to Havana, because it's here that several planets are aligned to help her find her true destiny," said Dora.

"Can anyone know their true destiny?" asked Guitarte.

"I owe you your present," I said. "All week talking about this and today..."

Then I realized that my error wasn't too great, because the day was just beginning and in Luján, where she was born, it was still the previous night.

"What are you going to give her?" asked Guitarte.

"Whatever she chooses," I said. "I have told her to choose whatever she wants."

"Go for it," said the widow.

"Carlota knows how to choose; she's discreet," I said.

"Carlota is a Sagittarius and you don't know a thing about her," said Dora.

I was surprised at her statement but I guess it wasn't too unexpected, given her temper and so much alcohol.

"The sign of the traveler. The sign of the artist. Her sun is in Venus. The moon favors her," said the Syrian.

"How is that?" asked the widow.

"The passage of the moon favors the woman," added the Syrian. He spoke with absolute conviction.

"Of course I'm going to choose," said Carlota.

"Right. A good present," I said.

"I'm going to choose. I'm going to do what I never dared to do until this moment. That's why I have come here."

I remembered when I used to go to the country, as a kid, and at dawn I would see some little sleeping bird waking up, and it gave me something like the chill I felt then.

They look at each other like accomplices.

"Of course. That's why you came," said Dora.

They looked at each other as accomplices.

"Sagittarius, the sign of fire," pronounced Dora.

I looked apprehensively at the red hairs that sprouted all over the Cuban but my look also tripped over Dora's tousled mane; a gust of wind stirred it like the fire of hell.

The bearded one got up, went toward the edge of the sea, took off his pants, his underwear and his shirt and dove into the water.

Then Dora shouted: "To the sea! To the sea!" She grabbed Carlota by the hand and the two ran off.

The Syrian wasn't far behind. He said: "That's a good idea," and after he had gone a distance, he also had stripped to his balls. Guitarte looked at me as though asking for help. I shrugged my shoulders. They say that this is done on all beaches except those in Argentina. As for me, I would never take off my clothes in front of everyone else, not even with all the rum I had inside me. Down deep, the sea doesn't attract me much. I stayed and made an idiotic remark, which I immediately regretted. I said:

"One needed a lot of water to put out so much fire."

I lit a cigarette and offered one to Guitarte and the widow, and I wanted the earth to open up and swallow me.

"I don't know what the hell is going on with those two," said Guitarte. He seemed ten years older than in the afternoon, when he had left the hotel freshly shaved and bathed and wearing half a bottle of cologne.

"They've gone to the other side," I said, as if it were up to me to offer explanations. In fact, the two men could be seen swimming toward the breakwater.

The two women were helping each other take off their dresses.

"Is it dangerous?" I asked, when I saw them advancing hand in hand, and I felt lower than a cockroach. I can't imagine diving in to save anyone. But to calm myself, I affirmed: "Carlota knows how to swim, and this sea isn't as rough as ours . . . And what about Dora? . . ."

"For all I care she can drown," said Guitarte. The women were laughing and leaping over the waves that were lapping at their knees. The moon illuminated them. Carlota seemed like a statue, like those they used to make: full-bodied, a moving statue. The Syrian and the bearded one were two little points heading out to sea, the madmen.

The widow said: "I want to leave."

Guitarte threw the cigarette butt to the ground angrily. "So that was it," he said, and he got up to leave. I kept smoking in silence.

"Let's go," said Guitarte. The Catalonian Englishwoman followed him. I still didn't understand what Guitarte had said. I stayed by myself. And I saw them. I watched them for a long time. I saw them kissing each other. I couldn't leave, watching how they caressed each other's nipples, breasts, falling slowly, slowly, while the water caressed their legs.

I saw the Cuban and the Syrian return and get dressed and head toward the car. Perhaps Guitarte and the widow were waiting for them there. And I remained where I was, tied to a dark thread that stretched from the earth.

I saw the sun come up beyond the sea, and then I began to walk.

Elvira Orphée

Elvira Orphée was born in San Miguel de Tucumán, Argentina, in 1930 and was educated at the University of Buenos Aires and at the Sorbonne, in Paris. She has traveled and resided in several European countries, spending eight years in France, three in Italy, and one in Spain. She has published novels, stories, and newspaper articles. As a writer, she has received many honors, including Honorable Mention in the Fabril Editorial Literary Contest for her novel *Uno;* Second Prize in the Municipality of Buenos Aires for *Aire tan dulce;* First Prize in the Municipality of Buenos Aires for *En el fondo;* and Honorable Mention in the 1970 short story contest sponsored by *Imagen.* She also received the Regional Prize for *La muerte y los desencuentros.* She has published short stories and articles in *Asomante, Cuadernos, Razón, El Tiempo, Revista de Occidente, El Tiempo, Zona Franca* e *Imagen,* and others.

Publications

Dos veranos (Two summers). Buenos Aires: Sudamericana, 1956.

Uno (One). Buenos Aires: Fabril Editora, 1961.

Aire tan dulce (Such sweet air). Buenos Aires: Sudamericana, 1966.

En el fondo (In the back). Buenos Aires: Galerna, 1969.

Su demonio preferido (Her preferred demon). Buenos Aires: Emecé, 1973.

La última conquista de El Angel (Last conquest of El Angel). Caracas: Monte Avila, 1977.

Las viejas fantasiosas (The fancy old women) Buenos Aires: Emecé, 1981.

La muerte y los desencuentros (Death and the missed connections). Buenos Aires: Fraterna, 1990.

Ciego del Cielo (The blind man from heaven). Buenos Aires: Emecé, 1991.

Basura y luna (Trash and moon). Buenos Aires: Planeta, 1996.

Secondary Sources

Alvarez Sosa, Arturo. "Su demonio preferido." *La Gaceta,* 8 July 1973.

Baracchini, Diego. "El retrato inalcanzable de Elvira Orphée." *La Opinión,* 15 January 1978.

Bastos, María Luisa. "Review of *Uno.*" *Sur* 272 (September–October 1961): 107–9.

———. "Tortura y discurso autoritario: *La última conquista de El Angel* de Elvira Orphée." In *The Contemporary Latin American Short Story,* edited by Rose Minc. New York, 1979.

———. "Una escritora argentina: Elvira Orphée." *Zona Franca* 3/44 (April 1967): 24–26.

Castillo, Abelardo. "Polémica sobre *Uno:* Carta abierta a David Lagmanovich." *La Gaceta,* 16 July 1961.

———. "*Uno,* novela de Elvira Orphée." *Ficción* 32 (1961): 78.

Chacel, Rosa. "Un libro ciertamente nuevo." *Sur* 245 (March–April 1957): 111–17.

Chevigny, Bell Gale. "Ambushing the Will to Ignorance: Elvira Orphée's *La última conquista de El Angel* and Marta Traba's *Conversación al sur.*" In *El Cono Sur: Dinámica y dimensiones de su literatura, A Symposium,* edited by Rose Minc, 98–104. Upper Montclair, N.J.: Montclair State College, 1985.

———. "Conversación con Elvira Orphée." *Zona Franca* 3/2 (July–August 1977): 24–28.

Clark, Maria Brigitta. "The Feminine Fantastic in Short Fiction from the River Plate." *Dissertation Abstracts International* 54.3 943A 44A (September 1993): DA9319185.

Correa, María Angélica. "Review of *Uno.*" *Señales* 131 (July–August 1961): 29.

Crespo, Julio. "*Aire tan dulce.*" *Sur* 307 (July–August 1967): 47–49.

De Miguel, María Esther. "La mujer en su literatura y su responsabilidad como escritora." *Revista de la Universidad Nacional de Córdoba* 10/1–2 (1969): 321–37.

Díaz, Gwendolyn. "Escritura y palabra: *Aire tan dulce,* de Elvira Orphée." *Revista Iberoamericana* 51/132–33 (July–December 1985): 641–48.

Dujovne Ortiz, Alicia. "Los demonios de lo cotidiano." *La Opinión Cultural,* 27 November 1977: 10–11.

———. "Elvira Orphée." *Journal of Latin American Literature* 51 (1979): 3–23.

Fares, Gustavo, and Eliana Hermann. "Exilios internos: El viaje en cinco escritoras argentinas." *Hispanic Journal* 15/1 (Spring 1994): 21–29.

Ferro, Helen. "*Uno,* en un libro de Elvira Orphée." *Clarín* 14 (July 1961): 2.

Flori, Mónica Roy. *Streams of Silver: Six Contemporary Women Writers from Argentina.* Lewisburg, Penn.: Associated University Presses, 1995.

Gómez Paz, Julieta. "*Aire tan dulce.*" *La Prensa,* 3 September 1967.

Hermann, Eliana. "Elvira Orphée. *Ciego de cielo*" *Hispanic Journal* 12/1 (Fall 1991): 350–51.

———. *Viajes en la palabra y en la imagen.* Buenos Aires: Gaglianone, 1996.

Justo, Luis. "Elvira Orphée y sus novelas." *Sur* 315 (November–December 1968): 88–89.

———. "La seducción de lo prohibido en un sagaz libro de Elvira Orphée." *La Opinión,* 22 July 1973.

Loubet, Jorgelina. "Lo cotidiano, el fulgor y el signo en la obra de actuales escritoras argentinas." *Zona Franca* (September–October 1980): 7–23.

———. "Tres miradas en trascendencia." *Boletín de la Academia Argentina de Letras* 51/201–2 (July–December 1986): 343–58.

Moctezuma, Edgardo. "Para mirar lejos antes de entrar: Los usos del poder en *Aire tan dulce,* de Elvira Orphée." *Revista Iberoamericana* 49/125 (October–December 1983): 929–42.

Olaso, Ezequiel. "*Uno.*" *La Nación,* 4 June 1966.

Picón Garfield, Evelyn. "Desprendida a hachazos de la eternidad: Lo primordial en la obra de Elvira Orphée." *Journal of Latin American Literature* 51 (1979): 3–23.

———. *Women's Voices from Latin America: Interviews with Six Contemporary Authors.* Detroit: Wayne State University Press, 1985.

Tompkins, Cynthia. "El poder del horror: Abyección en la narrativa de Griselda Gambaro y de Elvira Orphée." *Revista Hispánica Moderna* 6/1 (June 1993): 179–92.

Valenzuela, Luisa. "La belleza que lastima." *La Nación,* 2 August 1969.

Vázquez, María Esther. "Entre demencias y ángeles." *La Nación,* 14 June 1978.

Interview

1. Which authors have had the greatest influence on your work?

   I can't speak of influences, at least of conscious ones. I can speak of preferences which, since they are so varied, resist influences. That should be paired up with my aversion to whatever happens to be in fashion, because of the pressure it implies. I'll list my preferences: Japanese fiction writers, Akutagawa Ryonusuke, Tanizaki Junichiro, Ishikawa Takubobu, whose work I know only in fragments; Isaac Bashevis Singer, Isaac Babel, Elsa Morante, Colette, Emily Dickinson.

2. When did you begin to write, and why?

   As far as I remember, my first literary creation were some little verses that had nothing to do with truth nor with literature: "Una noche, noche muy bella / tu hermoso rostro yo contemplé / y en esa noche, noche de estrellas / a amarte mucho ya comencé." [One night, a beautiful night / I saw your handsome face / and on that night, a starlit night / I began to love you dearly.] I think I can be forgiven for them since I was only eleven years old. At twelve, the motivation that led me to write a novel—that never reached twenty pages—was boredom. You can imagine what it was like if you just think that at twelve years old one has no experience to write about anything. That attempt at a novel had a lot of forests and a character named Rolando, probably because of the influence of my French family, with its Song of Roland. What motivated me to write later, seriously, I don't know. What I know is that I should have been a poet. That, I believe, was what I really wanted.

3. How does the political situation influence your writings?

   When politics is incorporated into daily life and keeps us off balance, as it happens in this country, it stops being politics and becomes a kind of metaphysics, with the supreme power that metaphysics has over lives and souls.

4. Have you encountered difficulties, as a woman writer, with publishers?

With publishing houses I find all sorts of difficulties, even with the price of paper, which sometimes delays the edition of a book perhaps indefinitely. Before, the publishers were people who thought about business, yes, but also about quality. Now, here, that has almost disappeared. Besides, they don't reissue out-of-print books, no matter what they're worth, not even Sarmiento's books! Instead they put all their emphasis on what's new, even if it's mediocre at best. Finally, the publishers don't publicize their authors.

5. What do you think of feminism?

I think that feminism is a necessity. It opened the eyes of intelligent people; and the others will never open theirs.

6. How would you describe Argentina's women readers?

Women read much more than men do. But today I believe that it must be very difficult to spend money to buy the books that one would want.

Selection from *La muerte y los desencuentros*

La muerte y los desencuentros is about the life of a family in a town at the foot of the mountains. Although no countries or places are named, two different sites are mentioned: the narrator's place of origin, where the town is located, and the place to which she migrates. The first one is the town where her family has always lived, where she receives letters, and to where she eventually returns with a foreign husband. The second place is a chilly country described in these words by the narrative voice: "I went. I exchanged my warm land for a cold country." Upon returning to her native land she finds it dominated by a climate of terror and persecution. These are clear allusions to the political situation of Argentina and other Latin American countries during the decade of the 1970s and the beginning of the 1980s. At the time, all over the continent a so-called war occurred between self-styled "armed movements for liberation" and military governments, which took to themselves the task of restoring order in the community, an order which resulted in the imposition of a police state, silencing the majority of the population. Such events are reflected in the text chosen, which does not mention any political faction, but refers to a constant climate of violence, which caused the narrator's father to disappear. Towards the end of the story, the main character refuses to go back into exile and, also at this point, her husband begins to act strangely towards her. She decides to return once more to her childhood through her imagination, playing at being an angel and rediscovering the ties that unite her to her native country and to her family. She then leaves the adult world, and her husband with it, to follow the uncertain destiny of her father, precisely through literature, through the notes he had left behind, similar to those that she, too, will leave. As she puts it: "In the house of the grown-ups my notebooks will remain. Someone will hide them, as they did my father's" (168). The allusions to, and the descriptions of, the political situation in Argentina make this a critical and "angry" work that deals with the themes of terror and of the Dirty War from a perspective that can be considered typical of the circumstances that the whole of Argentine society once had to face.

Selection from *La muerte y los desencuentros*

My husband was in the doorway of the house when we arrived. The foreigner veered his automobile so as not to have to speak to him. On the threshold Manuel took my arm.

"When you were in my country, you wanted to be here. 'Always faithful to the absence,' as that poet says, the one you quote sometimes. Since you arrived here you wish you were there. Nothing here makes you happy. You feel wretched. We will leave, if you want, even if things are better in the country-side now. If you really want to, we'll return to my country. I'll begin again there, with a new job, although it may be harder."

"I don't want anything, not right now. I've put all my dreams in a forgotten corner somewhere."

In the dining room Clacó was waiting for me.

"Manuel wants to leave because he is afraid."

"How do you know?"

"When he heard on the radio what happened yesterday in the city, he got up so suddenly that he knocked over his chair. He went to the back of the house, and a little while later I heard him arguing with Florence. I'm afraid, too."

I flew to turn on the radio and I heard. Some criminals had created an absurd tragedy in the city square. Women with swollen bellies and baby carriages, fruit carts, station wagons carrying mattresses or furniture. Suddenly, from the baby carriages, from under the fruits and the mattresses, machine guns appeared. The people were falling dead, like ants under human feet, but they took control of their police station. For just a moment. Only to abandon it immediately. In the square there were cadavers of all kinds. Those of children with expressions of shock about to turn into smiles, as we saw later in the magazine pictures.

Like Manuel, I also got up, knocking over a chair, and I ran to confront Florence. Manuel was with her. I ordered her:

"Get him out of here. I will not tolerate a murderer in this house. Get him out, let them kill him."

"We can't go now. They'll see him. You'll all be exposed if he leaves."

"Why didn't you think about that when you brought him here? You! The two of you are as guilty as the ones who took my father away. And surely you are thieves like they are as well. Or perhaps you don't rob banks? Perhaps you don't kidnap for ransom? Perhaps you don't use bombs and machine guns to kill three-year-old babies? And here we are, right in the middle, making ourselves as shock absorbers for their bullets and yours too."

From one of the rooms off the abandoned patio came a sarcastic voice:

"But you have pity still. You would even open a dispensary if you had the wherewithal. We don't believe in charity. We let the people die of hunger so that they'll understand that they can only get bread with bullets. No, we don't practice bourgeois charity."

"Only at times, for propaganda purposes," I shouted at him. "You rob a food-truck and distribute it."

From a window the voice continued:

"You know so much! And we believed that these things didn't worry her. Enchanted Refuge sometimes escapes her spell. Perhaps she plays dumb like her brother in order to be able to spy more efficiently on the people's fighters."

Melitón hasn't hurt anyone from the people. He only fights for his snakes and for his love.

"Melitón doesn't spy on anyone. Don't be stupid. And I wouldn't spy on you. I would do things that are much worse, if only I didn't have to touch you. You disgust me as much whole as with your brains scattered on the pavement."

Florence pushed me, and I clearly sensed her intention, the way Arlequina feels or knows things: she wasn't trying to hurt me, she was pushing me out of the line of fire through a window.

But I couldn't keep quiet, and I kept on talking that way, more and more removed from the moderate words of my infancy.

"If anyone spies, it's you and your friends. How many times have you been here before? How many times have the others been here? Where were you hiding when you heard me talking with Melitón about his plans for a dispensary? Come on, Manuel, let's leave Common Place with his Common Place. But if you don't leave as soon as night falls I'm going to make you regret it."

"A snake?"

"Worse. But if it occurs to you to return, you'll find one in each empty room."

I withdrew shouting, followed by Manuel with a look of entreaty on his face.

"Yes, I know a lot!" I shouted. "I've known a lot ever since I studied in the cold country and my aunts and uncles talked about recovering my brothers. Not that anyone's told me; I'm guessing. And I have decided not to borrow any theory, any set phrase that be given to be repeated like a broken record. Death isn't effective in changing anyone's thoughts. Murders don't work. Yes, Manuel, you have to return to your country. Without me. I'll sell your animals and your seeds to some institute. Take Florence with you. I can't stand her."

"What right do you have to throw her out of this house?"

"The right of might. Isn't that what you practice daily? Well then, one does have to look at it with good eyes, whoever be exercising it."

"Don't you understand that Florence got involved with this because no one has ever loved her? She's pretty, she has a brain, and no one has ever loved her. Except for that one. Or at least he has made her believe that, so he can have her complete loyalty."

I shut up suddenly. Instantly, and for the first time, I felt Florence as if she were my sister. No one lives without the presence of the supernatural. And love, even misguided love, illuminates the meager entrails with its great brilliance. She was like me, someone else who could freeze from pure pain in the summer sun. One by one Melitón, Clacó, and now Florence have come to be my brother and sisters. Perhaps among all of us the secret ties of hatred, love, similar essences were elaborating an anxiety, a necessity, a goddess. Even Clacó, in love with stories, with the moon, with voyages, is more my sister than anyone else's. And once I thought that all the people around here were like them! In their indolence, yes, in believing that it is fun to injure others, as they did in their cruel game with Peteté. But no matter how far or how near, how beloved or how despised, any brother or sister is always a stranger. And in between me and those that are mine there are death and the missed connections. I turned, and from far away in the patio Florence looked at me and I looked at her, deeply saddened.

I didn't ask Manuel why he too had entered into the sinister plot, how they had convinced him. In his country they are very altruistic with the lives of others. Once a professor entered class saying: "I had a marvelous dream; all of Latin America was burning in flames." And I wanted the flames to reach them, too.

Beyond the dream, broken crystals from a pale mirror that reflect me break down. Pain and sleep break the unified image of the mirror and with each fragment a different mask destroys the limits of another one.

What pain that night! What pains tearing me to pieces! Each one, a major player that electrified with a floodlight the few dreams of the silent night, inhabited by perfidy and magnolias.

The next day, while the morning was still full of the perfumes of dawn, and I was the only one awake, I had a visitor, Date Lilina's son-in-law. The antman from the moonlit roof, dressed in a uniform. Oily, friendly, speaking with little pleasantries: he would like to see the place where a person as enchanting as I lived.

Again death was coming to visit us.

"Everyone's asleep."

"We could wake them up."

"My house is not fit to be seen. It's destitute, run-down, abandoned."

"The land is worth something."

He was telling me that this time they wouldn't take only the refrigerator, they would take away the house, with its deed and everything else. And they wouldn't leave anyone behind to hold them accountable. Like Roman emperors who ordered people killed, with the pretext of them being traitors, in order to claim the inheritance for themselves.

My heart seemed to lose its rhythm and its temperature. His ant-like protruding eyes calculated the worth of my body. The emissary of misfortune wanted to add humiliation to the torment and the pillage.

Surely he spoke, surely he said that courtesy obliged me to invite him to sit down because, suddenly, we were in the patio, with him in a chair and me standing. Perhaps only after the moment when I no longer spoke because the confused condition of my mind was total, he wanted our complete submission so that he could feel that he had the rights of the affronted one, on top of the rights for being the obedient emissary of his country. My mind was blank, like absent, and I knew that this attitude would have offended even a peasant accustomed to abuse.

Finally Lilina and Keto came out of their house; and a little while later, Clacó and Manuel from ours, all converging on the patio like points from a star into its center. Or, better still, like curiosity-seekers in the middle of a fight with wounded people.

"Well, it seems that they've awakened. Now I can see the house. And you can recover your speech. Will you tell the soldiers whom I left outside that I will take a little while still? I can go through it all, can't I?

A rush of fear. It's not me, it's Manuel. My fear does not show because it's preparing to fight.

"If you asked courteously, it would be discourteous not to show it all to you. But it would be discourteous on your part to pose a demand under the pretense of courtesy. We are not friendly enough for me to have offered my house to you."

He is surprised that I would confront him, the one with power.

"How old are you, *young lady*?" he said with irony, knowing perfectly well who I was. "Your brother is more capable than you to interpret. I'd say that he sees one's intentions and makes the proposals himself."

Gaps. He knows Melitón. Melitón always anticipates his intentions. Gaps make everything a mystery.

"I don't want anyone to see our poverty. I don't want to be ashamed."

"Pain or shame, which do you prefer?"

He half-closes his ant eyes.

"Let him see our house if he wants to," says Lilina.

She is a fool, but not to the point of proposing that they trap her sister. Florence is not there, then.

"Go with him."

"You come too."

"Our custom is to respect the house of the youngest. I can't go in."

"You, I believe, are younger than some of your sisters."

"Lilina will explain what the rule is when we marry."

We watch him walk with Lilina and Keto towards their house. Manuel radiates fear. Let it not be an impatient fear, one that has an urgency to betray itself! Let it not explode. I take his hand, I look at him without saying a word. Oh, God, let him take refuge within my fighting walls!

We're no longer speaking. Time seems to stand still. The children's house is becoming distorted in front of our eyes. There they are! They have come out.

Instead of coming toward us, they go toward the patio in the back of the house. It's over. They'll find them. And who knows what orders has the one with the knife face, Florence's *companion*. I go into the house with Manuel and Clacó.

"I'm escaping," Manuel's fear breaks out.

"Don't be a fool. They're waiting outside. There's a possibility that Florence and that individual have left without leaving anything compromising behind. I'm going to look for something we need."

I collect seven razor blades and a knife.

I return with it all to Manuel and Clacó.

"If the ant colonel finds Florence and that man, we won't let him leave. Those outside will start shooting. Someone might kill us. But if they don't manage to kill us? Don't let yourselves be taken alive. One-time pain is better than what they'll do to us, day after day, infuriated. If they take us, they'll do things to us that only a monster can imagine. Clacó," I hugged her, "I will cut you. I'm stronger."

"What a stupid plan! Razor blades. Be practical!" says Manuel. "Use your father's revolver. The one that your grandmother hid when they went with the Ibargurens. They won't give us the time to bleed to death from razor blades. Florence, her companion, and I have cyanide capsules."

Rapidly he looks for the revolver. I look outside and in, startled by everything, and suddenly my eyes deceive me: they see Colonel Anselmo, the ant son-in-law, walking calmly between Keto and Lilina. I calm my heart. Still incredulous, the hope that we might be saved returns to me. It makes me say:

"A revolver! They'll say that we have hidden weapons, if it occurs to them to search now. Where will we hide it?"

"On me," says Clacó, perhaps playing heroine, perhaps already heroic. "We have forgotten our grandmother. She's dangerous. Who knows what she'll come out with!"

It's true. There's no time to find out where she is. My heart won't remain quiet. I go out to meet the "ant colonel."

"You were right, young lady. The house is not fit to be seen. It is neglected. There's even a room with overturned furniture. That's not a matter of poverty."

"No. It's a matter of laziness, which isn't against the law. A question of laziness or of forgetfulness."

But, why am I challenging him? Who's setting out to open the door to tragedy?

"Let's see the rest of the house."

What rest does he want to see if he's already seen everything? Ah, our part, that from the older folks. The smart thing is to act like I'm resisting.

"It's not for sale."

"It could be, any moment now."

"Not as long as we live. We wouldn't have any place to go."

"Lately people are dying young. Drugs, subversion, affairs, you know."

"Yes, people die at all ages, yours and mine."

"Well, since everything is possible, I will look at the house. It would be worse if others came to look at it. I only came with the curiosity of a friend who can obtain the best price for you, if you should want to sell it, and I was counting on your cooperation. One supposes that a beautiful woman should be friendly, right?"

"No!" Manuel explodes. "A woman should be only the way she wants to be."

"What will happen," I interrupt, "if I refuse to let you see our poverty?"

"Just imagine."

Now it is all clear. I drop my veil.

"Then, go ahead. Come in. It's true, you have been pretty considerate, not ordering them to search it. Although I don't see why they have to keep going through it again and again when that business with my father happened so long ago."

"Parents bequeath their teachings to their children."

"Not to me, never did I or my brothers and sisters put up with anything except laziness."

"I will go to see the house. As a friend, of course, who trusts that you will respond to that friendliness."

Another threat. But one easier to void. The man with blue eyes could do a lot for us.

He searched the rooms tile by tile. We knocked at grandmother's door, no one answered. We entered. No one was there. The colonel looked under the bed, which had a long bedspread, and there one could hear a clucking. A hen came running out. We moved closer. One could see only my grandmother's eyes in the darkness.

"Come out from there. What on earth are you doing?" we said.

"I'm only brooding that hen to teach her to comply with her duty."

Peteté appeared, from some place where he must have been sleeping, and frightened the hen. It was an uproar. All of this madness convinced the military ant. At times it is good to have a loony grandmother. He said goodbye, full of insinuations, among them that he awaited my visit to his tower.

For the first time we were all together, planning together, deciding together. My grandmother, calm and astute, let out a little laugh:

"Brooding that hen was the best thing to do to make him leave."

The rest of us decided: an immediate departure for Manuel and arrangements for us in the first government office of his country that he could find; once there, more arrangements and the press; hounding anew his Ministry. If he could, he would make Florence leave with him, but he couldn't wait long enough to find her. She shouldn't return here for anything.

I remembered that yesterday she and I had looked at each other in the patio, as sad as when the specter of Victor Ibarguren met that of the guerrilla fighter, who wasn't God, in the street.

"Who will take care of her?" someone asked.

"Her friends."

"What did she hide in her belly?" asked Clacó.

We looked at each other, remembering her dirtiness, her deformed clothing. Pamphlets perhaps, perhaps other documents.

"Or perhaps a revolver," she said. "Look how the one I'm hiding makes me look funny."

The svelte Clacó had an almost pointed stomach. She took out the revolver and gave it to Manuel, and a notebook which she gave to me.

Mabel Pagano

Mabel Pagano was born in Lanús Oeste, in the Province of Buenos Aires, on May 6, 1945. Early in her career she took literature courses from the writers Marta Lynch and Isodoro Blastein. She still lives in her hometown of Lanús, actively researching and creating highly original works of literature.

She has received several awards for her work. The most important include: The Premio Fondo Nacional de Las Artes for *En Setiembre y por agua* and *El país del suicidio;* the Prize Faja de Honor de la Argentine Writers' Society (SADE); the Fortabat Foundation Prize for *Enero es un largo lunes;* El Cid Editorial Novel Contest for *Primera quincena de mayo;* the Medal of Honor from the Argentine Writers' Society (SADE) for *La familia es lo primero;* Emecé Publishers Annual Prize for *La calle del agua;* the Chivilcoy Municipal Prize; the Prize from the Greek Institute of Culture for *Los griegos no existen;* and the 1993 Alfredo Roggiano Prize for *Agua de nadie.* She was also a finalist in the 1994–95 Prize for Novels sponsored by LUMEN, in Barcelona. Since winning the Municipal Prize in 1994 she has been able to write full-time. In February 1997 she received the First Prize in the "XX Encuentro de Escritores Patagónicos" for the book *Ocho misterios*. The work will be published by the Fondo Nacional de las Artes. Her stories have appeared in *Vosotras, Para Ti, Nocturno, Letras Argentinas, Coyuyo, Creativos Argentinos, Oeste, Amaru, Ateneo, Letras de Buenos Aires, El Tiempo* (Azul), *El Día* (La Plata), *Convicción* (Buenos Aires), *Mayoría* (Buenos Aires), and *La Prensa* (Buenos Aires).

Publications

Liberación hundida (Sunk liberation). Buenos Aires: Odin, 1976.

En setiembre y por agua (September and by the water). Buenos Aires: Ramos Americana, 1979.

La familia es lo primero (Family comes first). Buenos Aires: Grupo Editor de Buenos Aires, 1980.

"Un baldío en octubre" (An empty land in October). *Amistad, divino tesoro*. Buenos Aires: Orión, 1980.

"El barrio" (The neighborhood). *Borrón y cuenta nueva*. Buenos Aires: Grupo Editor de Buenos Aires, 1980.

Eterna. Biografía novelada sobre la vida de Eva Perón (Eternal: Novel on Eva Perón's biography). Buenos Aires: Nuevo Sol, 1982.

Primera quincena de mayo (The first fortnight in May). Buenos Aires: El Cid Editor, 1983.

El cuarto intermedio (Interval). Buenos Aires: Celtia, 1983.

Nacer de nuevo (To be born again). Rosario: Fundación Rosario, 1985.

Enero es un largo lunes (January is one long Monday). Buenos Aires: Fraterna, 1987.

El país del suicidio (Suicide country). Buenos Aires: Catálogos, 1987.

La calle del agua (The water street). Buenos Aires: Emecé, 1988.

Trabajo a reglamento (Working according to the rules). Buenos Aires: Marymar, 1990.

Martes del Final (Historia de la Guerra de la Triple Alianza) (Final Tuesday: History of the Triple Alliance War). Asunción, Paraguay: Intercontinental, 1991.

Lorenza Reinafé o Quiroga, la Barranca de la tragedia (Lorenza Reinafé or Quiroga, the gorge of tragedy). Buenos Aires: Ada Korn, 1991.

Los griegos no existen (The Greeks do not exist). Buenos Aires: Almagesto, 1991.

"País de veintisiete otoños" (Country of twenty seven autumns). *El cuento argentino*. Buenos Aires: Editorial de Belgrano, 1993.

Niños que hicieron historia (Children who made history). Buenos Aires: Marimar, 1994.

Agua de nadie (Nobody's water). Buenos Aires: Almagesto, 1995.

Secondary Sources

Fares, Gustavo. "Mabel Pagano. *Los griegos no existen*. Buenos Aires: Almagesto, 1991."
Hispamérica: Revista de Literatura 64–65 (April–August 1993): 200–202.

———. "Mabel Pagano. *Trabajo a reglamento*. Buenos Aires: Marymar, 1990." *Revista
Iberoamericana* 155–56 (April–September 1991): 765–67.

Hermann, Eliana. "Mabel Pagano. *Lorenza Reinafé o Quiroga, la Barranca de la tragedia*." *Chasqui: Revista de Literatura Latinoamericana* 23/1 (May 1993): 91–92.

———. "Mabel Pagano *Agua de nadie*." *Chasqui: Revista de Literatura Latinoamericana* 25/2 (November 1996): 138–39.

Interview

1. Which authors have had the greatest influence on your work?

I consider it true what someone said, that "in literature we are all children
of someone." In my case, and although our styles are very different, the Argentines Marta Lynch and Haroldo Conti have influenced me. In the case
of Conti, whom I never personally met, through his books and, in Lynch's
case, besides her works, through her lessons, since I was her student.
Through them I was able to better understand my literature, to improve it,
to open new roads and, at the same time, understand better the literature
of everyone else. Of course the "great" Latin American writers have also influenced me, García Márquez, Rulfo, Vargas Llosa, Scorza.

2. When did you begin to write, and why?

I began to write when I was around sixteen. I wrote poems of which I am
now embarrassed. I began because, being confronted by all that was beginning to happen to me, nothing of which I could explain, writing seemed to
be a great consolation, allowing me to examine my own feelings. Afterwards, when I was about twenty-two, I began to write stories and later
novels, and then there were other motives that motivated me to write. Although I believe, deep down the first motive persists as something essential
and profound: the need to express my feelings.

3. How does the political situation influence your choice of themes?

It does not, although in a country where there has been a type of repression as brutal as in Argentina, this preoccupation, undoubtedly, is unavoidable. But I try to get beyond it and not be concerned with the immediate turmoil.

4. Have you encountered difficulties, as a woman writer, with publishers?

In Argentina men and women have the same difficulties finding publishers. It isn't a problem of sex, but of the economy. They're publishing very little and only the best known writers. The rest, me for example, are published when we win prizes. Broadening the topic a little bit, I should be honest and say that years ago, when the crisis wasn't so deep and they published more, I didn't have those kinds of problems.

5. What do you think of feminism?

Feminism, like all movements of that sort, is positive. At any rate, I try to raise my vision above whatever sectarianism there is, and my sermons, when I express them, are directed towards the attainment of better and more just conditions for human beings in general.

6. How would you describe Argentina's women readers?

Argentine women are avid, lucid, and intelligent readers, who demand from the writers an answer to their worries, even if it produces new turmoil. This is evident at book signings, when and where one has the opportunity to meet the author. First timidly, and then frankly, the female public asks questions, quotes other works, doubts, agrees with certain judgments or offers alternatives and, at times, they'll even say that they, as readers, have identified with some character from the book.

Selection from *Trabajo a reglamento*

Trabajo a reglamento gives a vision of humanity on the verge of death, failure, or disintegration but, in spite of that, still striving to survive somehow, anyhow, even if only in a dream or, in the worst of cases, a nightmare. In order to adequately describe those instances when finally "we understand," the collection of stories establishes a sequence of passions, events, dialogues, oblivion and nothingness that have managed to lead the woman, or the man, to the very instant in which they recognize themselves for what they are. Likewise they force us, as readers, to be responsible for their situation and for ours, to realize our own little miseries, our selfish betrayals, our abandonments, in short, our destiny. If, as Borges affirms, the aesthetic act consists in the immediateness of a revelation that does not become real, that act is found embodied in this work by Pagano. The title story from her collection reminds us of Kafka's anticipated nightmares, this time in a bureaucratic sector of Buenos Aires: the familiar hallways of the Main Post Office. Therein the narrator lives a world of nightmare, flight, and finally, acceptance. His/her final surrender can be seen as another type of internal exile, the life according to the rules, "to the letter" that the Argentines have had to practice as a means of precarious survival.

Working According to the Rules

I am convinced that I never would have found myself in this situation if Elisa had behaved like a normal woman, but asking for that would be like sitting under an apple tree, thinking that we were going to eat figs. And I have no right to complain, nor to reproach her, because she was always that way, special for everything. However, not once in our relationship has the idea of leaving her crossed my mind, and I even worked out some plans for our future together, which she once shared with considerable enthusiasm, although later she began to lose that initial zeal when, for one reason or another, the plans began to be delayed. But, in spite of that, I don't think she ever thought of breaking up with me either. Perhaps that's why her distant behavior, maybe even a little reticent, surprised me so the last time we saw each other, which was one evening at her house. After a pause in which we both remained silent, she spoke to me about the letter. First she told me about her trip—it's work-related, the Institute is sending me north for an inspection, I don't know how long I'll be away—and immediately, when I asked her to call me, or write, she mentioned that she had sent me a letter that very morning. It didn't seem strange to me because that's the kind of person she was. At the beginning of our relationship she used to send me cards decorated with flowers or little animals, which I liked a lot, although I never told her so. Afterwards she stopped doing that, although she maintained her habit of correspondence, in which she began to share her questions and her doubts. Later, she also abandoned that practice. I paid no attention to the change, because I thought that, finally, she had come to understand my position of not answering any of them, not even of acknowledging receipt on some occasions, in the belief that compliments as well as reproaches, should be uttered in person. The latter, to give the person the opportunity to defend him or herself, and the former, to share the occasion. We would always talk heatedly about it and then we would branch out to other themes regarding which we also disagreed, which were in the majority. For some time now, however, we haven't argued but, it seems to me, analyzing things in detail, that was not because I had convinced her, but because she no longer desired to keep going over and over the same thing. Now that I think about it, what I remember most about Elisa from those last months are her moments of silence, and that sentence she came out with one day, in response to my habit of reminding her constantly about her strangeness, be careful, it might be that the abnormal one is you and you're using me as a mirror. I know that I deployed an arsenal of arguments to rebut her affirmation, but when I finished she only added, you see? There's no way to make you recognize what you already understand very well, but don't want to accept.

And all of that is what I am remembering here in this basement of the Main Post Office, where I have ended up in my search for the letter that never arrived.

Elisa, just before we said goodbye, had handed me the slip of paper, saying, this is the registered receipt, in case you have any problems, since the mail is so slow. And it was with that document that I presented myself, three weeks later with no news from her and still no letter, at my local branch post office. The employee told me, when I entered, what I didn't know, as disinclined as I am to read the newspapers, that is, we are working according to "Rules and Regulations," and there was no way to induce him to explain to me what was the content of that "Regulation," thanks to which—judging from what I saw, crowds and crowds of people and sackfuls of undelivered letters—everything was getting even worse than if it didn't exist at all. Since people may outdo me in many ways but never at hard-headedness, finally I got an employee to pay a little attention to me. Even if she listened to me with the indifference of a rainy winter Monday, at least I managed to get her to answer: For that you have to go to the Main Post Office. Since that idea didn't exactly appeal to me, I decided to wait one more week, in order to give the local branches a reasonable time to make it up to me and to see if the delivery of mail figured somewhere in the famous "Regulation," even if a few days late. On the other hand, I still had the idea that Elisa's letter could be, perhaps, a message without great importance, which wouldn't be worth the bother, and that, perhaps, in the end she would call me on the telephone.

Neither of the two things happened though, so that, in the end, I made the decision to head to the Main Post Office, seeking to determine the destination of the letter that was meant for me. Pleasantly surprised, I found out that, as of that morning, everything was working normally. In effect, sir, the conflict has been settled, although, as you will understand, it's going to take some time before we catch up with the work, a suspiciously friendly young woman explained to me. Then she added that, unfortunately, the window where she was working wasn't the one where one has to go to file a complaint, what a shame, in spite of the little sign above her head, where one could clearly read "Complaints and Information,"—yes, sir, but not the complaints to which you refer—. I didn't have the time for her to explain in detail exactly which were the complaints that she took care of there—my desk at the bank was already waiting for me—so I tried to find out where I should go. She replied, now without such friendliness, returning things to their natural state that even if on the sign—which I indicated peremptorily with my index finger—the word "Information" was included, it wasn't the kind of information that I needed and I should try asking at the end of the hall, at window thirty-five. So that's where I went. Window thirty-five was deserted. I waited in vain for several minutes for someone to appear, until my impatience got the best of me and I shifted to thirty-six, where indeed there was a gentleman, whom I asked about the fate of his co-worker, the one from the neighboring window. He answered that he hadn't seen him for a while, without establishing if a while was an hour, a day or a week. Of course, since the two windows dealt with totally different matters, lamentably, he didn't have the slightest idea about what I wanted to know. He added, as if it were a brilliant idea, behind which I perceived a passing of the buck, that I should ask that gentleman over there, who knows all about administrative functions. I didn't doubt the statement, because the gentleman in question—from what his attire permitted one to deduce—was a janitor! a species that, as is public knowledge, always knows more than everyone else, although he's not always inclined to share his information. I looked all around and up seeing a multitude of windows with long lines waiting before each of them, I lost heart and I thought that, damned if I do, damned if I don't, after all it didn't cost me anything to consult the aforementioned individual, who had already stepped a few meters away, carrying a paper in his hand and dragging his feet heavily. I reached him in no time. It took a while for him to catch what I was saying; it seemed to me that he was half deaf, but he finally understood. Of course, neither was it easy for me to clarify what his answer was, because the words were confused between his lips, first, as a result of loose-fitting dentures and second, because the words had to fight their way through a dense, graying mustache. Finally, I seemed to understand that, because of the prolonged period of working according to the Rules, those questions dealing with delays and losses were being taken care of in the basement, where he invited me to go. What he didn't tell me, or at least it didn't register with me, was that I myself would have to take charge of finding the information, something that I figured out a little while after having descended to the aforementioned basement.

The first thing I saw was a mountain of letters and, on top of them, a gentleman busy placing them, one by one and with extreme care, into a great black bag. Since it was impossible for me to keep trying to ascertain anything concrete through the janitor, I approached the man who was on top of the pile of envelopes and I expressed my concern about the certificate whose receipt . . . he didn't let me continue; extending his open palm to me, he said wait a moment, please, this isn't where you should complain. I breathed a sigh of relief, considering it highly improbable that I would manage to locate my letter in that mountain of correspondence. But it turned out that the new location wasn't anything to celebrate, since the employee informed me that the letters he was putting in the bag—this is number ten, he clarified, showing me a corner where the other nine were—were from the period of working according to Rules and Regulations from December of the previous year—it was now June—that is to say that the overwhelming majority were Christmas cards, with good wishes for the holidays and a prosperous New Year for you and your family, almost all the same, sir, people aren't at all imaginative, he added, and at my surprised reaction, he shrugged his shoulders and finished by saying what do you expect? sometimes I open one, to break up the routine. We were in the middle of that explanation when another employee came up and, without paying a bit of attention to my presence, proceeded to tell the one on the pile that, according to what he had learned from a colleague in the Division of Labor Relations, the atmosphere was getting heavy, because the Administrator had received a list according to which, in the last week, of the three thousand agents who were supposed to work in Distribution, one thousand two hundred were out sick, six hundred were off with special permission for problems of diverse types and one hundred and fifty justified their absence availing themselves of Article 48, Section 2 of the Internal Regulations of the Institution, which is the one that says that, by invoking it, one can miss work without giving a reason. Undoubtedly, that statistic had to have been planted by some saboteur, but be calm, we've already organized a union assembly for tomorrow, in which we have decided that, if the Administrator tries to take any measures, we'll immediately announce a state of alert, followed—in the worst of scenarios—by the declaration of another period of working according to the Rules. As I saw that this wasn't going to be a short conversation, because the agents then moved right away to the topic of yesterday's soccer—something that made me remember my mother's advice, never to go to a public office on Monday, and I regretted, first, not paying any attention to her and second, that she wasn't around any more to recognize my mistake—I asked the one on the mountaintop where one might find the letters that were accumulated during the last labor dispute. Bothered by the interruption, he pointed vaguely and returned to his own thing, that is, to the sleepwalking forward who had missed a goal in the stupidest manner. On my way over there I was intercepted by a gentleman who, with hair uncombed and an unfastened tie, asked me if there in the basement, besides delayed letters, one could find applications addressed to the post office, telling me, before I could answer that I didn't know, that he was the President of the Impossible Doesn't Exist Philatelic Society, whose members specialized in the international exchange of hard-to-find stamps, and that a month earlier he had sent a letter, naturally, to the Head of the Section of Special Concessions and Franking Privileges, trying to procure a reduction in the tariff for shipping at the institution over which he presided, since its work made an undeniable contribution to the culture and to the integration of nations by means of promoting mutual acquaintance. Finally, I made him listen and then I told him, look, ask anyone, except those gentlemen—and I indicated the one on the pile and his informant—because they are doing something else. He thanked me and after waving, he headed toward another employee behind a counter to the right, and I then set out to tackle a fellow who was on the opposite side of the enclosure, lighting a cigarette, an extremely dangerous activity, if we consider that he was surrounded by several black plastic bags, overflowing with letters. It didn't seem opportune to me to point out to him the risk that his match entailed, since I didn't want to offend him, and I asked if that was the correspondence delayed by the recent period of working according to Regulations. He looked at me and he took his time to answer me that, as I could see, everything was in perfect order and, therefore, what I was asking was absurd. Seeing my uncomprehending face, he hurriedly pointed out that those were the letters from the conflict of last June, which he had recently finished classifying. It had taken a great effort because, as you will remember, my friend, in that unfortunate moment in our country there had been a real fever for contests and the people were sending coupons to all of the television stations, radios and businesses, solving all kinds of puzzles.

While I was striving to find out where I should claim a month-old certificate, I was interrupted by a gentleman carrying a big package, which he proceeded to put on the floor and, while he dried his perspiration with his handkerchief, asked where he should deliver a shipment of papers for the Division. The Gentleman of the July Conflict pointed to a window that I hadn't seen because it was behind a column and that's where the man headed, after shouldering the package again. On seeing the employee that I was about to consult get up to head to the bathroom—something I deduced by noticing that he was taking a towel out of his desk drawer and putting it over his shoulder—I thought that I should also go to the window where the man with the paper order was going or to the counter where the man from the Philatelic Society had gone, so that either of those two agents might orient me, and I tried to decide which way to head. There was no need, because the President of The Impossible Doesn't Exist was now coming toward me, saying that the individual at the counter wasn't there to answer questions nor to receive complaints—according to his own words—but to count the number of conflicts that the Post Office personnel had been involved in without the government ever seeing fit to satisfy their just complaints. Therefore, he was charged with informing his colleagues about the most propitious moment to launch another protest, by means of working according to Regulations, basing himself on the respective statistics, the ones that reflected faithfully which was the exact date on which such a situation would cause the most havoc. The conclusion was that he was no more able than the others to tell us where we should go for our problems to be resolved. The Man with the Package had the same luck—he was returning wearing a disheartened expression—with the employee at the window on the right, who told him that he was there substituting for someone else for two days and that for such a short period of time, it wasn't worth acquainting himself with anything. In the instant when we were about to ask ourselves what to do next, we were joined by another man, very agitated, who was trying to locate a telegram of dismissal that, according to the information he had been given by the company where he worked, had been sent to him, but that had never reached his hands, for which reason, when he had gone to work the previous day, as it was his custom, he was told that you don't belong to the personnel of this factory any more. The greatly afflicted character waited until that same morning and then presented himself at the postal branch in his neighborhood, from where he was sent to the

Main Post Office. After a few dead ends, he went to the Telegraph Sector. There, a young woman who waited on him informed him that the telegrams from the period of conflict were now being distributed, although not all of them, so that she couldn't assure him that his would be one of those delivered, and that only time would tell. She added that those that never arrived—something that didn't matter too much, considering that a telegram that arrives after the fact isn't worth much—were in the basement. He decided to come down because, if his was among those being delivered it would be better if he wasn't at home to receive it, since he couldn't bear his family's anguish and, besides, as long as the written notice didn't arrive, there was still hope that it was all a mistake. If, on the contrary, it was one of those that never would be delivered, he wanted to convince himself, by finding it, that he really had been fired, after so many years. At that moment the janitor who had sent me down there appeared, and we decided to approach him, for lack of a better alternative. Loose teeth, mustache and deafness notwithstanding, we learned that his shift was finished and that we should wait until his replacement arrived who, perhaps, would be able to suggest something. Before leaving, he reproached us for having asked him questions at the last moment.

Fifteen minutes later, in effect, another janitor appeared, much younger and very alert, although somewhat ambiguous and a little slippery. He answered our requisitions by showing the President of The Impossible Doesn't Exist the correspondence addressed to Distribution that had arrived during the dispute and pointed to a mountain of envelopes that nearly touched the ceiling. There were claims and applications of all kinds, related to the total sum of the services that the Post Office executed and, therefore, his should be there among all of them. To the Man with the Package he said without beating around the bush that his was a very complicated case, given that, to begin with, it was necessary to verify if the purchase order authorizing the request for those papers had come from the General Direction of Providers or from the Warehouse Division. Besides, neither destination was located in the Main Post Office but in other buildings, although perhaps just recently, considering that they assured you that it was here where you should make your delivery, it could have been authorized by some receiving office for small orders, one that he wasn't aware of—as probably would be true for the entire Distribution Section, except for the one who gave the order for such a shipment—because since the dispute and surely due to a lack of attention imputable to it, their only photocopier still in use gave no signs of life and, therefore, the internal memo providing information about the new office would never have managed to circulate. The solution was to look for it in that pile of papers waiting to be photocopied, see? and it's most likely that they never will be, because by the time the work can be done, their content will be out of date. Check anyway, so that if you locate it, we can find out where it is and what functions the alleged new department has. When the Man with the Package tried to inquire why they didn't fix the broken photocopiers, the janitor answered him that, in reality, they weren't broken down, but dirty, that is, it was a question of maintenance. What happened was that the appropriate division, that is the Quartermaster's Department, hasn't been able to decide which was the best estimate to accept, according to the terms offered, including the commission and, due to that fact the representatives of the two firms that presented the estimates had been wandering aimlessly from office to office for a month, seeing one person and consulting another. He himself has passed them in the hallways several times a day and he noticed that they were already talking to themselves. The Man with the Telegram was shown a box so big that it had a ladder beside it, and he was told that there he would find inheritances, dismissals, evictions and notifications of that sort. Addressing himself to me, he asked Regular or Certified Mail? Certified, I answered with a certain cockiness. Bad luck, my friend, it's that one, the largest pile, the one in the corner. What happens is that in periods of working according to Regulations, the people send all their correspondence by certified mail, believing this will force the personnel to fulfill their duties, a sort of pressure exerted through a higher fare leading to a guarantee, do you understand? But, as you'll see, here we maintain a strict observance of the Code of conduct and there are no pressures that can be effective. At that point, and when the four of us intended to head to our respective destinations, the janitor told us that it was now lunchtime and offered, for a few pesos, to bring us sandwiches and soft drinks right there. And so it all began.

I'm sure that none of us has counted the days that we've been here inside, because that doesn't matter now. I've begun to forget about the bank and I'm almost convinced that no one there has even noticed my absence. Besides, what meaning could it have to keep counting the hours? In the end, what is time? An illusion, something that conditions us to do things at a set hour, and something that, when we notice it, has already passed. What's certain is that we have formed a quite close-knit group, and things aren't going so badly. With the passing of the days, others have been added to the four of us who were there at the beginning. The Money Order Boy, who came looking for the money that his parents had sent him from the province to pay for studies that he hadn't even begun; the Dreamer about Other Countries, who arrived looking for a big envelope with several cassettes that his friends abroad had sent him, telling him wonders about far-off lands, where everything works, and where, when it doesn't, it gets fixed immediately and even with an apology. His friends were telling him what procedures to follow to leave this republic, where no one is ever going to fix anything, you'll see. He says that in the International Sector they told him that if the recordings aren't here below, it's because they were never sent or else they were lost in the foreign mail, statements that he, of course, rejects flat out. Then came The Mysterious Woman, of indeterminable age, who hides her eyes behind enormous black sunglasses. She appeared one afternoon, trying to locate a file that, according to the Office of Permits to Third Parties, Article 8 Law 20.126, could be there among many others, whose procedures have been pending since 1950. The woman in question wouldn't explain why she was looking for the file, nor what it was that the above-mentioned office permitted through that Article of the famous law. We also watched an older man coming down the stairs one day, very well dressed, who said he was a lawyer and was there at the suggestion of the Department of Judicial Transactions to try to locate, on the shelves behind the rear counter, a lawsuit that the firm he represented filed against the Post Office for misplacing some checks in 1972. In truth, the firm, as The Juris Doctor always explains it, wants to withdraw the lawsuit, but it can't if I can't find the pertinent documentation, according to the information I received from the Legal Affairs Division of Distribution. Another who's going around in circles is The Mechanic from the South, who in January of 1985 repaired one of the Post Office's trucks in his shop, solving their problem in a hurry and who, ever since, has been trying to collect for his services. According to what they told him in the Division of Vehicles and Transportation, in order for the sum in question to be paid, he has to locate the whereabouts of the original bill, which he swears he submitted to the "Admissions Table," where they certified having passed it on to "Accounting," where, in turn, they testify that they sent it to the "Treasury," where, finally, the trail is lost. The Mechanic has shown the duplicate, properly notarized, to whoever would care to look, but since the original hasn't appeared and without it he can't receive payment, if he wishes he can look for it in the basement, in the drawers of the Unverified Documents since, as you will understand, sir, the Post Office Personnel cannot concern themselves with this, because we are busy with other things, so if you decide to do it … down those steps. Thus here he was, going through the drawers and so dizzy now that he confused the ones he had checked with those that he hadn't and he had to start all over again. The Old Man of the Analysis appeared a few days ago, very worried because the Health Division refused to assist him, as a retiree from the Division, if he didn't present the appropriate card that accredited him as such and which he had lost somewhere in his house. He explained, to whoever would listen, that it wasn't going to be possible to find it because, since his wife had died a few months before, everything was topsy-turvy and he couldn't bear to organize things following such a calamity. The final answer he received was that they were going to issue him a new card, but that he should give them the corresponding file. When he went for it, they told him that the Personnel Manager has too many problems with the confirmation and verification of medical certificates and licenses and with awarding permits, plus the study of possible holidays, to spend time searching for that file, which has already been placed among the files in the basement so that you, who are at home here … and so here we have him, fairly well entertained, in a section labeled Documentation of Retired Personnel, shoving around papers and remembering old colleagues, with whose files in his hands he wonders what's become of their lives. The one who bores us a little is The Theory Salesman, who works for a company that sells methods for the Development of Communications Systems and who says he has a way to solve all the problems of the Post Office, for which reason and, with the possibility that his idea might just be true, he was sent to the basement by the Department of Special Projects, so that he can try to locate an organizational chart of the activities of the Division prepared in 1960, on the basis of which he should present his plans, which otherwise couldn't be taken into account. The last one to arrive is a woman writer, who came last week, telling us that she was sent from her branch post office to one of the windows of the Main Post Office, to discuss the possibility of sending an envelope without a return address, something that—according to what they told her, totally shocked—is expressly forbidden by a statute of the Institution. She has tried to explain, in vain, that the envelope to be sent mustn't have any identifying information on it, because it has to do with a work she's submitting to a contest, whose rules state clearly that the author should sign with a pseudonym. They sent her to the basement, after long conversations in which she couldn't convince either the employee, nor her supervisor, nor the manager, nor the Section Director, to look for a copy of the resolution regarding the subject of return addresses, in order to resolve her doubts.

As I said, it's not so bad here and, to be honest, we have been so distracted with our tasks that we didn't even realize it when the employees who were here to begin with stopped coming. When it occurred to us to ask the afternoon janitor, there was a meaningful silence, although for us all it meant was that we had free access to their desks. He continues providing us with sandwiches and soft drinks, varying the menu sometimes with a good cheese pizza, accompanied by a bottle of wine. Since most of us have run out of money, he gives us credit, in a notebook where he writes down the debts and where we sign below. When we expressed our concern for his budget, he explained that the money comes out of the Post Office Treasury, through debits from an account called Special Emergencies. This account is used frequently by diverse government officials, since it isn't necessary to explain the destiny of the funds that originate from it. Pressed by everyone and in confidence, he told us the whole truth. A big boss with access to that account owns the corner bar, where almost all of the Post Office staff place their orders. The regular staff has to pay cash, but the upper-level staff is billed monthly and they pay with the funds designated for Special Emergencies. So that for the official in question—with whom I get along marvelously—the greater the consumption, the better for him, without it mattering who the consumers are, do we understand each other? I carry this notebook for my commission. It's fair, don't you think? Of course. This janitor, a true friend, has also provided us, for a few pesos, with pillows and a couple of blankets, since we sleep where we search. Likewise he furnishes us, at a really bargain price, with clean towels, which each one of us takes to the bathroom in the basement, in regular shifts, to wash up the best we can, so that we can be presentable. Of course we men decided not to shave our beards, to limit our expenditures. Since he is, besides, very nice, he takes charge of entertaining us a little in the afternoons, when he serves us coffee—on the house—telling us anecdotes and gossip about Division. The latest news is the romance between the Head of the Masculine Shipping Office and the Head of the Feminine Shipping Office who, utilizing the services of personnel under their command, send each other letters in code, and are known to have romantic encounters in the building's most unforeseen places, as for example The Broom Closet or the Cabinet for the Correction of International Cables.

Of course, we don't know how much longer we'll remain here, and I think that we all have reasons for not showing any hurry to leave. The President of The Impossible Doesn't Exist Society has decided to divide up his days, so that in the mornings he looks for his application and, in the afternoons, he tries to locate rare stamps missing from his collection. He has confessed, further, that he is now alone in the Society, because the other members of his club resigned one by one, tired of always seeking the impossible to demonstrate its nonexistence. The Man with the Package says that rather than walking from here to there carrying bundles, he prefers to stay here in the basement, looking for the authorization memo about the new receiving office, something that, at any rate, gives him a good excuse for not returning to a job where he is perpetually mistreated. The Telegram Man continues to maintain that as long as it doesn't appear, he can think that he still has a job and, on the other hand, if he stays here, he won't have to face the reproaches and laments of his wife. The Office of the Telegrams that Will Never Arrive is a good place to live. The Money Order Boy prefers to stay here, as a way of avoiding opening his books and answering the letters from his parents, who are worried about the progress of his studies. The Dreamer about Other Countries affirms that if he doesn't find those recordings, he won't know how to carry out the procedures of the embassy and, besides, he needs the incentive represented by the voices of his friends, telling him of the wonders that wait for him in those lands, where he will be received with open arms, since he's not quite convinced in his quest, to leave behind that stupid nostalgia that keeps him holding on to the place where he was born. At times he likes to think that perhaps, when he returns to the outside world, everything will have changed and then he won't need to leave. The Mysterious Woman has finally confessed that now she doesn't really remember why she's looking for the permit file, but she feels comfortable with us, and that's better than returning to a house where no one is waiting for her. The Juris Doctor, for his part, doesn't want to return to the Courts without having located the documentation of the trial, because that would subject him again to the hard time caused to him by the tiresome jokes of his younger colleagues, in relation to his age and his efficiency. The firm wasn't worth worrying about; the recently arrived law clerks were very anxious to advance, which is an attitude that the management seemed to look upon with much favor. The Mechanic from the South, who at first was worried because he had left his car double parked and his garage unattended, finally said that if the tow-truck takes it away, the Municipality loses money and, with regard to his job, lately there were almost no cars to repair, because the people don't have a cent to their names and, before fixing an engine, they prefer to buy something they can put in the oven. Besides, I'm already like two months overdue on my rent, so that it wouldn't be advisable for me to return. The Little Old Man has almost forgotten now about the analysis and if he should have to choose between the plaza with its inclement weather or this basement, he opts to stay here, where he hit it off well with the Morning Janitor, whom he seems to understand without great difficulty, when the janitor tells them that he already should have retired, but considering that with what they're going to pay him he won't be able to do anything, he acts absent-minded and tries to keep out of sight, so they won't remember that he's still working. The Theory Salesman still hasn't found the organizational chart, but he doesn't want to leave either, because he has found such a quantity of pending projects, each one with an infallible solution, that he is very entertained and he consoles himself seeing how so many people wasted time in the past, on the same things that he is wasting it now. The Writer's contest deadline has passed. She has had no other choice but to resign herself to be excluded from it, but she considers that here she will find good material for her stories and that is the reason she stays, she assures us, and not because this unreal atmosphere helps her to bear more easily her progressive detachment from reality. She has also determined that for future contests in which she decides to participate, she will hand carry the envelope, no matter where. Writing is a difficult business and there's no need to make it even more trying. As for me, I'm assaulted by two opposite sensations. At times, I feel like running to my house because, perhaps, Elisa will have returned, or may be calling on the phone, shocked that she can't find me. Or perhaps, in the time that I've spent here, the letter that I'm looking for has arrived. But at other moments, what I want most is to stay here in this basement, thinking that she misses me and that she asks about me every day. While I'm here, I can cling to the idea that she still loves me and that she never intended to leave me.

Things being as they are, none of us has set a time limit for our stay together; and as I said, neither have we mentioned the urgency of departure, because we have been finding new pastimes. I know that there inside the box, for example, the Telegram Man has begun to read, minutely, each telegram, to check how many people are being fired or evicted or notified to pay their debts. Meanwhile, the President of the Impossible Doesn't Exist Philatelic Society, with his initial scruples vanquished, has devoted himself to the task of cutting out the stamps that interest him, perusing the different piles and bags. The Man of the Package no longer remembers where he put it and devotes himself, together with The Mechanic, to reading the magazines that never arrived in the hands of their subscribers, especially the sports magazines that various institutions from diverse countries exchange. The Money Order Boy has already opened a fourth of the envelopes from his mountain, and he fantasizes about what he would do if he could collect all that money. The Mysterious Woman gets along well with The Theory Salesman and the two of them become involved in long discussions about the permits that can't be obtained and the projects that never are put into practice. Seated on a desk, The Dreamer about Other Countries elaborates his plans for the day when he leaves this one, provided that he finds those cassettes and this country hasn't solved all its problems by the time he gets out. The Writer and I have discovered each other, with a certain shame, doing the same thing and then, in confidence, we began to share our respective experiences. We open letters haphazardly from some bag or from the pile that happens to appeal to us. On occasions, we compete with each other to see who finds the most interesting story, but now we are excited because we have found the answer to a letter we encountered earlier and we are trying to see if there is more correspondence exchanged between a couple who, according to what we've learned up until now, is separated because of various misunderstandings for which, we fear, the Post Office is not entirely blameless.

The Afternoon Janitor has commented to us that a new period of Working according to the Regulations is imminent, this time because the government has not complied with the provisions of Law 14.217 b, in accordance with the documents signed during the last Collective Bargaining Agreement. This news has us very excited, since, surely, new bags will arrive and perhaps, new companions in our searches, given that—according to the same source—there will be several important events in the Republic: an International Dissidents Symposium, a World Spiritist Encounter, a Summit Meeting of Opposing Lodges and a Latin American Congress on the Incidence of the Consumption of Soybean on the Economy of Developing Nations, all of which will generate, undoubtedly, a profuse exchange of correspondence which, on not arriving at its destination, promises misunderstandings and setbacks in the most diverse surroundings and on a grand scale.

Some nights, when the silence is interrupted only by the distant rumor of street traffic, I realize that the world continues out there, but I don't feel nostalgia for it, and as I think about my situation, I can verify that, deep-down, I don't find it strange that I've come to stay here—now I am The Certified Mail Man—or that I find myself immersed in this singular episode because, as long as I remember, I have spent my life living according to the Rules and Regulations; I constantly avoided definitions and I never asked questions, so as not to have to answer them. Besides, I have always wanted to find a place like this, in which there are no mirrors, or clocks, or radios, or televisions, and everything that happens, in reality, has already happened. Where no one asks for what one is not inclined to give, and where no one demands that I be someone, so that I can simply stay.

Alicia Régoli
de Mullen

Alicia Régoli de Mullen was born in Buenos Aires on July 19, 1934. Her parental home fostered a climate where art was a fundamental part of everyday life. Her father, a musician and a painter, was interested in all artistic manifestations. Her mother was a writer. Alicia was the only child. From the time she was a very young girl she studied piano, speech, dance, French, English, and voice. She married at the age of twenty and during the next ten years her six children were born. This was the time in which she published her book *El mundo de los otros,* which obtained the National Beginning Prize from the Ministry of Education and a subsidy from the National Arts Fund that allowed its publication. She was president of the Association of Catholic Writers and Publicists between 1965 and 1967. She has served as a juror in poetry and short story contests, given lectures and courses on literary themes, and participated in radio and television programs. Her books have been used as classroom texts.

In 1983 she received a special recognition from the Secretary of Culture for her narrative production from 1979 and 1982. In 1984 she was given the task of writing the prologue to the book *Juventud y Familia,* about the relationships between theology and human sciences, edited by the Center for Social Research and Action. Her second book, *Una naranja, el mundo,* is the story of her family's life: five generations appear in the book, from her great-grandmother to her children. In 1964 she received the National Initiation Prize, and in 1975 an award from the National Arts Fund. She is a professor of French literature, a commercial translator and interpreter of French, and a member of the editorial board of the journal *Letras de Buenos Aires.* Currently, as she has for the last fourteen years, she resides on an old colonial estate that dates from 1886, a few miles from Buenos Aires.

Publications

Una naranja, el mundo (An orange, the world). Buenos Aires: Guadalupe, 1975.
El mundo de los otros (The world of the others). Buenos Aires: La Mandrágora, 1985.
La ciudad sumergida (The sunk city). Buenos Aires: Guadalupe, 1985.

Secondary Sources

Dubecq, María Elena. "Un libro para abrir sin miedo." *Esquiú* 9 (June 1975).
Fares, Gustavo. "This Text Which Is Not One." *Hispanic Journal* 12/2 (Fall 1991): 277–89.
Giovannoni, Héctor. "*La ciudad sumergida.*" 69 *Criterio* (March 1988).
Noriega, Néstor Alfredo. "*Una naranja: el mundo* de A. Régoli de Mullen." *La Capital,* 25 June 1978.
———. "*La ciudad sumergida* de A. Régoli de Mullen." *La Capital,* 3 February 1980: 5.
Peltzer, Federico. "Poesía, testimonio e imagen." *La Prensa,* 3 February 1980: 7.

Interview

1. Which authors have had the greatest influence on your work?

    When I was very young I began to read French poets, and I would recite poems and fragments of poems. Later, I read the complete theatrical works of O'Neill and of Chekov. The Cortázar of *Final de juego* and *Todos los fuegos el fuego* awakened my enthusiasm for the brevity of the short story. Afterwards, that brevity became more accentuated when I came to know certain aspects of Eastern literature that fascinated me; for example, the stories of *A Thousand and One Nights,* the greatest concentration in the most minimal space. I would like, further, to mention as influences Bradbury and Lord Dunsany. If I must speak of a mentor, I'll name Borges. Reading his work opened up for me the vastness of the horizon that literature can reach.

2. When did you begin to write, and why?

    I would begin by telling you why I write. I know, without any doubt, that it is my means of expression. My work reflects what I feel, what I think, what I am. All literature that boasts of such intent springs forth from layers that are unknown by the person who writes. Therefore I can say that literature, before it communicates with anyone else, communicates with me, me with myself. Without that previous step, without that essential becoming honest, what we write can't possibly interest a sensitive reader, who is, definitively, the ultimate audience.

3. How does the political situation influence your choice of themes?

    I would like to answer that question with Sábato's words from *El escritor y sus fantasmas.* Sábato says: "Every now and then one forgets that there is only one valid dilemma: profound literature and superficial literature. Obsessions have their roots in profound zones of the I, and the deeper they are, the less numerous they become. The theme should not be chosen: one must let the theme choose you." From that perspective, there are no options. Because the theme doesn't arrive alone: it comes dragging with it the demands for focus, for times, for contexts. If an author thinks that her obligation is to write about the present day, she should probably do it by means of the essay. Fiction, on the other hand, is tied closely into what Sábato says and, once in its context, we can no longer choose the setting.

4. Have you encountered difficulties, as a woman writer, with publishers?

The situation of the country, in my case, doesn't influence the act of writing, but it exaggerates the difficulty of publishing, which I don't think has anything to do with the fact that I am a woman. Writers, in general, have no other means of publishing but to send their manuscripts off and pray to the celestial powers that they won't be swallowed up in some desk drawer. Publishers lack imagination and they prefer, I know this well, to make second and subsequent editions before they'll risk publishing a previously unpublished manuscript. It would seem that also for the experts the printed word has a prestige that the unpublished word lacks. "Prophets of the past" is what Sábato calls them, speaking of this situation. With respect to the system of publicity, I only know a few partial aspects. For example, when one signs the publishing contract, the publisher reserves the right to print 10 percent more than the number of copies agreed upon, which will be used for publicity purposes in magazines and newspapers, or for donations to libraries.

5. What do you think of feminism?

Look, I am in agreement with the general nature of the changes that the movement has been demanding since its beginning, although one should make the distinction that feminism is not the same all over, not even in different parts of the same country. At times our problems are more immediate than the fight for the equality of the sexes, when men as well as women should fight tooth and nail to move forward.

6. How would you describe Argentina's women readers?

I don't know the current data.

Selection from *El mundo de los otros*

Alicia Régoli de Mullen embarks on an adventure of intimacy, home, children, and the observation of nature—themes traditionally considered "feminine." Her book *El mundo de los otros* is a collection of short stories. The narrative form Régoli de Mullen inaugurates in this book doesn't follow the "Borgesian" tradition of the short story, with plot complications, winks of complicity to the reader, or philosophical and metaphysical arguments developed from an external perspective, all of which can seem more like intellectual games than palpitating realities. On the contrary, for Régoli de Mullen, the transcendent, the metaphysical argument, is not exposed by being debated or examined, but rather is meant to be perceived in all its everyday intensity. The contemplation of an archetypal model, of the transcendence of an idea, is already a given fact before one begins to write or to read; it is this presupposition that offers meaning to the narrative and to Régoli de Mullen's work in general. In her book, chronological reality is questioned in diverse ways, from merely doubting it, to radically denying its existence. In our selection, the title story, the text invites the reader to question which is the world of the others, which is the sane world as opposed to the insane one, and from this ambiguity emerges the capacity for the alienated imagination to deny the passage of time and to have precarious access to one's essence, if there is such. The narrator's time is contrasted to that of the "world of the others," a world which never fulfills the expectations of happiness of what seems to be an alienated intelligence. The parameters of reality are called into question in the stories of Régoli de Mullen's volume, which invite the reader to look a little further than at what the immediate surroundings show.

The World of the Others

She felt the presence of Inés behind her, but she didn't move. She remained next to the window as if she hadn't noticed. Inés always entered the room like that, perhaps wanting to surprise or disturb her.

Whenever Inés approached, she used to think of Ana. Sweet Ana. Good Ana. Remembering Ana meant feeling protected and fearless; the thought annulled the disturbing, viscous presence of Inés.

Her life with Ana would have been so different . . . The two of them were capable of living together without bothering each other, without even bumping into each other. But there Inés was, always between them, between her and Ana, between her and her modest happiness, between her and her small, everyday peace. Inés loomed suddenly beside her, overflowing with dark words.

"I don't understand how you can sit there for hours beside that window."

(She was thinking about the plaza in front of her and about the tireless children chasing the sun.)

"I would like to know what pleasure you find in watching all afternoon that grey, water-stained wall."

Those wasted, pallid, meaningless words were returning. As they returned every afternoon at the same time, they were losing their relief and their contours. Or perhaps Inés spoke using symbols, or metaphors, or allegories. Perhaps "window" meant eyes, or curiosity. Perhaps "water" meant freshness and springtime and green. Perhaps Inés simply hated her and wanted to upset her. Perhaps her means of expression were as strange as her ways of being and living.

She continued looking at the plaza, motionless. The sun fell toward the horizon behind the trees and the children were forming clusters of color around each bench where their coats were buttoned, preparing to leave.

Soon the stars would come out.

It was at that moment when Inés handed her the envelope. "Marcos wrote me to ask if I would tell you that he's not coming back." The voice was opaque and hard. Perhaps in that moment she didn't want to be sour, but she always was; she couldn't help it.

The news didn't trouble her, didn't even surprise her; she thought her own indifference strange.

When Inés left, she repeated out loud: "Marcos is gone; he will not return."

She said it slowly, breaking off each word, making an effort to be anguished, or at least upset. It was useless; she recognized that it didn't matter to her.

Afterwards, she turned and recovered her past. She thought about the little Marcos from her childhood memories; about Marcos stirring her adolescent dreams without respite; and, closer in her memory and in time, she thought about that austere and distant man—was it Marcos?—who was watching her one afternoon from her doorway. An unsituated being, strange to his own image, disagreeable, who was waiting for a word from her to enter and stay. She remembered herself being inexpressive, motionless, incapable of uttering that word or of articulating his name. And then . . . silence. And now . . . this letter.

She took the paper out of the envelope and folded it in many directions until she had made a little bird. When the stars came out she would open the window and throw it out so that it could fly.

Afterwards, she continued watching the plaza that was slowly emptying of children. A while later Inés opened the door and left a tray with her dinner.

She perceived the steaming soup and also the severe gesture and the forced favor. She didn't budge.

The night was interposing a curtain of shadow between her and the plaza.

The bowl of soup cooled little by little. Through the open window the little bird took off for the stars.

When she awoke, the slats of the Persian blinds filtered elongated threads of sun over the rug. In the half-shadow she could see the figures on the ceiling losing their outlines. She felt quite capable of finding their blurred contours or forging them again. She recovered a hand from the warmth of the sheets and from far away she outlined the familiar silhouettes with her index finger. She saw her arm lengthened by the perspective, and beyond, her finger, like a sign or an arrow.

All around her, the floor and the rug began to be transformed into a cloud, into an immense cloud floating through an anonymous sky. She felt herself transported by the wind and the rain.

And then she fell into the sea . . .

The steps of Inés resounded on the patio and headed toward the kitchen; afterwards they crossed the patio again and finally stopped at her door. She heard her knocking as she did every day. Each morning with renewed thunder, with tenacious impetus, she forced her to leap brusquely from sleep into the vacuum.

The sea was calm and the wind rocked the ships in a soft swaying motion.

Through the door came the enormous voice divided into words. She seized one word and retained it to think about it later, in detail. In the air the vowels remained, floating on a sunbeam; colorful vowels vibrating on a thread, like notes on a rudimentary scale. Then came the consonants, and they rushed headlong into a heap on the rug. She squeezed the rescued word in the palm of her hand, she drew it close to her eyes and examined it between her fingers. It was there, encompassing its real dimension, circumscribed to its limits, small, timid, violently stripped of its voice and tone.

She got up soundlessly, fearing that something would collapse when she opened the shutters. But everything continued as before.

She sat next to the window and looked at the plaza.

Suddenly she noticed that the trees had grown during the night; doubtless it had been a very long night. No one knows what strange changes, what evolutions, what dark and surprising metamorphoses take place in the secret space of the night.

And the plaza had also grown.

The cobblestone streets stretched indefinitely toward the horizon; the little central statue that the children had climbed effortlessly was a gigantic monument whose apex perforated the clouds; the symmetrical flower beds were extensive valleys irrigated by the water from the pond. Everything was transformed.

Now the street no longer existed, or the corner, or the boy who hawked the afternoon newspaper.

Everything was plaza.

Perhaps the very children who were playing yesterday were new plants today. Perhaps the wind that rocked the ships had pushed hers to remote shores and this plaza wasn't the same one as always.

From the other side of the door she heard a brief creaking, and saw the doorknob turn and then, somewhat shyly, the child entered.

She smiled, gestured, and the little boy kneeled on the rug, careful not to knock down the letters. Dazzled, he contemplated the vowels that were still floating on the sunbeam.

They conversed ceaselessly. She, with tremulous hope; he, with that candidness that makes the friendship of children simple. The words were born, searched for each other, wove among each other with elation.

She wondered if it was Marcos who was returning as a child to recover some remnant from the past or if a boy from the plaza had come to her, attracted by her unchanging figure next to the window.

Her arm was raised to the invisible stars under the sun, to indicate the site where the little bird would be flying.

Later, they played on the rug, intermingling the letters and trapping the colored vowels, which trickled between their fingers as if made of water. They argued in the midst of laughter, gesticulating in the vacuum. They rolled around the rug, scattering the consonants towards all the corners of the room.

Then, lying facing the ceiling, they were silent, as if everything that had happened had been staged only in the depths of their minds.

She thought of Ana.

Hurried steps advanced down the hall and stopped at her door. A thousand arms pounced on the boy, who was imprisoned as in a cage.

The enormous words returned and she managed to recuperate each disparate letter. The boy was motionless, perhaps asleep in that labyrinth of arms.

Suddenly the boy abandoned his lethargy and spoke.

The letters fell on the rug, unconnected and neutral. She made an effort to put them in order, give them meaning. Then her own distorted, strange words reached her; " . . . a little bird has been flying since last night, higher than the clouds . . . the children are plants . . . the letters are touching . . ." and nervous laughter cut the air.

Afterwards, she was alone, trembling from her own fear of herself.

Afterwards, the stars came out.

From that day on, he began to persecute her in an obstinate dream. It was always he—that ungraspable creature—but he was never the same.

A while ago . . .

He was running, disoriented, down a strange street in an interminable city climbing and descending long narrow stairs to the seashore, disappearing suddenly and becoming diluted in the darkness.

A long-ago night . . .

He was the little prince of a borderless country inhabited by children.

Another time . . .

In a shady plaza, other children were playing. He, with a blanket on his knees and his hands painfully lax, contemplated them continuously running from the slide to the pond where the boats navigated; from the swings to the field where they were kicking a ball.

She dreamed about him, always in different spheres. One night . . .

He was lying in a hospital bed, pale and solitary.

His unfrightened eyes ran over the convulsed faces of the other sick people.

She approached him slowly, silently, and when she thought she could reach him, she found herself next to his empty bed.

That was yesterday . . .

An unmerciful winter dawn, she saw him in front of her window.

She saw his limp arms.

She saw his closed eyes.

She threw herself without thinking across the yard that separated them. She reached him. But she found only a snowman.

The last time . . .

She found him in the vortex of an old labyrinth, trapped by an intricate hedge of illusions and dead-end passageways.

That versatile being—from beyond the space in which humans move, from the wretched time counted out by the hours—dragged her every night toward the threshold of the fantastic.

The reiterated dreams threatened to become an obsession.

But that night she felt him nearby, within reach of her desperation. Defenseless. Cornered. She felt that for the first time it was within her power to break the incantation that brought him to her side every night in a strange rendezvous.

She made her way through the labyrinth with incredible lucidity. She had him next to her. It was he and he could not flee.

Frenetically, with a long cane, she destroyed his body and she followed him beyond the agony . . .

She wakes up without remorse, without uneasiness. Definitively free.

She sits up.

The boy is seated on the overstuffed velvet sofa.

She only remembers that she shouted until she was hoarse and that she fell on her back again, without thinking, without feeling, only wishing to die.

One morning, much later, or perhaps only the following day—time had ceased to have any meaning—she heard Inés' footsteps. The kitchen, the patio, the entire house was saturated with the noise of her footsteps. Each tile of the patio floor, each plank of the floor, each corner, quietly suffered the echo. But today she thought she noticed in them an unusual rhythm, a resonance that she didn't quite understand.

Later, confused by the murmurs, noises and unfamiliar footsteps and by the sound of doors closing, she heard Marcos' voice, as if from far away. Disconcerted, she tried to reason serenely, to justify his presence.

Since that dream, since that boy, she didn't remember anything; she couldn't coordinate her thoughts. She wasn't even capable of vaguely calculating how many days had passed. She didn't remember the sun through the blinds or Inés' hands with the tray.

She looked around.

The closed shutters filtered the familiar tenuous clarity from the windows. Within the room, the atmosphere had a rare empty transparency. There were no letters or palpitating shadows on the ceiling.

She breathed deeply and felt a deep peace invading her.

Suddenly the door opened and in burst Inés and Marcos and two men with impenetrable eyes.

Marcos approached slowly, cautiously, perhaps fearfully. She thought about the hunter, who must exercise all his cunning on approaching his prey.

Like a thunderbolt, the truth hit her.

From the other side of the bed she saw the men advancing, while her eyes remained on those of Marcos. They pounced on her and something spun around her. She couldn't move any longer.

Like a subdued animal, she threw herself backwards and closed her eyes, conquered.

Then they took her away from there.

Nearby, a siren rent the air with its piercing sound and she felt Marcos' presence beside her in the darkness.

She didn't ask where they were going. Perhaps she knew, even before Marcos left her. Perhaps she had always known that this trip was waiting for her in some twist of time.

She remembered the garden of the old house where she and Marcos had played and on summer nights invented names for the stars. She remembered the ship that took them to distant landscapes, cutting through clouds and streets and deserts.

Then, weary, she fell asleep.

The car stopped and she felt herself being carried through a garden. The sky, at the very edge of her vision, was intensely blue.

Ahead, opening before her, were some enormous doors, made gigantic by her uncertainty. White walls, interminable white ceilings, endless white corridors and Marcos' hand, cold to the touch, deepening the solitude.

Afterwards they left her alone, with blankets and straps imprisoning her body, immobilizing her, crushing her. With an effort she managed to recline; immediately the woman entered.

The letters returned, the consonants and the vowels; they hadn't been forgotten in a corner of her room, she had them again in this new place. But here the sun didn't shine and this woman was not Inés. She noted, however, the same neutral look, the same indifference; this woman brought a syringe and plunged it into her arm.

She felt herself falling into the precipice. She could continue falling indefinitely without ever stopping, without ever touching the bottom.

Suddenly she was an adolescent again. Marcos was by her side and Inés much farther away. And she, with pigtails still bouncing along her back.

She continued falling. She crossed a threshold.

She was in that house with the sunny patio, with her parents and her little brother. And life was fragile and uncertain, an ambush waiting somewhere.

She continued falling.

She almost didn't recognize herself. She was a baby and she was playing with cardboard letters that later would be letters of light vibrating on a sunbeam.

She continued falling. She crossed another threshold.

It was a dark and silent environment. It was pre-birth.

She continued falling.

It was eternity.

The door that opened to the hallway didn't have a lock. The straps were on the chair.

She leaned out silently, fearing that they would tie her up again.

Everyone was in the corridor. Some posted against the wall, others walking slowly, very erect, as if the rigidity of their bones would translate into a conventional order in their brains. She imagined them making extreme efforts to achieve a determined pattern in their breathing and in their footsteps, to feign a serenity that they didn't possess. It made her think of a group of hypnotized people who responded as to a single will.

Suddenly, in the air, she felt a storm approaching. The windows were closed and a peal of urgency shook the bell.

Those beings lost their rigidity, their slow pace, their serenity melted into their fear.

All of that world began to shake, to vibrate, to grow ... And the corridor was filled with screeching bodies, and the bodies with gestures, and the air with shrillness; as if birds of different plumage and songs had invaded it; as if each one were unaware of the others' languages, of the others' existence.

She retreated to her room. From the window she saw old Roque who was smiling in the garden, and calling her. On seeing her approaching, he went to meet her, as if he had been waiting for her for many years. Together they explored the new flower beds and looked for still-unopened buds.

A line of grey clouds got tangled up in the crown of the trees. The wind picked up suddenly and then abated again, stirring the timorous and thirsty plants. Anguished, she picked up the petals of the exhausted flower from the floor where they had fallen.

The bell continued ringing in the shadows.

A small and timid rebellion was growing inside her. She took old Roque's rugged and comforting hand. When the first drops began to fall she followed him to the greenhouse. It was a tiny paradise of flowers and greenness; it was the site where she would have chosen to remain.

Outside, the branches collided, disturbing the shadows of the pool. It was that uncertain hour in which the wild animals descend to drink the fresh water from the spring, when the beginning of the night shields them; that hour, perhaps beyond time, beyond clocks, in which the wolf and the squirrel whisper on a tree stump and the fox makes a nest for the dove; that hour in which the heavens become human and descend and become mud as in the beginning of creation.

From the vestibule she saw the stairs, and beyond the gate, the street. She picked up her little suitcase, almost sorrowfully.

She was alone again. More alone than ever.

She crossed the garden without haste, without joy. From the other side of the tall gate the world was waiting for her, the world of the others . . . For months they had prepared her for this moment. With painstaking patience they had analyzed each deed, each thought, each reaction, until converting them into dust. Later, they had chosen logical thoughts, serene deeds, normal reactions, and they had put together the puzzle.

And there she was, painfully lucid, with a lucidity without darkness, arid, exposed, deprived, feeling each shiver of the world in her open wounds.

She continued advancing without listening to that something inside her that anchored her to what remained from this side . . . Ana . . . her intimacy . . . old Roque . . .

She opened the gate and walked through it painfully.

She began to walk by the great wall and her footsteps resounded in the quiet with a distant echo.

Inés opened the door and her face reflected an indecipherable astonishment. Upon entering, she felt a long gaze following her to her room.

Everything seemed the same and yet, what profound changes in the deep structure of things.

The ceiling was nothing but a smooth square. The rug, now deserted, had lost its relief and its depth.

On the sidewalk across the street she saw Marcos coming. Precipitously Inés crossed the street and walked up to him; then she returned and the man continued on down the street without turning his head, like a fugitive.

She also felt, somehow, like a fugitive.

. . . the immense plaza . . . the colorful letters . . . were distant, as if an enormous parenthesis had squeezed them into some corner of her memory. She couldn't allow them the possibility of the most fleeting return.

Not even Ana.

Especially not Ana.

In the clinic they had placed Ana, her image of Ana, on an operating table, with a disconcerting white light illuminating her from above. They dissected her, they ripped her up, they cut her into tiny fragments, unrecognizable, impersonal ones. They tried to show her that Ana was no one, simply a friendly figure that her imagination had invented to make the solitude more bearable.

Ana had joined the world of the others, where she had been forced to acquire her tangible dimension of nonexistence.

She went to the window.

There was no plaza.

There were no children.

The corner was there and the kiosk of the boy who hawked his afternoon newspapers. She saw for the first time the grey, water-stained wall.

Everything became suddenly strangely simple. Ana was evaporating in a world of logic. Inés and Marcos together, hidden in the shadows. The wall in front of her, no doubt, had always been there.

The plaza that never existed.

She closed her eyes and imagined the vacuum . . . the absolute Vacuum in the rondo of the uncertain, unstable whirlwind. She felt that not even that little world, forming slowly on top of the tortured rubble, would be saved from the chaos, because its essence was the same as the world of the others.

And she thought about the hot ashes of her deluded world.

She thought about its intangible truths.

She bent over the edge of the window and blew away the ashes.

Then, her world began to yawn and stretch as if awakening from a prolonged dream.

Then she reached out her hand and grabbed it.

Then she launched the Vacuum from within herself. She opened her arms and reclaimed Ana.

(She picked up her untouched suitcase, crossed the patio and entered the plaza. From a remote bench she contemplated, far away, the confused stirring of the world.)

Reina Roffé

Reina Roffé was born in Buenos Aires in 1951. The author says of herself: "During her high school years, she asked a teacher from school to read her first novel. That teacher turned out to be Haroldo Conti. With a 'Miss, you are condemned to be a writer all of your life,' Conti, for better or for worse, made her aware of her destiny. Her first novel was published in 1973 with the title *Llamado al puf* and with it she obtained the Sixto Pondal Ríos Prize in 1975 for the best book by a young writer."

In 1973 she published a book about the Mexican writer Juan Rulfo, *Juan Rulfo: autobiografía armada*. In 1976 she published the novel *Monte de Venus*, which, in spite of a very favorable reception by the critics, was banned by a municipal decree in that same year, beginning thus a long period of silence for the author. Roffé won a Fulbright fellowship in 1981 and participated in the International Writing Program at the University of Iowa, in the United States. There, she resided for three and a half years, published a book of interviews with Latin American writers, and worked on another novel. In 1984 she returned to Argentina and in 1987 obtained the International

Prize for Short Novel for *La rompiente*. "Reasons of economic exile moved her to Spain in 1988 and she has lived in Madrid since that date. Her current novel is unpublished and she continues to think, as she did in adolescence, that life is an uncomfortable place" (letter from the author).

Publications

Llamado al puf (Called to puf). Buenos Aires: Pleamar, 1973.

Juan Rulfo: Autobiografía armada (Juan Rulfo: An assembled autobiography). Buenos Aires: Corregidor, 1973.

Monte de Venus (Mount of Venus). Buenos Aires: Corregidor, 1976.

Fuera de foco. Antología. Ultimos relatos (Out of focus. Anthology. Latest stories). Buenos Aires: Nemont, 1977.

"Preface." In *Espejo de escritores: Entrevistas con Borges, Cortázar, Fuentes, Goytisolo, Onetti, Puig, Rama, Rulfo, Sánchez, Vargas Llosa* (Mirror of writers: Interviews with Borges, Cortázar, Fuentes, Goytisolo, Onetti, Puig, Rama, Rulfo, Sánchez, Vargas Llosa). Hanover, N.H.: Ediciones del Norte, 1985.

"Manuel Puig: Del 'kitsch' a Lacan" (Manuel Puig: From kitsch to Lacan). In *Espejo de escritores: Entrevistas con Borges, Cortázar, Fuentes, Goytisolo, Onetti, Puig, Rama, Rulfo, Sánchez, Vargas Llosa*, 134–45. Hanover, N.H.: Ediciones del Norte, 1985.

"Omnipresencia de la censura en la escritora argentina" (Omnipresence of censorship in the Argentine woman writer). *Revista Iberoamericana* 51.132–133 (July–December 1985): 909–15.

"Diversidad y dispersión en la narrativa actual argentina" (Diversity and dispersion in contemporary Argentine narrative). In *El Cono Sur: Dinámica y dimensiones de su literatura, A Symposium,* edited by Rose Minc. Upper Montclair, N.J. : Montclair State College, 1985.

"Revelaciones" (Revelations). *Present Tense* 12 (Spring 1985): 24.

"Alta marea" (High tide). *Puro Cuento* (1986).

La rompiente (The breaker). Xalapa: Universidad Veracruzana, 1987; Buenos Aires: Puntosur, 1987.

"Qué escribimos las mujeres en la Argentina de hoy" (What women write in Argentina today). In *Literatura argentina hoy: de la dictadura a la democracia* (Literature today: From dictatorship to democracy), edited by Karl Kohut and Andrea Pagni. Frankfurt: Verbuet Verlag, 1989.

"No entres dócilmente en esa noche quieta" (Do not enter docilely into that quiet night). *Feminaria* (1990).

"Una ciudad gris y beige" (A grey and beige city). *Hispamérica: Revista de Literatura* (1993).

El cielo dividido (The divided heaven). Buenos Aires: Sudamericana, 1995.

Secondary Sources

Fares, Gustavo, and Eliana Hermann. "Exilios internos: el viaje en cinco escritoras argentinas." *Hispanic Journal. Journal of the Indiana University of Pennsylvania* 15/1 (Spring 1994): 21–29.

Flori, Mónica Roy. *Streams of Silver: Six Contemporary Women Writers from Argentina.* Lewisburg, Penn.: Associated University Presses, 1995.

Foster, David William. *Alternative Voices in the Contemporary Latin American Narrative.* Columbia: University of Missouri Press, 1985.

———. "The De-mythification of Buenos Aires in Selected Argentine Novels of the Seventies." *Chasqui: Revista de Literatura Latinoamericana* 10/1 (November 1980): 3–25.

Gramuglio, María Teresa. "Aproximaciones a *La rompiente.*" Estudio Posliminar. *La rompiente.* Buenos Aires: Puntosur, 1987.

Martínez de Richter, Marily. "Textualizaciones de la violencia: *Informe bajo llave* de Marta Lynch y *La rompiente* de Reina Roffé." *Siglo XX 20th Century* 11/1–2 (1993): 89–117.

Szurmuk, Mónica. "La textualización de la represión en *La rompiente* de Reina Roffé." *Nuevo Texto Crítico* 3/1 (1990): 123–31.

Tierney Tello, Mary Beth. *Allegories of Transgression and Transformation: Experimental fiction by Women Writing Under Dictatorship.* Albany: State University of New York Press, 1996.

———. "From Silence to Subjectivity: Reading and Writing in Reina Roffé's *La rompiente.*" *Latin American Literary Review* 21/42 (July–December 1993): 34–56.

Interview

1. Which authors have had the greatest influence on your works?

None, and all. I think that each time I have read something, fiction, poetry, theater, essay, it has left a very important impression on me. If we can call these "influences" I will try to concoct a list of authors to which I always return and which I could call "my tutoring angels." In the first place, Jorge Luis Borges. In second place, I'm going to take the license of naming a handful of writers to make direct use of my right to discriminate positively: Virginia Woolf, Djuna Barnes, Carson McCullers, Katherine Mansfield, Marguerite Yourcenar, Marguerite Duras, Flannery O'Connor, Silvina Ocampo . . .

2. When did you begin to write, and why?

I don't remember exactly when I began to write, because I have always written, but I do know what was the catalyst for my decision to be a writer. I was around fifteen or sixteen years old when a girlfriend lent me Simone de Beauvoir's *The Broken Woman*. I read the book all at once, in one afternoon, and it made a strong impression on me. Everything the reading provoked, especially the title story, with regard to its insights on life and the place of emotions, helped me discover the capacity that a writer can have to provoke "something" in others. This was what motivated me to want to evoke my own experiences through literature, with the idea of producing in others what I had felt so intensely myself. That's what I've tried to do ever since, but I don't know if I have succeeded all the time.

Regarding why I write, besides what I have already noted, the answer is in the foreword to *La rompiente* in the Punto Sur edition: "I know that one writes for many reasons: to become famous, to alleviate anguish, to have a place, for pleasure, out of disgust, for vanity, to annihilate the ghosts, to give them life, because one speaks very little, because one wants others to talk about her, or to cover their mouths, because one failed as a ballet dancer, out of audacity, in order not to die, or to die peacefully, to pass the time, so that something will happen, for no reason. I don't know exactly why I write, or even if it's right for me to do so, but what is certain is that since the 1970s, when I wrote my first novel, I've never abandoned writing, although sometimes I have felt that writing has abandoned me."

3. Has the political situation influenced your choice of themes?

I am more interested in the internal processes of the characters than in writing about political situations. Nevertheless, and since in Argentina the sociopolitical question is so overwhelming, politics are present in all the stories I narrate, despite the fact that my primordial intention is to make the treatment of human behavior more relevant than anything else. As you can see in *La Rompiente* I don't confront the political situation face on, but from an angle. I utilize elusive strategies to tell that other story, the political one, within a fictional framework. I should recognize that in *La rompiente* as well as in my latest novel, provisionally titled *No entres dócilmente en esa noche quieta,* the fictional plane is mined by a determinate and recognizable political climate, which is that of the Argentina of recent times.

4. Have you encountered difficulties, as a woman writer, with publishers?

Currently I have no problems with publishers. But I don't know if this situation is part of an editorial policy that is going to continue, or if it responds only to a commercial "boom": women writers, suddenly, "sell."

5. What do you think of feminism?

Feminism in the 1970s was a fountain of illumination for women: a very useful tool to open doors and make us conscious of our position in history; to arm ourselves with courage and to settle accounts. In this sense, I hold in high esteem what feminism has done for women. But, like all "isms," the Women's Liberation Movement is now passing through moments of estrangement and confusion. I feel closer to the women who act as feminists without joining any particular organization than to those who are militant in a movement that seems to have ended up without acceptable strategies for the majority of us, since those strategies come from a theory that is still poorly elaborated. I identify with feminism's connection to a pending revolution.

6. How would you describe Argentina's women readers?

I think Argentina's women readers have attitudes that are similar to those of any reader from the so-called civilized world. I have the impression that they are avidly seeking new voices that represent them and in whom they can perceive a rapport with their current problems and desires. If indeed the buying power of the Argentine reader has diminished a lot in recent years, for reasons that are public knowledge, I think that this same situation has generated a very interesting phenomenon. Now women pitch in together to buy a book, or to exchange books, to talk about them, et cetera, which has brought them closer together and enriched them enormously. The proliferation of study groups and workshops attended primarily by women is not a coincidence but an imperious necessity of moving forward against all odds. At this time, as I understand from my experience as a leader of literary workshops in Argentina and in Spain, I can state that women are the ones who are most interested in reading, in reading groups, and in learning about the fine arts.

Selection from *La rompiente*

The work of Reina Roffé prior to *La rompiente,* for example the novel *Monte de Venus,* is particularly interesting from a feminist perspective due to the iconoclast vision it offers of women's role in Argentine society in general, and in "porteño" life in particular. *La rompiente* can easily be considered an experimental text. The road toward the examination of experimental narratives was signaled by Julio Cortázar's *Rayuela.* Since then, however, the fragmentation of characters' voices and identities has not been very common in Argentine narrative. It is even less common in the works written by women. This fact, among many others, renders this novel by Roffé extremely interesting. In this work we see once again the motif of the journey, already noted in the works by Diaconú, Mercader, and Orphée. This time, the journey could be to exile, it could be that of a group of students, it could have no return. We say "could" because one of the characteristics of this work by Roffé is the ambiguity with which facts are presented. They are narrated from several points of view, with different voices that alternate in the leading role, and whose identity is constantly questioned. The work is divided in three parts and contains several stories. The first part presents a journey to a foreign country; the third part relates a persecution previous to that journey and, within it, there are other histories, journeys, and illnesses. Between these two, we find the second part, also made up of several different stories that are alternated, mixed, lived through the same characters of the other parts, but with different names and identities. So the "I" of the main character sometimes is called Rahab; the Professor is identified with a former seminarian; Boomer is also known as "the critic." The passage selected belongs to this second part and it tells a love story in a series of short fragments wherein the narrator and Boomer participate. This text is at times revealingly autobiographical, as when the narrator says that she is worried over having betrayed her own "voice" in order to please those who had allowed her to collaborate in a magazine. This passage reminds the reader of the statements Roffé made concerning her search for an identity that would allow her to find her own "voice" ("Qué escribimos las mujeres en la Argentina hoy" [What women write in Argentina today]). The very title of the work, *La rompiente* (The breaker), alludes to the identity of the narrator, formed by the traces that her own story has left in her, and thanks to which she can now write.

Turn the Page

"Turn the page," that was the title of one of the poems that so enthused the former seminarian on that humid afternoon, in a neighborhood coffee-shop, when he put me in the hands of my destiny. Yes, let's say it was my literary destiny, but also the other one, which you're going to like: that of a love story. The critic adopted me immediately, and don't think it was for my pretty face or my pretty verses, but for what I promised. Publishing in the magazine made me feel like a chosen one; it wasn't so much seeing my poems in print, it was the possibility that I was being invited to join. Having access—even if it were just as a spectator or an apprentice—to the scenario where people discussed and elaborated on the so-called "Cultural Continuity of the Nation" was something that made me feel on top of the wave. And this was the reason why I owed them such gratitude and fidelity; first of all, to the former seminarian who had put me in the hands of the critic; and second, to the critic who had opened for me the doors to a world and to its makers, engaged in battle with neocolonialism and reactionary literatures. I was grateful, believe me, to have found a group I could belong to, finally. The magazine lasted for three or four issues. The former seminarian and the critic agreed on which of my poems they would finally publish before the magazine folded. It was a poem in the style of Pizarnik; the protest, if there was any, was rooted in the mocking of individual solitude. You see, although the tendency of the publication was to exalt collective sentiments, other purposes also had their place—if the truth be told. However, afterwards my "gratitude" became subservience, when, looking for approval, I renounced what I wanted to say and borrowed a voice that, since it didn't belong to me, turned against me. The necessity of responding to the expectations and demands of those that I believed to be my interlocutors—certainly, at that moment, they were the only ones I had—and who functioned as a frame of reference, produced a strange phenomenon: it deviated me from my path. If I was extremely productive then, my production caused me more dissatisfaction than happiness. And when I tried other routes, well, you can see the results. Now, will I be able to do this, leave behind these stagnant waters and find the course of my own stream? The question fills me with anguish.

Did I tell you that September presents me with surprises, encounters, changes? It was during that glorious month that the critic and I submitted to our love story:

I

The villa seemed desolated and that wasn't so strange at that time of the year. My body defied the authority of the sun. Among the dunes and under the warm rays of the late afternoon hours, I felt sure of something, of someone. Boomer had suggested that I lower the straps of my bikini so that the sun wouldn't leave stripes on my skin. I ignored him, wanting to be more daring: I took off the bra entirely and pretended to sleep, face up to the wide sky, but then I think I really did fall asleep. I dreamed that I descended to the sea. The waves rushed against me like a windstorm against a weathervane. The fury of the water lifted me, revealed my fragility. In spite of it, I swam beyond the breakwater. During my journey, the line of the horizon suffered waves, great wings roused to greet me and, when I turned my head, Boomer was above me, between the dunes and the pines; his look custodial, his lips pronouncing a mimicking call. Then I began the return journey. He encircled me with his arm. He dried my hair. He brushed from my eyes the soot of insanity while he said to me: "Oh, your orgiastic acrobatics."

II

We were alone for a moment. "The Soul of the Poets" made me whirl, holding tightly to my glass, or perhaps it was the world that was turning. The voice of

Ives Montand was the reason for that soiree. "Boomer is all men for me," I thought. I put my head on his shoulder and, from that position, the legs of the furniture and the friezes were transformed into excessive images. I told him: "I want everyone to know that you love me." I served myself another drink, and I wanted to dance alone with my glass full. Boomer threw himself into a chair. When I saw that people were approaching, I sat beside him and in a low voice I implored: "I want you to say it now that everyone's here." They served hot chocolate to sweeten the new day that was beginning and ease the emanations of the alcohol. "Boomer," I said, "I'm waiting." And I went to find my cup of chocolate. I maneuvered with some difficulty to the center of the room, but without spilling that after-midnight elixir, and from there I shouted with all my might: "Let's toast the couples of this new day," and I began to laugh mockingly, bitterly. "Let's toast the women and men capable of declaring their love with a cup of hot chocolate. I toast Boomer, who is now going to tell you all that he loves me . . . I toast all the eunuchs of this land." The faces observing me began to contort. The people standing began to shrink to the size of a handgun. "Let him speak, or remain silent forever," was the last thing I remember having said.

III

Now I could spy on myself; put myself, for example, in a corner of the room and observe myself languishing on the bed, see my face next to the crook of my arm and my five fingers on top of my head, like a crown. I discovered my breasts, damp like the muzzles of goats; my nightgown lifted to my knees, freeing one of my legs, which I normally kept withdrawn, to absolute abandon. Now I knew that something wasn't going well. Something turned flips and become lodged in my throat. I still couldn't lift my head or open my eyes. I was shaken by spasms produced by the fever, and double-edged blades were nailed to the walls of my stomach. Before continuing I could devour my own image—it is as hostile to me as it was then, when I submitted to a slow waking up: sighs, little inflections; my skin smelling like iodine, indicating the proximity of the sea. What had happened the night that preceded the day that was dawning? The alcohol caused me to behave shamefully. I was conscious of overacting, and yet I couldn't avoid it. I needed the others to believe that the basest instincts made the more noble ones resurge, flood through the hardest zones of the shell that shielded me, to give birth to an affectionate and generous woman. "I am a mediocre being," pounded my temples, "fairly pitiable. I try to find out what or whom I love in this desert, in this interior anarchy, in this repeated sentimental sabotage." Waking up this way was a coup, an act of violence. Who was taking me out of that sweet nothing of sleep to throw me into the debris of reality? I knew I was at fault and I hated to be wrong. I breathed with difficulty. The air brought pestilent waves. I imagined the skeletons of the fish with their crushed heads on the sand and the seagulls flying away from the remains they had just digested. Someone was softly, barely perceptibly, tracing the features of my face. Was it to wake me up or to bury me in a deeper sleep? Boomer's hand stopped on my neck and afterwards I heard some verses from Desnos—almost under his breath—*Corps et Biens*—for which it was worthwhile, finally, to open my eyes.

IV

The warm sand under my feet was a balsam; an abandoned dog followed me. It was always Boomer that the animals really loved. I didn't know why this one had glued itself to my heels. I led the pack. Boomer, behind me, was trying to seduce it, and our friend Asius—who was trailing in the rear—was practicing pirouettes and howling as he supposed the sea-wolves did. I reached the rocks, where the waves splash high, and the air wets one's smiles, a little. Boomer was saying, "come on, doggie, come to your old friend, come lick my boots. Come here," ordered Boomer, "you're lost, aren't you? I know what you need. Come with me and I'll pet you." The sea was the only part of nature that moved me; it inspired submission in me, it took control of my feelings. "I know you'll leave," recited Boomer, "that you're going to disappear, because you are a traveler and this place, just like I am, is merely one more stop on your long voyage." He took my arm and made me sit next to him on a boulder; he already had now conquered unconditionally the dog of unrecognizable breed that wagged his tail at his new master and scratched with his paw at the mollusks encrusted on the rocks. Asius climbed agilely over the stones, showing off his physical aptitudes. "Another vagabond, another acrobat," he said, pulling the ears of the dog that had reclined at Boomer's feet. "Perhaps descended from a Greek Hound," he added. While both of them dedicated themselves to examining him, I busied myself pouring a cup of tea.

Since I didn't want either of them to touch the food with their dirty hands, I wrapped the sandwiches that I offered them in paper napkins, but I couldn't stop Asius from rummaging through the basket looking for his container of whiskey, much less from drinking from the bottle. I strayed a little way from them; I liked to watch them eat together. From a certain distance, the shape of our friend's body—seated several centimeters below Boomer—and the exuberance of his movements made him funny and endearing; like the buffoon reciting a satirical poem to a great king who accepts the criticism honorably, only to forget them immediately in his laughter. Boomer had taken up his habitual pose as a thinker; to do that, he lifted the lapel of his hunting jacket. The dog licked his boots. The two men and the animal were dancing at the edge of the cliff. A shoulder rises, an arm reaches out, a yawn meets its echo. They are very far away, fine to the extreme of being barely an outline, a pair of lines whirling around the wide beach. Seen across a sun-dial, aged. The dog with Asius' same frank, roguish mouth, his lips smiling, his muzzle open wide, showing his teeth; and his eyes, which communicated an infinite gamut of messages, from the most tender to the most aggressive, were identical to Boomer's. All of this, and a poem by Alfonsina came to mind.

V

Silence is more voluptuous than the flattering sound of a voice. Boomer lingered with each bite of toast. I picked up the crumbs one by one with my fingertips, and I put them on the plate. We drank several cups of coffee. Carefully, I cleaned the stains on the tablecloth with a wet rag. He finished his toast, shook off the remnants of the bread and began to massage his temples and to form eddies with tufts of hair. I examined my nails, cleaned them a little, retained in my mouth the taste of the bitter coffee. "Words are not wasted," he said, "but one can waste himself in words."

VI

Sordidness was the frame of reference. It was almost noon when I went to see him. When he opened the door, the air current made the particles of dust float a few centimeters above the floor. There was a musty odor. Some of the objects were packed in fruit crates. Boomer was emaciated, and in his eyes I

could see the weariness and the desperation caused by insomnia and suffering. As I had suspected he had taken the telephone off the hook. He went directly to his bedroom and lay down on the bed that was rumpled and full of
crumbs; he said that he couldn't stay on his feet. I lay down beside him and
for a while we looked at the ceiling, watching the flight pattern of a fly that
opened its wings in the corners of the room—believing that there, perhaps, it
would find a window and fly away from asphyxiation. Since Boomer had decided to move away from that house and live with me he never did anything
but talk about feeling sorry for himself. I went to make coffee. Since there was
no tray in the kitchen, I served the cups and hand-carried them to the bed. I
arrived without spilling a drop on the way, but as I sat down I turned a cup
over on the sheets. Boomer called me an imbecile; it was the first time that he
had treated me that way. Then, he began to laugh with such gusto that I was
surprised to find out that he was capable of laughing that way. He helped me
to clean the stains and changed the sheets. He kept laughing, and it was contagious, but I felt offended and furious; I felt like killing him. I threw myself on
him, we struggled, still laughing, and I unfastened his clothes, and I took
mine off. Boomer hated it when I took the initiative, he hated any manifest
lasciviousness by women; he preferred that the dark prostitutes remain only
in his imagination while he possessed me. My nails clawed his back with too
much vehemence; I could see that his skin was turning red. I felt the disgust
that each act of voluptuousness produced, and the intimate perspiration. As
the disgust grew, so did the necessity of indulging in repeated contortions, in
repeated surrenders. I took his head between my hands and pulled him by the
hair; Boomer didn't complain, but he remained on top of me until I pushed
him away. I went out to the street, determined to walk, to purify myself.

VII

I recline my head against the glass of the little window, and only this is
enough for me. I go higher, I reach the nineteenth floor of an office high rise;
from there, the cats that walk around the cornices are tiny acrobats. The entire landscape in front of me now is another one—one like that which, for
some time, accompanied me. I find myself again in the apartment where
Boomer and I lived: "I am glad to be someone that happiness never touched,"
he would say mockingly when I proposed a truce, a simple walk to distract

him. Back then he invented games so as not to leave the house. That afternoon it had occurred to him to prepare an hallucinogenic brew that had the ability of inducing the faithful to confess hidden truths, I had to submit to it. I drank the potion confidently; although for entertainment, I controlled the content and breathed the aroma; the taste was pleasant, it seemed like coffee with grated cinnamon and chocolate. Lowering the blinds was enough to create the atmosphere. Boomer put on the record *The Candid Marksman* by Von Weber since, according to what he said, he was going to let loose a battle between good and evil, between the divine and the diabolical. He would be the devil's representative on earth and I the angelic and pure Agata. My beloved Max couldn't defend himself or defend me; consequently it was up to me alone to recover or to say goodbye to happiness forever. I ingested that thick liquid, savoring it with pleasure, because certainly it was a strong perfumed coffee, and I rested on the sofa to wait for its effect. Boomer was in a chair facing me. I closed my eyes and squeezed them until I felt creases forming around them; also the wrinkles on my nose. Violet points of light began to fan out, giving way then to a face of exaggerated features. "I'm looking at you," I said, "I'm seeing you as if you were holding right in front of me a burned, close-up photograph. The corners of your pursed mouth give you a cunning and perverse look. How is it possible that never, until now, have I seen your pointed goat-like beard that ends in such a funny ringlet . . . Oh yes, now I understand, you want to control me, it's not enough for you to possess me, you need for me to be something more than a simple pupil. Oh yes, now I see clearly, you want me to become your good double, obedient, even your clown. If I were an athlete, for example, a classical ballerina, the most skillful trapeze artist from the Moscow circus, then I would be a much more perfect double. Boomer, you erred, how badly you have chosen. I am not life, I am—rather— its negation, or a long agony. Oh Boomer, how horrible, I am so frightened. When does the music stop? Perhaps should I wait for my beloved Max?; we both know that he doesn't exist. After all, what does that Max matter to me; I will go out alone. Boomer, don't shake that way. Your beard has gotten stiff. Don't torture me, please. When will this end? Oh, this isn't a fair game, you're not playing by the rules. One might expect you to participate; you should answer me. The needle was scratching the record: I saw a light or a sun of tar. Then came the lament, the hugs, etcetera.

VIII

I moved away from myself, and I see myself as if I were someone else. A woman who walks with her head down, looking at the cobblestones or the tiles of the sidewalk. She's carrying a package. (I know that it is a beveled mirror wrapped in brown paper.) She looks very fragile. She is a woman to take a closer look at, more precisely a face for a close-up. She always looks at herself in the mirror of the medicine cabinet. She walks and looks at the feet of the passersby. She has just bought a large mirror (to see her entire body). A walk through the streets shows the facade of some old houses, one or two vacant lots and tall buildings; it is not a zone for appreciating the architecture—here few Parisian awnings adorn the businesses and the beauty and barber shops. But it's better to see her in a neutral setting, transporting with great care the object she's just bought. She approaches what is apparently her house. The entrance has nothing to distinguish it. There are people in the doorway, children who play. In the apartment the man waits for her, although he should be somewhere else. And his expression is disagreeable: his brow is severe. (I remember that when she returns from a long or short walk, the man gets surly and his sentences are dry and cutting. I know also that he used to tell her: "When two people are getting along well they fuse into each other." She respects the proclamations of the man, almost all of them. However, she considers that she is alone, and from time to time she needs to be alone. And at times she needs company, without ceasing to be alone. But she says nothing, because this embarrasses her.) Now she's going to try to put the mirror on the inner part of the closet door, hammering first some hooks into the wood. The man walks from the dining room to the bedroom. She drops the hammer, takes the mirror and tries to fit it between the hooks; two are weak. The man appears and disapproves. She places the mirror on the bed and picks up the hammer again. He follows each movement. She hammers the loose hooks, but one of her fingers, one of those supporting the hook, receives a blow that makes her open her mouth and breathe hard. Her open mouth describes the pain; her lips tighten, turn pale. The man grunts. And her eyes crystallize. He moves near her, tries to make her feel better. Now she cries and won't listen to anything. Trying to soothe her wounded finger, she caresses it, she wets it in her mouth and she cries. He says: Does it hurt? . . . At least you have fingers that hurt. She hammers the hook again. He stays there, watching her. And his gaze bothers her. She says: Weren't you going to visit a friend? He responds: Does it bother you when I stay in my house? She stops hammering, threatens to break the mirror with the hammer. He continues: Have you forgotten already that I hate looking at myself? Now she tries to leave but he stops her: Let's do things the right way. I'll show you how to put up the hooks. She disagrees. He says: You're hurting me. She remembers her finger and caresses it. I'm going to take a walk, I'll be back soon. And she goes. She only gets as far as the foyer and she returns. Now she is banging on the bathroom door: she is calling him. He doesn't answer. He is in front of the medicine cabinet. There is a glass of water. In his hand, in his only hand he has a strychnine capsule. He puts the capsule beside the glass. With difficulty, he lowers his pants and sits on the toilet. From the other side of the door, she knocks and pleads. She says: I won't stop knocking until you open. Then she remembers that her finger hurts, and she stops knocking and caresses it. He keeps sitting on the toilet and crying without uttering a sound. He gets up. He picks-up the capsule in his hand, looks at it, and places it on the basin. He turns over the glass. He drinks the only swallow that remains. Having his pants down prevents him from returning to the toilet. He picks them up, he sits down. He hears her saying: It is infantile, it is ridiculous. You're not going to do it; you never did it before, and you certainly won't now. So don't waste your time locking yourself up in there. She walks away from the door with noisy steps, then she collapses on a chair, and shouts: You are worse than a woman. He answers: I am like a woman and like a woman I'm going to kill myself. She doesn't say anything. He waits for her to say something. The wait is useless; then he says: If I were really a man, a whole man, I would have a revolver, I would load that revolver with a bullet, with a very real bullet and I would shoot myself. Now she waits for him to say something else, but he doesn't say anything. She sets a clock to the correct time and winds it. He fills the glass with water again. Finally, she says: I'm going to give you five minutes, no more than five minutes. When the time's up I'm going to hang myself from the chandelier with the clothesline. And I will I do it. When you decide to show your face I'm going to be sticking out my tongue at you, because that will be the first and the last image that you will have of me. Me, sticking out my tongue at you. He puts the capsule in his mouth, but immediately spits it out. Hurriedly he lowers his pants and sits on the toilet again. Now she heads for the bedroom. She picks-up the mirror and sees her reflection. She hangs it on the closet door. First she straightens one edge, then the other. The mirror is crooked. She backs up, turns a little to the right and looks at herself. She looks at herself and smiles. She stands up straight and begins a detailed examination of her face. One profile, the other profile. She looks straight at herself and sticks out her tongue. She looks at her tongue. Afterwards she inspects her neck, rubs it and smiles. Her finger moves down and disappears into the pit of her throat. She loosens the first buttons of her blouse. Her collarbones stick out a little. Then she decides to take off her blouse entirely. She looks at her arms. She studies her abdomen. She backs up and looks at her whole body. She folds her arms behind her and leaves them there until she manages to unfasten her brassiere. She crosses her arms in front of her breasts. Little by little she opens them and looks at herself, then touches herself. She closes them and smiles. Now her hands hurry to take off her skirt. She holds the skirt out of view of the mirror and drops it. She whirls and looks at herself. She whirls and smiles. (He is in the bathroom, she thinks, he's already taken the capsule. The strychnine is taking effect; he is collapsing. The odor of vomitive nut and San Ignacio Beans is acrid, repugnant. He falls and hits his head on the edge of the bathtub. His head splits in two like a pumpkin.) Now she is serious, naked in front of the mirror. She looks at the tips of her feet. She raises her toes. Some of the pores of her feet are dilated, a purplish-red color. She looks at her legs and remembers a dream that makes her smile again. In that dream she found herself nude on a table. Cornish hen eggs were coming out of the pores of her legs. She was taking them delicately so as not to break the shells. On each of her sides there was a box. Into one the healthy ones would go, into the other the worthless ones. Horrible bird fetuses were rotting in the box for the castoffs. A fetus, still alive, tried to raise its head, but it was too heavy; the neck remained doubled over. She thinks again about the man locked in the bathroom. She thinks about finally opening the door and finding him in his bloody vomit. She looks at herself in the mirror and the image erases the horror. Now she smiles and hugs herself: she has her head inclined on her own shoulder. Now she fuses with the image in the mirror. The warmth of her mouth clouds the image. In the mirror remain her imprecise lips, the mark of her lips, a breath that is vaporizing, a track in the sand that the wind erases. Now the doorbell rings. She covers herself and goes to listen to the electric doorkeeper. She can hear the voice of someone announcing his arrival. She hears the water from the toilet running. She understands that the man in the bathroom is flushing the toilet again.

IX

Asius goes straight to the refrigerator. "This is all you have?" he says. A glass of wine pacifies him. Boomer is pale; he seems upset. He asks me to pour him a cup of tea. Asius advises us to go out and buy groceries, saying that the best thing one can do is invest in food: cooking oil, bags of flour, cases of wine. He talks about the rumors: another possible economic catastrophe. He tells us that the people have gone out into the streets, invading the stores, clearing the shelves. A price hike of a hundred per cent or more is being announced. Boomer says that he has colitis, he is passing blood; he already took two charcoal capsules and he can't take it any more. And he is fed up with women running to the market at the first rumor they hear. I rush out in spite of his warning, but looking for a vent through which to breathe another kind of air. I board a bus, I arrive at the station, I buy a train ticket: my goal is to flee. In the seats across from mine two men are playing cards. He opens, I would have passed, I raise; the others pass and my opponent covers. I say that I am staying put and he says the same thing. He doesn't hesitate a moment and his certainty makes me suspicious. I make him believe that I know perfectly well that he has nothing. In reality I don't have much. He bets a great sum with a defiant attitude. I quadruple his bet. And it's a good move because the man folds.

I returned and I put what I had bought into jars. Organizing the kitchen was the way I had of beginning to organize the apartment. I finished the task and I locked myself in the room. I was anxious to have a moment to myself. When someone plays a hand of cards alone it's because the vice has begun to harm her faculties. For that they recommend hibernation or a sleep cure. However, the mechanisms of my reasoning were functioning correctly. I didn't see anything wrong with practicing a few moves on my green felt card table. I felt like the only one alive among the dead. Many times my opponents were fearsome, putting my shrewdness to the test. I would spend hours imagining challenges, planning strategies. The hands would follow, one after the other in my mind. I would deal the cards. Those who had hands in the first and second places passed, but the third tripled my opening bet with a slight smile beneath his mustache. I matched his raise and discarded two cards. I kept, of course, the three Jacks that I had in my hand. If I knew that my opponent was an expert in the art of bluffing, this fact would give me an advantage. I pick-up my two other cards. If nothing had been said but I suspected the existence of a high three in the other's hand, I was very prudent. I would always win somehow. Later, I would tell Boomer how I proceeded in those imaginary hands. He liked to make observations, share his knowledge; he would also attack my strategies, frustrate my ingenuity, laugh at my slippery reasoning. He would say: "The whole game can depend on the choice of a discard." He started calculating the probabilities to show me which was the best one from a mathematical standpoint. He also criticized my blind leads, with extreme cruelty. I defended my position, affirming that the normal lead bored me; in the other way I could raise the amount that I was betting. I ended up saying that it was he, in reality, who bored me.

We return inevitably to what I promised, to what the critic believed that I had promised. I now see my blind spot: the promise. And still I don't see what the others see or hope for. You were hoping, you tell me, for a love story, and you received a burst of machine-gun fire, sequences of a hand to hand combat. Perhaps the remains that were left don't belong in a love story; can one write about anything that hasn't left a mark?

In the novel the Professor is murdered and no one doubts it. Several chapters allude to a possible persecution suffered by the character which will lead to his death. "I have to get out of here," he says in one paragraph; "I don't want to die now, I can't, I mustn't. I want a free death, that comes to me when I ask for it. The baby will be born soon, and at the very least I would like to meet him. I should take care of my wife, send her to a safer place." In this passage the female protagonist, Boomer, and Asius listen to the Professor intently, although his paranoid anguish confuses them and raises their suspicions—especially when he tells them: "They called again. They spoke in code as if they believed that I can decipher it. They wake me up every day at three-thirty in the morning. They call my name with a very loud, very clear voice. They say: 'How happy it makes us to hear you. I am here, with a lackey, having a cup of tea with lemon. Tell me something . . . tell me, tell me.' Now they're also following me." As you can tell, the Professor's profile is drawn with traces of insanity; all the references made throughout his speech add up to pure delirium. Perhaps this is because the madness of others comes to and rests in the Professor, since certain inbred groups function that way. I don't know, the idea is just occurring to me now. If Boomer and Asius don't openly show incredulity at the statements of the Professor, since their acceptance responds to mixed feelings, it is she—the protagonist—who puts in doubt the credibility of the story she just heard. Due to that she is censured by the recriminatory look of Asius. That look tells her that she cannot comfort desperate people at the moment of confession; that her mere presence profanes the sacred place of masculine friendship; that to accept someone's overflowing with incoherent words, infected by verbiage and gestures, by truths or lies, by belief or disbelief, it is necessary to love and to have to share a part of the story; that to understand is to do an homage of surrender. The novel is constricted by certain referents. The fears from which the Professor suffers turn out to be justified. Boomer attempts an explanation: "Our friend," he says, "has a serious problem, but I wonder if each one of us doesn't carry a load of such magnitude that everyone else's load seems comparatively illusory. Anyway, I suspect—if I must hold to some logic—that someone wants to kill him. There are those who don't like it when a nobody fleeces them in the blink of an eye." Later, the Professor seems to identify his persecutors. In the dialogue that he begins with Boomer there is an abundance of metaphors, and the speech is markedly Nietzschean: "I know who they are," he says, "You also know them. They are the mediocre ones, Boomer. They have discovered me, they want to eliminate me. I can't allow it, you know, because of the baby. He's not even my son. I don't know how they managed to find out. And they're not going to let me be pure. They will submerge me in the impoverished happiness that they peddle, in the filthiest reason that they have imposed, in the lamentable well-being of the virtue they lack, in the scandal of a coerced justice that they don't even practice now, and in the vulgarity of compassion. Boomer! he shouted, they are cold monsters. Therefore, I'm going to fight back now." To this Boomer responds: "One man cannot fight the whole pack." The professor asks him to be his witness, the avenger, if they win. Boomer believes that it is an unreasonable request. He declares: "You're making a mistake with me. I'm not an ocean that can receive streams of oil and remain unpolluted. I am contaminated. Look at me," he says and reaches out his arms, "I haven't been able to overcome this violence." The Professor declares that no one will be saved from the nightmare. How strange. It wasn't then, when I was evoking fragments of my life and writing, that my organs were being paralyzed, even this particular one, so reviled, called the heart, but rather now, facing so many tricks, saying something seized by my fear. Now, I was telling you, at the time of reading, of exposing myself through a ridiculous text that barely attests to all that I was hiding: an ambushed memory in which one wouldn't or couldn't remember. One can be indifferent to reality, but not to the memory of that reality which is constantly unfolding. That must be why I keep on exploring the possible murder of the former seminarian, as if that death were predicted by a clue or meant to end a story. To extract a reliable fact from the confused murmur of the past is an heroic act, but it is insignificant. I prefer, if you agree, that the novel itself keep on speaking.

Boomer received a letter from the Professor in which he begged us to agree to let his wife stay in our house for a few days. Quenia arrived one afternoon without any further notice than the reference in that letter. Her appearance didn't betray any suffering; on the contrary, she seemed very healthy. In spite of that fact, during the week when she was our guest, I became very solicitous. I was always available to offer her my arm and to warm the milk she drank after meals.

Quenia spoke very little; in that way we were alike. However, the fact that we were in my house permitted me to converse with ease. Besides, if I didn't speak—Quenia, in general, didn't say more than thank you for what her hosts offered—her stay would have been very boring for everyone, and as for me, I would have been unforgivably discourteous. I wasn't so much interested in her, but in what she would tell the Professor about me—therein my painstaking care to please her, along with the effort to ease my feeling of being watched and perhaps even censured by an accidental witness to my acts and to my relationship with Boomer.

When we sat at the table, Quenia, at the head, looked at us before each bite; she turned her head like a spectator at a Ping-Pong match. Often my conversation with Boomer did turn into a Ping-Pong game—irrepressible in the moments when we forgot the roles that we had tacitly imposed on ourselves to play.

After the meal, Quenia would stand in front of the window and, while she rubbed her voluminous abdomen, she would become lost in the contemplation of the neighboring terraces. Boomer stationed himself for best view—in the armchair—and watched her. She, in turn, watched the neighborhood cats with the avidness of a trapeze enthusiast, until she would go to sleep. Fascinated, Boomer scrutinized the nocturnal landscape looking for a sign that would reveal our guest's frame of mind. "She must be waiting for the Professor, for some signal," he said. More than clues, he was looking for excuses to justify the fact that Quenia, or her condition, attracted him.

In the narrow bed that we had to share, Boomer's voice was whispering a story, the same story that he told me every night: "The Professor was going to the hospital accompanied by a friend who had a sick wife. He met Quenia there. She used to ask him for cigarettes, you know the Professor doesn't smoke," Boomer would tell me, "but to satisfy her, before entering the hospital, he bought a pack and gave it to her." Once they began to talk, she was fine—almost euphoric that day. The Professor began to comment about something that, on the other hand, had been in all the newspapers, the death of somebody named Menéndez, a famous psychiatrist. Quenia began to cry, inconsolably, according to the Professor. Although regretting that he had opened his mouth, now he couldn't stop talking, because he wanted to calm her, and he began to say anything, funny things that—because it was him—would have been for sure tragic and solemn. Quenia told him that she had seen Menéndez on several occasions and now he was dead, and when she said *dead* she would cry even harder. Disconcerted, the Professor took a cigarette from the pack he had bought and took two puffs—just to do something—and nearly choked. Then he put it in her mouth and she calmed down. Another day, the Professor went and found Quenia aglow. He understood that she was the most lucid woman he had known in his whole life. She started to confess and in her confession she spoke of some messages that she had received when her conscious restraints malfunctioned and of how she had deciphered symbols that have always been present forever and that no one sees them because no one takes the trouble to think about them as such. She said that she would never lose that divine grace, even if she regained her sanity. The difference in this woman, her capacity to utilize powers that those who aren't in on the conspiracy can't even dream of, dazzled the Professor. Quenia showed herself to him as a true mystic. Both coincided in the desire to reinaugurate the revelry and the joys of this world. The Professor, who had spent so much time repeating that in the best of circumstances women are cows, swooned in an abstruse devotion. He did nothing but talk about her, I mean, about that tender cow that she is now. Thus it was how I found out about the story that Quenia told him about her life. According to the story, she was in a clinic in New York for nearly a year. Quenia came from a wealthy family. She had studied in an English school, she spoke English as well as she did Spanish; that must be why they took her to North America, I guess. Once they had let her go out; she had a pass until six in the afternoon. Her room-mate was trying her new car that morning. Together they went for a ride. They went by way of one of those monstrous highways that take you to the ends of the earth in a few minutes. When they tried to return, they got into an uproar. Quenia sang psalms for two straight hours, believing that singing would raise the spirits of the people who, like themselves, were trapped in the cement and the night. She could never recover from the effect that such an effort caused on her vocal cords. You must have noticed her hoarseness, her muffled voice the few times when she does speak. Another time, she got lost in a Manhattan neighborhood. And, although she remembered perfectly well the address of the clinic, in order to return she had to give the directions to a taxi-driver, if she took a taxi, or ask someone which bus would take her there. But in that way, she thought, she would divulge the name of the clinic and with this she would reveal the location of her refuge and the refuge of her sib-lings and guardians. So she preferred to wander alone through the streets, in the snow. It was in February, I think, when it is very cold there and the snow blinds and causes hallucinations like the desert sand—especially after six o'clock. Because, after that hour, all the permits expire, and so does every-thing that is legal, and one is exposed and takes risks. And Quenia didn't want to expose herself, and even less to take any risks. In New York, where the tele-phones actually work and there are public booths all over the place, it would have been easy to call the clinic and ask them to come for her, but she had forgotten the number and she feared that an indiscreet operator would in-form the police. Finally someone found her. After a while, the family brought her back. They had her with them until they grew weary, and they abandoned her little by little. There is something else: when the Professor went to see her one afternoon at the hospital in here, they had discharged her and no one knew her whereabouts. They had rid themselves of her as if a certificate of good health exempted them of all responsibility. The Professor, indignant, grabbed a boot and with the boot in his hand, broke the windows in the women's room. He laughed when he told me that he began to break the windows and to shout—the Professor who never raises his voice—"On guard liars!" And into an enormous bucket, a kind of tunnel where they washed the dishes, he put his feet and incited the patients to wash themselves in that same dirty water. From that day on he looked for Quenia tirelessly. Exhausted, he came to see me, no longer knowing where to look. I took him in my car, and we covered the whole port, believing that perhaps she would leave for New York again. He told me: "Think, perhaps we are passing by the place where she was looking for me a minute ago; what worries me the most, Boomer, old friend, is this ridiculous failure to meet, this clumsy joke. Then, after his fruitless search, the Professor found her in the twilight of a luminous afternoon, as he told me. He said, I remember, that she was in the Cathedral doorway like a mystic, watching the people who entered and left again, puffing on a cigarette, burning it up in two puffs almost without perceiving the stupor of the lighted butt between her fingers." "I infer," continued Boomer under his breath, with that whisper that made one sleepy but didn't let one sleep, "that when the Professor found her she was already pregnant, although even she didn't know it. Who's to guess whose child he is, what happened in the hospital or on the streets while she was loose among those 'cold monsters,' as the Professor says. Do you know?" said Boomer, soothed by his own voice, "to love a woman, pregnant by God knows who, to make love to a poor, tender cow, to have her with oneself, to care for her. Have you seen how she stands in front of our window and caresses her belly?" Yes, I saw, I said before falling asleep, and I know.

Quenia didn't smoke any more, now that she was expecting a baby and the Professor. On the seventh day, after receiving a message she left our house. We accompanied her to a station; we watched as she boarded the train and disappeared in the car. After her absence it took a while for Boomer to recover from her stay with us.

Noemí Ulla

Noemí Ulla was born in the Santa Fe province of Argentina in 1935. She studied philosophy and literature at the Rosario National University, in Santa Fe, where she lived until 1969, when she moved to Buenos Aires. She earned a doctorate in literature from the University of Buenos Aires. In 1984 the University of Toulouse Le-Mirail invited her to participate in an International Tango Colloquium, where she spoke on "The Hybridization in the Tango Lyric: Marginal French." In 1987 she was invited by the Katolische Universitat Eichstatt to participate in the International Congress on Argentine Literature with her lecture "Inventions, Parodies and Testimonies: Argentine Literature from 1976 to 1986." In 1990 she was invited by the Universidad Complutense of Madrid (Spain) and also received a scholarship by the DAAD (Deutscher Akademischer Austauschdienst) in Berlin. In 1992 the University of Toulouse-Le Mirail (France) also invited her to speak. In 1993 she lectured at University Blais Pascal in Clermont-Ferrand (France) and in 1995 she taught at the University of Caen (France). She received the Premio Novela from the Direction of Culture from the Santa Fe Province for her novel *Los que esperan el alba;* and the 1995 first Prize for Essay from the Buenos Aires Municipality. She is a researcher for the CONICET (Council of Scientific and Technical Investigations) in Buenos Aires, and actively continues writing works of literature. She has taught literary theory at the University of Morón and Argentine literature at Rosario National University.

Publications

Los que esperan el alba (Those who wait for day break). Santa Fe: Dirección de Cultura, 1967.

Urdimbre (Warp). Buenos Aires: Editorial de Belgrano, 1981.

Encuentros con Silvina Ocampo (Conversations with Silvina Ocampo). Buenos Aires: Editorial de Belgrano, 1982.

Tango, rebelión y nostalgia (Tango, rebellion, and nostalgia). Buenos Aires: Centro Editor de América Latina, 1982.

Ciudades (Cities). Buenos Aires: Centro Editor de América Latina, 1983.

La ruptura de un motivo clásico: El amor cortés (The rupture of a classical motif: The courtly love). Bremen: Hispanorama, 1983.

Trayectoria y análisis de Silvina Ocampo (Trajectory and analysis of Silvina Ocampo). *Evaluación de la literatura femenina de Latinoamérica.* Buenos Aires: Siglo XXI, 1985.

"Macedonio Fernández." *La vanguardia de 1922.* Buenos Aires: Centro Editor de América Latina, 1986.

Después de la noche: Diálogo con Graciela Fernández Meijide (After the night: A dialogue with Graciela Fernández Meijide). Buenos Aires: Contrapunto, 1986.

"La escritura coloquial rioplatense: Escritores y críticos" (River Plate coloquial writing: Writers and critics). *Rio de la Plata: Culturas* 4/6 (1987): 377–83.

"*Hombre de la esquina rosada*" *de Jorge Luis Borges* (Jorge Luis Borges' "The man on the rose street corner"). *Alba de América: Revista Literaria* (1987).

"La recepción de la escritura coloquial rioplatense" (The reception of River Plate colloquial writing). *Nuevo Texto Crítico* 1/2 (1988): 353–360.

El ramito (The bouquet). Buenos Aires: Ultimo Reino, 1990.

Aventuras de la imaginación. De la vida y los libros de Adolfo Bioy Casares (Imagination's adventures. Adolfo Bioy Casares' life and books). Buenos Aires: Corregidor, 1990.

Identidad rioplatense, 1930. La escritura coloquial: Borges, Arlt, Hernández y Onetti (River Plate identity, 1930. The colloquial writing: Borges, Arlt and Onetti). Buenos Aires: Torres Agüero, 1990.

"Tradición y transgresión en los cuentos de Julio Ricci" (Tradition and transgression in

Julio Ricci's short stories). *Revista Iberoamericana* 58/160–61 (July–December 1992): 1065–76.

Invenciones a dos voces. Ficción y poesía en Silvina Ocampo (Inventions with two voices: fiction and poetry in Silvina Ocampo). Buenos Aires: Torres Agüero, 1992.

"Cuentas (Accounts)." *Violencia II: visiones femeninas.* Buenos Aires: Instituto Movilizador de Fondos Cooperativos, 1993.

El cerco del deseo (The desire's fence). Buenos Aires: Sudamericana, 1994.

Secondary Sources

Beccacece, Hugo. "Noemí Ulla y una infatigable labor literaria: El Centro Editor publica ahora *Ciudades*." *Tiempo Argentino,* 17 August 1983.

Campra, Rosalba. "Mappa della narrativa argentina." *L'Indice* 6–7 (July–August 1985): 6.

Camuffo, Marta A. "*Ciudades,* de Noemí Ulla." *Alba de América: Revista Literaria* 9/16–17 (1991): 85–91.

Carnevales, Jorge. "Noemí Ulla o el peso del silencio." *Clarín,* 8 March 1984.

Castagnino, Raúl H. "*Urdimbre.*" *La Prensa,* 24 October 1982.

Di Giovanni, Norman Thomas, ed. "Noemí Ulla, Afternoons in Buenos Aires: Meeting with a Balcony in the Background." Translated by Susan Ashe. *Journal of Literary Translation* 18 (Spring 1987).

Engelhardt, Daniela. "Argentinische Literatur heute. Der Uebergang von Exil und Diktatur zur Demokratie." *Argentinisches Tageblatt,* 29 April 1988.

Fares, Gustavo, and Eliana Hermann. "Y ahora? Reflexiones acerca de la literatura femenina argentina actual. *Forma oculta del mundo* de María Rosa Lojo, *Metáforas y reflejos* de Jorgelina Loubet, y *Victoria Ocampo* de María Esther Vázquez." *Letras Femeninas* 19/1–2 (Spring–Fall 1993): 121–34.

Frías, Esteban. "Podemos conocer la existencia de una tradición literaria (con la escritora Noemí Ulla)." *La Prensa,* 16 January 1983.

Gallo, Alejandra. "El arte no tiene sexo. Literatura. ¿Qué sucede cuando las mujeres escriben?" *El Cronista Comercial,* 19 November 1989.

Goloboff, Gerardo Mario. "*Ciudades.*" *Caravelle, Cahiers de Monde Hispanique at Luso-Bresilien* 42 (1984).

Sarlo, Beatriz. "Estar hecho de palabras." *Clarín* (December 1981).

Soares, Norberto. "Eluard decía que hay otros mundos, pero estaban aquí." *Tiempo Argentino,* 12 December 1984.

Thonis, Luis. "Tango, rebelión y nostalgia." *Convicción* 5 December 1982.

Interview

1. Which authors have had the greatest influence on your work?

   I don't know if I can talk about influences with much clarity. The memory of poems, stories, novels we have read and liked so much, forms a sort of literary fabric that certainly enters into dialogue with our own writings. From Cervantes to Italo Calvino, from Borges to Clarice Lispector, Juan Carlos Onetti, Felisberto Hernández, Katherine Mansfield, Poe, Silvina Ocampo, Henry James, Carson McCullers, Hemingway, Faulkner, or Flaubert.

2. When did you begin to write, and why?

   The truth is that I began to write when I was about eight years old. Back then, I thought I had written a novel, but of course, it wasn't one. The need and the pleasure of inventing, of understanding the world, of learning about the people and perhaps learning about myself, about being happier and finding happiness, were what captured me at first, and are what still lead me to write. In sum, I began to write because it fascinated me; now I do it because it is a way of becoming myself or of changing myself into the other that I will be.

3. How does the political situation influence your choice of themes?

   I never stopped working, even under the censorship and the repression of the last military dictatorship, which harassed our thoughts. There were books of mine that were much less favored, even ignored, than others. The book that we did with Hugo Echave, *Después de la noche,* a series of interviews with Graciela Fernández Meijide, mother of a "disappeared person" and a member of APHD, the Permanent Assembly on Human Rights, didn't have the expected reception, since the ghost of censorship is difficult to overcome.

4. Have you encountered difficulties, as a woman writer, with publishers?

It's enough to glance at any history of literature to find that women writers are almost absent from it. Publishers, in general, don't make up a world that is separate from the history of the country.

5. What do you think of feminism?

If you only look at the content of the histories of literature, you can see that women writers almost do not exist, which means that those books lack, obviously, real data. And this is only one example related to my profession, since the same could be said of any number of social and cultural activities from where women seem to be absent. This would demonstrate that our place in the social imagination continues to be, deep down, conflictive. Therefore, I believe that we still have a long way to go.

6. How would you describe Argentina's women readers?

I think that a sociologist should respond to that question, or perhaps a publisher. Sometimes I have met readers of a book of short stories I wrote, who have confessed that they seemed to find, in the female characters, reflections that felt like theirs, and that they could really identify with the problems that were raised in the stories. I cannot pass any kind of judgment about the Argentine woman reader, but I would remark that in the last few years there has been like a rising tide and that, ostensibly, women seem to have thrown themselves into literature.

Selection from *Ciudades*

Noemí Ulla states in the introduction to her work *Ciudades* that she would like someday to live in Montevideo, because, between Montevideo and the city of Rosario, in the Province of Santa Fe, "there is a weaving of memories and landscapes, corners that return when in the company of beloved people and voices" (7). Those are the cities of the book's title, located between the Paraná and de la Plata rivers, which provide a frame for the inner landscapes of the volume's characters. The story selected, "Encounter with a Balcony in the Background," narrates in an impersonal third person voice the relationship between a man and a woman. As in a painting, the title gives an explanation for their actions at the same time that it showcases the element that serves as a visual prop. The balcony is not an inert object, but a space inhabited by a woman first, and later by a couple unfurling a universe that belongs, at the same time, to the man who observes them and to his past. As if he were a voyeur, he recognizes himself in the couple in the balcony, as he and his former wife used to be years before, when their love was still new and they were young. The words "in the background" then, should not lead the reader to think that the background is merely decorative. On the contrary, it is the woman on the distant balcony who serves as a contrast to the one the narrator is talking to, so that we can better appreciate the unhappiness, perhaps born of indifference and ennui, that characterize the existence of members of the former couple, each one now trying, in vain of course, to remake their lives.

Encounter with a Balcony in the Background

The woman looked at him sweetly. He raised his eyes and settled them on a fixed point, there, in an apartment building, which first was only a stain, transmitted by that balcony to him the vague sensation of well-being, some geraniums with white blossoms and the woman shaking out her bathing suit. Then she told him no, that she had made other arrangements for that day but it could be any afternoon the next week. The woman on the balcony was brushing her hair now and she seemed to be living a moment of special happiness, unconcerned with anything that was happening around her, but her gestures and head movements indicated her agreement, her acceptance, her confidence in herself, waiting patiently for something that was unknown. While they were speaking, she never abandoned for a moment the sweet and even cheerful expression in her eyes; he studied her perfect hairdo, her manicured hands, the inexpensive necklace that lent a happy and informal touch to her otherwise serious clothing. The woman on the balcony brushed her hair again and again and tossed her head back as if she had just left the water after swimming. The woman looked into his eyes; now she had abandoned all her earlier sweetness and was reproaching him for things, too late and inopportunely, he thought. He preferred the freshness of the balcony, the woman who continued tossing her head back after each brushstroke, without a past, wearing a light, sheer robe, destined for an unlimited future. She was putting on her coat and then he felt the newly fresh air, from a recent storm. She continued talking to him of a distant time, which he received in images that were very sharp but totally fleeting, as the long, almost violet fingernails stopped uncertainly on one of the painted beads of her necklace. Her neck, long and rigid, was like another face of her face: solemn, decided, in permanent pursuit. The woman on the balcony turned her head to talk to someone, laughing and stretching out her arms as if to embrace the entire city. He, spontaneously, smiled. It wasn't too difficult to imagine the attitude of the man with the woman on the balcony: nude or half-dressed, drowsy and satisfied from his recent shower. She did not excuse his smile, she demanded a little common sense, at least now, when they were talking about disagreeable and even dirty things; but she could see that he would never change, not letting himself even be touched by problems that, without question, concerned both of them. He couldn't explain anything, he felt the truth of his imagination and the placidness that feeling gave him, because the woman on the balcony and the man, in underwear or bathing trunks, were hugging, breaking apart laughing, and hugging again. Turning around violently, she examined the scene, and then she continued pushing things as always, ancient and distant things. He looked openly at the time on his wrist watch and offered her a cigarette that they lit in a climate of nerves. Now the man on the balcony extended to the woman a colored pitcher, perhaps flowered; she was all happiness and the geraniums received their afternoon watering. Immediately he felt thirsty and the urge to be nude, or at least sitting with a frosty glass of beer at one of the nearby tables. But she would not accept, and even if she did, the burden, the dirty things she was saying, could be interminable. Still, those white geraniums receiving the fresh and generous water from the pitcher made up his mind. The frosty beer was now an irresistible urge. She changed the purse to her other hand and caressed again the beads of her necklace, putting one in her mouth with a delicious flirtatiousness that he received pleasantly. Now, from the table, the woman on the balcony could be seen in greater detail, and she was a vision shared by the two of them. The woman and her man, the laughter, the hugs, the games of touching and then retreating to make certain that the moment was real. She sighed, showing her discontentment, a memory, perhaps nostalgic one, he supposed, and because, just because, he found himself squeezing her hand, that manicured hand with long, perfect nails, almost as a sister or brother would. The air was turning cooler and he suddenly decided to clear the air before the storm broke loose. Why not today? he insisted, and added, lying: next week I'm going to Montevideo. Urgent matters, he specified. So many years without seeing them, as if they weren't your children, and now such haste, she reproached with an emphasis that faded into indifference. And next she returned to more concrete reproaches, to parental obligations, to the times they were living in, to the need for a man to talk to them, not advice perhaps, only a little communication. Your husband? he asked with the aloofness that permitted him to hide, barely, his aggressiveness. I have never allowed it, she said rapidly and firmly, as though not wanting to grasp the meaning of his words, always with so much of that indescribable irony to which she had now gotten unused to responding. It began to mist and she buttoned her coat, as if that could protect her from the water. The woman on the balcony threw her head back again to receive the mist on her face, with delight, while he, at her side, contemplated her possessively and with steady pride. So much time had passed, they had been growing up almost without knowing him, because one knows each other out of dealing with one another, when one worries about someone else's life, she said in an almost philosophical tone with which she was endeavoring—he felt—to scold him with severity and like a child, making evident to him the impossibility of his having any hopes, or at least, giving him the secure knowledge that any hope he had, he would have to pay for some day. For a moment he thought about pressing on with the same philosophical tone she had used, it was so easy to leave her without more arguments, but all that distance and the alienation without alternatives that he had manifested, in spite of himself, he realized now, had hurt him too much. It had begun to rain hard and he wasn't sure that she would be willing to take refuge in the tea room. When he suggested it and she assented, he thought then that she was enjoying her reproaches with all the force they had acquired in the distance of those years. She returned to the same matter and asked defiantly if he knew, if perhaps he had worried about knowing what his children were up to, being so young, just children, given the fact that she had done everything possible to give them an education, an education like the one that she understood was the only possible one, the one that she herself had received and had seen, through her parents, that it was the true one, the one that her own children should have. He felt disconcerted and also bored: although it was true that before, when they had been together what she understood by good was the contrary for him, and never had they been able to agree, now there was such an abyss between that proximity and this distance that arguing lost all meaning, bringing examples, demonstrating errors, pointing out values, the values he understood as the true ones. He felt defeated, his own invalidity was exposed; she, simpler, more constant and perhaps stronger, didn't exhibit anything but proofs, and those proofs were in a way irrefutable. He felt alienated now from the pair on the balcony—seeing love was a form of reconciling oneself with life, and now the awning impeded any suspicion of happiness. All around them, at the other tables, there were men alone, two men together, four men together, over there a circle of men and women, and in a corner a sad and silent little couple. They, once, had been the couple on the balcony. But that was so long ago, when she didn't wear her nails the way she did now and he had less of a stomach. He thought about his wife, so happy and without tracks on her face, not because she didn't have them, he mused, but because she knew how to erase the roughness, forget what is forgettable of the past, get up every morning to live the new day. His wife was wise, indeed she was, although at times he said that living the way she lived, with a smile just because, seemed foolish and even inhuman; but that wasn't it, she had reasons for living always in the present, secure, desiring to live. But what are they up to? he dared to ask, realizing that he was doing it with a somewhat superfluous security, because the memory of his present situation of a moment ago had showed him, he supposed, frankly defeated when compared to her. Well, she said sighing again, I don't have too much time to worry about it either. And she put her hand on her heart as if absolving herself of the guilt that memories also brought to her, the time that she had to run out on the masseuse because their youngest had broken a leg playing soccer on the playground, when she knew very well that she should have skipped her appointment for a massage because he was still little to be running around alone. But that was so long ago and she didn't know why she was remembering it now. I spend so much time away from home, my commitments, you know, she said thinking of the long hours that she had to pass at her clerk's desk, because only the time for work existed, and the early passion that had permitted her to bear the office schedule had been disappearing, together with the hasty embraces, the promissory encounters, the burning looks of suspicions and shivers. All of that had ended, as had her admiration, her sacrifice, her love for that man who now was across from her and who was, without any doubt, a stranger, just like the one in the clerk's office, who had been a mere equivocation, a junction for her drawn-out matrimonial agony, becoming afterwards nothing but oblivion, because things were that way, fleeting, and she had the certain conviction, the bitter, eternal certainty, that everything in this life was totally transient. Another beer? he asked unenthusiastically. She said no with a soft movement of her head and added: thanks. The group of men and women at the table in the center wasn't there any more; the sad and silent little couple was still there, animated now by the arrival of a third party. He thought about his other son, the one who was about to be born, the one he expected now from that happy and wise woman, who was his wife, his wife that he loved more than ever, than always, than before. He didn't know since when. He paid the bill. One day next week, when I return from Montevideo, he lied, we'll talk.

On leaving he looked toward the balcony: the woman wasn't there any more. No, he said, why lie. Some day I'll see them, when I choose, not by chance; I'll pick them up, definitely, he said convinced, and he glanced at the white geraniums, wet from the recent rain, as if foretelling the cool droplets that in the last dampness of the afternoon opened to the avenue, to the grand cloudy sky and the warm night that was breaking out all over the city.

María Esther Vázquez

María Esther Vázquez was born in Buenos Aires in 1934. She is married to the poet and academic Horacio Armani. She has been an essayist, poet, fiction writer, and journalist since 1965. She studied at the University of Buenos Aires. Since 1972 she has been in charge of the section of the Literary Supplement of *La Nación: Instantáneas*. She has traveled on fellowships to Europe on several occasions, and has been invited to the United States and Canada by those countries' offices of cultural affairs to give seminars and lectures. In 1978 she participated in the Interamerican Colloquium of Women Writers that took place in Ottawa, Canada. From 1959 to 1965, and from 1972 until his death, she collaborated with Jorge Luis Borges, with whom she edited a collection of fantastic literature for a publishing house in Milan, Italy. In 1992 she participated in the Lieja Poetry Biannual; in 1993 the Xunta de Galicia invited her to take part in the Eduardo Blanco Amor Congress, in Orense, Spain. In 1994, commissioned by the Fundación del Banco Mercantil, she researched, taped, and filmed testimonies on the Argentine writer Julio Cortázar. She has received numerous prizes and awards for her writings, including the 1995 Comillas Prize from Editorial Tusquets for her book *Borges, esplendor y derrota*, the 1980 Dupuytren Foundation Grand Prize; and the first Municipal Prize for the biennium 1980–82.

Publications

Los nombres de la muerte (The names of death). Buenos Aires: Emecé, 1964.

Everness (Everness). Buenos Aires: Falbo, 1965.

Noviembre y el ángel (November and the angel). Buenos Aires: Kraft, 1968.

Para un jardín cerrado (For a closed garden). Buenos Aires: EUdeBA, 1970.

Soldi por Soldi (Soldi by Soldi). Buenos Aires: EUdeBA, 1970. 2nd edition, 1977; 3rd edition, 1980.

Borges: Imágenes, memorias, diálogos (Borges: Images, memories, dialogues). Caracas: Monte Avila, 1977. Translated into Italian: Palermo: Novecento, 1982; translated into French: Paris: Seuil, 1985.

"Generaciones antagónicas: Entrevista con Silvina Bullrich y Héctor Lastra" (Antagonistic generations: Interview with Silvina Bullrich and Hector Lastra). *Diálogos*. Buenos Aires: Emecé, 1978.

Diálogos: Libro de reportajes (Dialogues: Book of interviews). Buenos Aires: Emecé, 1978.

"Victoria Ocampo, una argentina universalista" (Victoria Ocampo, a universalist Argentine). *Revista Iberoamericana* 110–11 (1980): 167–75.

Invenciones sentimentales (Sentimental inventions). Buenos Aires: Emecé, 1980.

Butler, conversaciones con María Esther Vázquez. Vida y obra del maestro Horacio Butler con 150 reproducciones (Butler, conversations with María Esther Vázquez.). Buenos Aires: Gaglianone, 1982.

"L' homme Borges" (Borges, the man). Translated by Julian Garavito. *Europe: Revue Litteraire Mensuelle* 637 (May 1982): 40–48.

El mundo de Manuel Mujica Láinez. Conversaciones con María Esther Vázquez (Manuel Mujica Láinez's world: Conversations with María Esther Vázquez). Buenos Aires: Editorial Universitaria de Belgrano, 1983.

Borges, sus días y su tiempo (Borges, his days and his times). Buenos Aires: Javier Vergara, 1984.

"Recordando a Güiraldes" (Remembering Güiraldes). Suplemento Literario de *La Nación*, 9 February 1986, 2. With others.

"Homenaje a Jorge Luis Borges" (Homage to Jorge Luis Borges). Suplemento Literario de *La Nación*, 22 June 1986. With others.

"Sábato: El sentido de la existencia" (Sábato: The meaning of existence). Suplemento Literario de *La Nación*, 3 August 1986, 1.

"Diálogo con Ernesto Sábato" (Dialogue with Ernesto Sábato). Suplemento Literario de *La Nación*, 28 September 1986, 1.

"Vasko Popa: Con la estirpe del lobo" (Vasko Popa: With wolf's lineage). Suplemento Literario de *La Nación*, 30 August 1987, 6.

Desde la niebla (Out of the mist). Buenos Aires: Emecé, 1988.

"Sábato: La ciencia, la novela y el arte" (Sábato: Science, novel, and art). Suplemento Literario de *La Nación*, 27 March 1988, 1–2.

"Sábato: La vida se hace en borrador" (Sábato: Life is made as a rough draft). Suplemento Literario de *La Nación,* 14 August 1988, 2.

"Bioy Casares y Denevi: La novela y sus secretos" (Bioy Casares and Denevi: The novel and its secrets). Suplemento Literario de *La Nación,* 10 April 1988, 1.

"Encuentro con Carlos Fuentes" (Meeting with Carlos Fuentes). Suplemento Literario de *La Nación,* 18 February 1990, 6.

"El terror a la lectura y al silencio" (The terror to reading and to silence). Suplemento Literario de *La Nación,* 13 May 1990, 2.

"'La memoria de Shakespeare': El último juego de Borges" ("Shakespeare's memory": Borges' last game). *Revista Iberoamericana* 56/151 (April–June 1990): 479–87.

"El factor sentimental como aventura" (The sentimental factor as adventure). Suplemento Literario de *La Nación,* 9 December 1990, 2.

"La realidad nacional desde la sátira" (The national reality as seen from the satire). Suplemento Literario de *La Nación,* 23 December 1990, 2.

Victoria Ocampo. Buenos Aires: Planeta, 1991.

"Fervor de Buenos Aires" (Fervor from Buenos Aires). Suplemento Literario de *La Nación,* 24 January 1993, 2.

"Desarraigos y encuentros: Entrevista con el narrador paraguayo Augusto Roa Bastos" (Displacements and encounters: Interview with the Paraguayan author Augusto Roa Bastos). Suplemento Literario de *La Nación,* 6 November 1993, 6.

Borges, esplendor y derrota (Borges, splendor and defeat). Barcelona: Tusquets, 1996.

In collaboration with Jorge Luis Borges

Introducción a la literatura inglesa (Introduction to English literature). Buenos Aires: Columba, 1966.

Literaturas germánicas medioevales (Medieval germanic literatures). Buenos Aires: Falbo, 1966. 2nd. edition, Buenos Aires: Emecé, 1978. Both included in *Obras Completas en Colaboración.* Buenos Aires: Emecé, 1966.

Secondary Sources

Borges, Jorge Luis. Prologue to *Los nombres de la muerte.* Buenos Aires: Emecé, 1964.

Fares, Gustavo, and Eliana Hermann. "¿Y ahora? Reflexiones acerca de la literatura femenina argentina actual. *Forma oculta del mundo* de María Rosa Lojo, *Metáforas y reflejos* de Jorgelina Loubet, y *Victoria Ocampo* de María Esther Vázquez." *Letras Femeninas* 19/1–2 (Spring–Fall 1993): 121–34.

Hermann, Eliana. "María Esther Vázquez. *Victoria Ocampo.*" *Chasqui: Revista de Literatura Latinoamericana* 22/1 (May 1993): 94–95.

Marcos, Juan Manuel. "María Esther Vázquez, Helena Araujo y el canto del cisne." *Plural: Revista Cultural de Excelsior* 15/11 (August 1986): 16–20.

Interview

1. Which authors have had the greatest influence on your work?

There were many. I will tell you that my surname is Vázquez; I'm from a Galician family. My father, a former professor, had books in Galician, travel books. After my family migrated here, he became a businessman; but still, Valle Inclán was a great influence. Everything in Galician, everything they told me, stories, a little family history . . . I used to read Alvaro Cunqueiro, but I read him in Galician, because in my house I heard Galician spoken, and so I learned it. The Argentines also influenced me a lot, Mujica Láinez, Borges, and Mallea, as well as Mansfield, Kipling, Henry James, Hermann Hesse, I read the German writers a lot. I read a lot of German poetry. I was lucky enough to meet the great writers of this country when I was very young. For example, I met Borges when I was sixteen. I met Mujica Láinez at a dinner. I sat at a table next to a relatively young man who said to me, "And you, what's your name?" and "What do you do?" I answered him that I was in school and I liked literature a lot. "And what writers do you know?" "Well, I know Borges, Mallea . . ." "Ah, and you don't know Láinez?" "No." "And how do you imagine him?" "As a very fat old man." Of course I must tell you, that man was Mujica Láinez, who wasn't either old or fat, he must have been around forty then. He became a friend of mine for life. I wrote a book with him. But I also had the luck of having very good teachers. For example, Angel Batistessa who, in my first year of college, had done his own translation of Goethe's poem *The Mignon*. It seemed to me so fascinating and fantastic that the next day I enrolled in German class and learned the language. Of all this mixture, in reality I always return to the Galician, the Celtic element. I studied Celtic poetry; I became an expert on the theme when I was around twenty. I have forgotten a lot, but deep down I have maintained my love for that kind of literature. I recognize that all of these things are present in the way I write, in my works.

2. When did you begin to write, and why?

I began to write when I was very young. In elementary school I wrote a play that was presented at school. It was assigned as homework by the sixth-grade teacher and my play was the one chosen. It was very important for me also that, in one of so many illnesses I had when I was a child, as I was convalescing, my mother gave me a set of books by Jules Verne and another by Dickens. The first book that she gave me, which I read with fervor, was a book by Verne called *Dos años de vacaciones*. The plot was about some children who are going to make a trip around the world in a boat, and who are getting ready to leave. During the night the boat breaks free of its moorings, and the children, by themselves, go here and there on the boat. Of course the book is from the nineteenth century. The children, who were between eight and fourteen years of age, have a series of adventures, and many things happen to them. Anyway, I was so excited by the theme that immediately I began to write my own version of *Dos años de vacaciones* in which, instead of being all boys, the protagonists were all girls. One of the most important characters was my dog.

It was in secondary school when I won my first prize. I was very undisciplined, somewhat mischievous, petite, and troublesome; I imagine that I caused problems for everyone. I wrote poems, playing jokes on my teachers. One day the director organized a contest. The theme was "Write about the great books." I remember that I wrote a fragment about the Bible, but in first person, as if I were the Bible. And my paper won the contest. At that time there were about 900 students in the school. I can tell you that the director couldn't understand how that girl who was so disobedient and rowdy could have won the contest.

In my first year of college I met Borges. I had also read Mallea and Gálvez. I guess I did not understand much, but I felt a true adoration for all the writers, who were sacred figures to me. Then, well, beginning to write for myself was a very natural step.

3. How does the political situation influence your choice of themes?

The political situation has not affected my work because I have never worked in a government job. I did work for a while for the Municipal Radio, but as a contract worker, not as a government employee. I was always terrified of working for the State, because one cannot criticize one's employer; that's not ethical. I can tell you that politics were harsh during the time when I was very young, and then came the military, and Perón's first period. The situation was very hard, indeed. My husband and I were spied upon, watched, we knew it all along, first because we were journalists and second because in one of those arbitrary interventions, they put a dear friend of ours in jail, Mr. Di Benedetti. We sent him letters to jail saying "this is an injustice," "don't worry," "it'll all work out." Later we found out that the letters never got to him. We had sort of personal spies, who knew our names, what we did, our schedules, the names of the people who worked in our house. However, I continued writing and, well, it turned out more or less all right.

Besides, I believe that a writer should omit the political situation. On principle, she should support the principles on which democracy and freedom are based, but she should stay away from political matters. She should support a sense of democracy and freedom and the idea that we are all equal under God; the writer should always defend the truth and the rights of others. But she should abstain from participating actively, I mean getting involved in politics, because then she stops being a writer and becomes a politician. Now, as to the case of Vargas Llosa who has a long career as a writer and who feels called to politics to help his country, that seems fine to me, but he can't do anything else, he can't do both things well. Either you're a writer or you're a politician, either you're a doctor or you're a politician. Politics requires exclusive attention, and so does literature.

4. Have you encountered difficulties, as a woman writer, with publishers?

No, I haven't had any difficulties, either as a woman or as a writer. I haven't published any of my books on my own. My publishers are Emecé, EUdeBA, Editorial Belgrano, for my works in Spanish. Of course, I have had the same problems as everyone else does due to the economic crises that Argentina suffers more or less frequently. But as a woman, I haven't had difficulties and perhaps that's due to my education.

5. What do you think of feminism?

I grew up in a matriarchy. My father died when I was very young. The role of father figure was played by an uncle of mine who was very old; he died at almost one hundred years old, in 1960. He was actually a sort of patriarch who was consulted as a last resort. My mother and my grandmother raised me with a very Galician concept of life, Galician in the sense that women in Galicia have always practiced a sort of matriarchy; they are the ones who have been in charge of the home; the men, and especially the peasants, emigrated, left the country to work, and that took place also in the upper classes, since Galicia was always very poor. So the women remained in charge of everything. So much so that women didn't use their husbands' names when they married, the maternal surname was followed by the paternal surname, so the family name was given by the mother. Anyway, these two women, my mother and my grandmother, raised me the same way they raised my uncles and nephews, who were the same age as I was. The only condition we had to live by at home was not to tell lies; we were all raised under a system that was more or less strict, but also very soft because one was allowed to do whatever one wished. I think that my grandmother was ahead of her time. She cursed when the occasion called for it. She used to say, for example, that it seemed to make much more sense to her for a girl to live with a man without getting married than for one to marry an old man for his money. My grandmother was born in 1894 or 1896. Anyway, I never realized that women were on unequal footing with men until I began to travel around the world and I noticed the differences. I was shocked when, in Canada, someone told me that women earn less money than men, because here, in Buenos Aires, there is seniority, and that's it. A male teacher earns the same thing as a female teacher, a male journalist the same as a female journalist, and so on. In a commercial situation, perhaps there are differences. Argentine women are very intelligent. Many times men don't want to accept that a woman can do anything as well or better than they can. On the other hand, Borges helped me a lot, my husband helped me a lot, that is to say that even today he gives me a hand when I need it, we read each other's work, and we give each other advice, and we also respect each other, but I have not, honestly, had problems because I am a woman. In the end I think that mutual respect is the formula.

6. How would you describe Argentina's women readers?

I think that they are the best readers possible, because Argentine men read very little. In lectures or classes, for example, 90 percent are women, and not only old women who have nothing else to do, but young women as well, and girls who often take notes. Women are the ones who make the culture in this country. Nowadays no one can spend too much money on a book, but women check it out from libraries, or they buy it with two or three other people and read a lot.

Selection from *Desde la niebla*

From her collection of stories *Desde la niebla* María Esther Vázquez chose "La visita" for our volume. In her collection, the stories deal with themes as varied as abandonment, love, fear, violence, and death. Everyday matters prevail in these texts where details are presented with great freshness. "La visita" portrays the lives of two spinster sisters who spend their empty hours helping the parish priest and trying to perform deeds of charity through their prayers rather than with money, which they lack. The marriage of their nephew Luisito offers them the occasion to offer him a splendid tea, a banquet to remember, and which culminates in an unexpected way. The details of the sisters' lives are associated with the Buenos Aires of the decade of the 1940s, which María Esther Vázquez details using the names of streets and buildings, such as the Eagle Cafe, now gone, and by noting customs that she surely observed growing up in her childhood home. According to Jorge Luis Borges, with whom Vázquez collaborated on a fundamental study of medieval Germanic literatures, these stories possess "the passion, the imagination, and that appearance of eternity that all creations of art should have."

The Visit

To the memory of Manuel Mujica Láinez

The man was old and lame. It was difficult for him to walk; therefore, not to have to go from the vestry to the door, he shouted, rattling the keys in his hand: "Ladies, it's eight o'clock, I'm going to lock up." His voice resonated among the columns, against the marble floor, and was lost with a solemn echo up in the gilded cupula. It was really twenty minutes before eight, but he knew that the Castro sisters would take quite a while before coming down from the altar and leaving. Way up high, almost hanging, like two spiders, at the highest point of the double stairway, they were tidying up the small gold-colored brass crown and the brownish ringlets of the Child Virgin. The two answered simultaneously: "Just a moment, Basilio, we're coming."

The church was dark; on the main altar one little lamp was shining and only the chapel to the right, where the ladies were repairing the damages caused by time and dust, was illuminated. The light, focused and limited, casted giant shadows and made the place seem gloomy and shadowy.

The irritated voice of the old man called again and they descended reluctantly. They were thin and dressed in black. The older one, Eulalia, had her white hair gathered up in a low bun over the nape of her neck; the younger, Rosita, knotted two gray braids on top of her head, like a diadem. They put on their coats and their hats and walked to the door, putting on their left-hand gloves so that the bare fingers of their right hands would receive the cool holy water. Outside it was cold and foggy.

"It's really gotten late," murmured Rosita, taking the arm of her sister, who didn't answer. They descended the four steps that separated the atrium from the street and silently walked home. Living so close to the church seemed like a blessing. They used to go there every morning to the early mass, still in the darkness in winter, and they lit a candle to the Holy Child, and they returned at noon to help put things in order, and then, before the rosary, they were already attending to the altars and dressing the saints and the Virgin and Saint Ana, and they washed and starched the lace and combed the curls; those of Jesus more lovingly and with more patience than those of Mary Magdalene, not because she had been a sinner before she was a saint, but because hers were much longer. They cleaned the dust from the plaster and wax statues carefully, so as not to strip the paint off, and once every two weeks they put kerosene on the wooden carving of John the Baptist to hinder the advances of the moths. But, above and beyond all of these tasks, they went to pray. They prayed a lot for the souls in Purgatory, for their dearly departed ones, for the storekeeper's wife (they suspected her of adultery) so that God would have pity on her soul and lead her down the right path, they prayed for Father Carlos and for the Pope and, with the greatest fervor they could muster, they prayed for God to end the cruel war that had been laying waste to Europe for three years now, and which no one knew when it would end.

Each Saturday they made anise biscuits and took them to Father Carlos, who put them in a can so they wouldn't get stale.

On Tuesdays and Thursdays, before the rosary, they taught catechism. Rosita loved the children; Eulalia, not quite as much. Rosita was the one who answered the difficult questions; fornicating was, of course, a form of lying, and perhaps that was what she thought about it. After the catechism, out of her sister's view, she secretly handed out candies to the children. Candies were expensive and they lived on very little money. So little that they barely managed; however with punctual dedication, they saved a bit every month from that pittance to have something for extra expenses "like going to a doctor or God knows what unforeseen event," as Eulalia used to say.

The Castro sisters spent more time at church than at their home, a huge, ancient run-down and cold mansion with three patios, fourteen rooms, a covered cistern and a fig tree that yielded a few skimpy figs at the end of April. They had lived alone since their parents died and Manuel, their brother, had married and moved away from the neighborhood. Manuel, Carmen, his wife, and their children knew them as the aunts from Mexico, because the house was on that street, in the south of the city.

They didn't have a telephone. The storekeeper, husband of the presumed adulteress, had offered them his, and they used to use it when, once in a long while, they called their sister-in-law or Luisito, their favorite nephew, on his birthday. Carmen called them, in turn, right before Christmas to invite them to supper on Christmas Eve. They never went; they went to Midnight Mass, as they had done for as long as they could remember, with their parents and their brother first, alone now. On Christmas day, during the afternoon, they would visit Manuel, bringing Carmen a little tray of anise biscuits and a great flask of homemade fig jelly, prepared with last season's figs. Carmen would put everything in the kitchen and offered them a splendid tea where hot scones shone on the silver tray, along with small pastries and sandwiches brought from the Eagle Cafe, and offer the two lay saints their only occasion to commit a sin: gluttony.

It was precisely on that Christmas of 1942 that Carmen gave them the news: Luisito, who had been seeing someone steadily for a year now, was getting married. And marrying well, to the only daughter of a rich man, very rich, whose name appeared often in the society pages of the newspaper *La Nación*. Even more importantly, the photos of the girl and her mother adorned month after month the pages of the magazine *Home*. Truly enough, the girl was a cute little thing. Luisito, the two sisters agreed, deserved it all. So young and already an attorney, for a fashionable firm, and so good looking, the most handsome among the nephews, and also the best one.

"When he was a little boy, I would look at him and think that the baby Jesus must have been like that," assured Rosita with sweetness.

"Don't talk foolishness," Eulalia interrupted her dryly. "Baby Jesus must have been fair and Luisito is dark."

"Girls, don't argue," said Carmen. "I have a surprise for you. The fifth of January we're going to Mar del Plata, but the second or third, whichever day is more convenient for you, I'll come by with Luisito and Marta, his fiancee, so you'll know her and she can meet you; after all, you're the only aunts on the father's side."

"The best day is Wednesday, which falls on the third, I think," answered Eulalia.

Eulalia and Rosita looked at each other and understood without speaking. It was the best day because on Tuesdays they cleaned house and then, before lunch, they washed their hair and, the most important thing: on Tuesdays they collected their meager annuity check.

"Come on Wednesday for tea, we'll expect you at five-thirty," concluded Eulalia.

"And when is the wedding?" asked Rosita.

"May fourth, at the Cathedral."

"A beautiful church, Carmen, very good choice," approved Eulalia. "I know the parish priest, a real saint."

Once in the street they decided that they would give the newlyweds their sterling silver candelabra, the most valuable thing they owned. Naturally they would go to the church, but not to the reception. A long time ago, they said without looking at each other, they had overcome the vanity of worldly parties and, besides (each thought without confessing it out loud), they didn't have appropriate clothing for worldly parties.

The state of excitement and nervousness in which they lived during the eight days before the visit was tremendous. Even Father Carlos noticed that they were strange and distracted and, for the first time in many years, his anise biscuits arrived burned on the bottom.

With the money from the annuity check they decided to throw caution to the wind. The rest of the month they would live on boiled rice and, as a last resort, they could take something from their Savings Box; the occasion warranted it. They looked for the best embroidered tablecloth they had and they sent it to the cleaners. They polished the silver candelabra and took out the Limoges service, which they still had, for tea. A service that hadn't been used since their mother died, twenty years before, when they still had servants. They opened the big dining room, which no one ever entered except to clean, and took the dust covers off the chairs and polished the chandelier with its eighty crystal prisms. They asked for an estimate from the Gaslight Tea room for a little lunch; after all, there were going to be only five people. They thought, at the beginning, that they would invite Father Carlos; then they agreed that although the Father was a very good person, who deserved everything, his humble origins wouldn't allow him to fit in well with the fiancee. Besides, five eat less than six and the Father liked to eat a lot and, finally, they had only five Baccarat crystal cups left for after tea sherry. Because of course, they would serve everything, from little salmon and caviar canapes to sweets of dates and nuts. Everything would arrive punctually at four o'clock, so they would have time to prepare the table, which would shine splendidly with the lights from the candles playing on the tablecloth, which, ever since the day before, when they retrieved it from the cleaners, had been stretched so it wouldn't show any creases.

At four the caterer arrived; there really was everything that the imagination of the caterers could conceive, even a walnut cake topped off by chocolate doves and another one of *sambayón* with the names of the happy couple written on it with cherries. At the center of the table, a dish of Bohemian crystal displayed morsels of frosted chocolate wrapped in gold papers.

They decided that Eulalia, as the eldest, would preside at the head of the table as their mother would have if she had lived; to her left the engaged couple, first Luisito, then the girl; to her right, Carmen and Rosita.

The two sisters got dressed, as always, in dark clothes. Rosita, as the youngest, indulged herself with a little white collar over her blue blouse, and a drop of perfume on her temples.

At five-thirty they put on the water to boil. But the visitors weren't punctual. When they heard the wall clock strike six, they were so anguished that they didn't dare to look at each other. Rosita, seated in the darkest corner of the dining room, wringing a handkerchief in her hands, repeated silently, to herself: "Dear God, let them come, please!" Eulalia, standing with her back against the dining room door, looking toward the patio, perhaps did the same. A disillusionment, an infinite sadness had wilted their earlier excitement, the solitude of the room was growing in the darkness of the dusk, and the two remained quiet, one in her corner, the other against the wall, defeated. One minute after the clock struck six-thirty, the doorbell sounded. At first they didn't react, then they ran toward each other and hugged, almost crying. The second bell produced the expected reaction. Rosita flew through the patio to the front door and Eulalia lit the fifteen candles of the dining room chandelier, which shone on the Limoges, the candy dish, the silver of the candelabra and the china and the platters brimming with food. Eulalia looked at all of it and couldn't suppress a smile of pride and happiness, which grew even broader when she saw the astonished and incredulous faces of their visitors when they entered the dining room. She kissed her sister-in-law, Luisito and Marta, who seemed almost cowed at such magnificence. There was a moment of silence, until Carmen, smiling happily, said, looking at everything: "What a table, how wonderful, how many delicious things we are going to eat!"

Luisito seemed to them more delightful than ever; the girl, whom they didn't know, was cute, but without exaggeration. Somewhat shy, yes, but better timid and not forward like so many others. The Castro sisters liked it that they had to insist that she eat; the same thing happened with Luisito, but they knew how he had been brought up, with such modesty, with such prudence. The conversation, carried on by the older people, revolved around other encounters, other reunions now distant. They spoke of the dearly departed, whose almost forgotten faces still lived in the photographs. At the end, when they served the sherry, Marta praised the silver candelabra. Then, Eulalia, very moved, told her that was the wedding present they planned to give them. The girl kissed the aunts. Luisito also kissed them and Carmen said that it was extravagant for them to give away something of so much worth. They toasted, raising their glasses, and the Mexico aunts seemed so happy that the visitors were also taken by that excessive happiness, somewhat pathetic and also somewhat ridiculous. When it was eight o'clock, Carmen got up and at the insistence of the sisters, put a chocolate in her handbag, because she hadn't tried any, and Marta and Luisito did the same, he putting his in a pocket.

With the leftovers from that memorable Wednesday, January third, they ate for four days; but, with the minute by minute review of the hour and a half that the visit had lasted, they lived happily for six months. Their vacant days, dedicated to dressing saints and to dying slowly in poverty and in denial of all that was really living, their innocently wilted days, their frosted nights, their lost youth; all of it they saw as compensated, suddenly, by that visit. Feeling that they were important to the family, and that they could entertain them as they deserved, had filled their souls to overflowing. They remembered and commented on stray phrases, gestures, expressions, above all the gracious shyness of the couple. They detailed to each other the pink dress of the girl, so young, still such a girl, with her beret, also pink, inclined over her long, flowing hair. And Carmen, always a lady, with her mother's pearls complementing the light gray dress and wearing a very strange but nice hat on the top of her head. And Luisito, so elegant, carrying a walking cane that he couldn't even dream of needing.

As the weeks passed, sometimes in the middle of the rosary or the mass, Eulalia would smile, and Rosita knew that she was thinking about something from that afternoon and that she would tell her later. It was Rosita, the more gifted of the two, who wrote down all the impressions of the visit and kept them in an envelope, which, after they died, appeared among their old papers and photographs. The envelope said: "To our dear niece and nephew, Marta and Luisito."

Even Basilio and Father Carlos knew detail by detail everything that had happened.

But what they didn't know and couldn't imagine, any more than could the Castro sisters from Mexico Street, is that Carmen, anticipating the poor ritual of the anise biscuits with fig jelly, had treated them to tea and cakes at the Cafe La Suiza, before coming to visit. The spectacle of the table set for them filled them with real horror, but at the warning words of Carmen: "How wonderful, how many delicious things we are going to eat!" like shipwrecked sailors who throw themselves into the sea to die, they accepted the ceremony and tried everything, except for the frost chocolates, because by then it was physically impossible.

And if for the Castro sisters the afternoon was glorious and memorable, the visitors couldn't ever forget it either.

General Bibliography

Abeijón, Carlos, and Jorge Santos Lafauci. *La mujer argentina antes y después de Eva Perón.* Buenos Aires: Editorial Cuarto Mundo, 1975.

Alarcón, Norma, and Sylvia Kossnar. *Bibliography of Hispanic Women Writers.* Bloomington, 1980.

Albalucía, Angel. "Notas sobre un libro hablado por escritoras de América Latina." *Discurso Literario* 4/2 (Spring 1987): 583–94.

Aonso Fuentes, María Elena. "Towards a Feminist Reading of Latin American Women Writers." *Dissertation Abstracts International* 47 (1987): 2572A–73A.

Anderson Imbert, Enrique. "Victoria Ocampo. *Testimonios. Tercera serie.*" *Sur* 139 (1946): 72–73.

Anderson Imbert, Enrique, and Eugenio Florit. *Literatura hispanoamericana: Antología e introducción histórica.* 2 vols. New York: Holt, Rinehart and Winston, 1960.

Arancibia, Juana Alcira. "El descubrimiento y los esplazamientos: La literatura hispanoamericana como diálogo entre centros y periferias." *Proceedings of V Simposio Internacional de Literatura, Universidad Interamericana de Puerto Rico, Recinto de San Germán, Puerto Rico, November 14–17, 1988.* Westminster: Instituto Literario y Cultural Hispánico, 1990.

Araujo, Helena. "¿Cuál literatura femenina?" *El Espectador* (September 1981): 5–6.

———. "Escritoras latinoamericanas: ¿Por fuera del boom?" *Quimera* (April 1983): 8–11.

———. *La scherezada criolla: Ensayos sobre la escritura femenina latinoamericana.* Bogotá: Universidad Nacional de Colombia, 1989.

Arcidiacono, Carlos. "Silvina Bullrich: *Un momento muy largo.*" *Sur* 275 (1962): 109–11.

Arizpe, Lourdes. "Interview with Carmen Naranjo: Women and Latin American Literature." *Signs: Journal of Women in Culture and Society* 5 (1979): 98–110.

Avellaneda, Andrés. "Argentina militar: Los discursos del silencio." In *Literatura argentina hoy: De la dictadura a la democracia,* edited by Karl Kohut and Andrea Pagni. Frankfurt: Verbuet Verlag, 1989.

———. *Censura, autoritarismo y cultura: Argentina 1960–1983.* Vols. 1–2. Buenos Aires: Centro Editor de América Latina, 1986.

Balderston, Daniel. "Dos literatos del proceso: Horacio Bustos Domeq y Silvina Bullrich." *Nuevo Texto Crítico* 3/5 (1990): 85–93.

———. *The Historical Novel in Latin America.* Gaithersburg, Md.: Hispamérica, 1986.

———. *The Latin American Short Story.* New York: Greenwood, 1992.

———, ed. *Fición y política: La narrativa argentina durante el proceso militar.* Buenos Aires: Alianza, 1987.

Barr, Marleen, and Richard Feldstein, eds. *Discontent Discourses: Feminism/Textual Intervention/Psychoanalysis.* Chicago: University of Illinois Press, 1989.

Barrett, Michele. *Women's Oppression Today: Problems in Marxist Feminist Analysis.* London: Verso, 1980.

Bautista, Gloria, ed. *Voces femeninas de Hispanoamérica.* Pittsburgh: University of Pittsburgh Press, 1996.

Bergamin, José. "Carta abierta a Victoria Ocampo." *Sur* 32 (1937): 67–69.

Bermann, Sandra. "Looking to Particulars: Feminism and the New History." *Yearbook of Comparative and General Literature* 39 (1990–91): 100–12.

Bierre, Anne. "Victoria Ocampo et l'étrangere de Saint-Jean Perse." *French Studies* 29 (1975): 434–39.

Billman, Lynne Lois. "The Political Novels of Lucila Palacios and Marta Lynch." *Dissertation Abstracts International* 37 (1976): 1580A.

Birkemoe, Diane Solomon. "Contemporary Women Novelists of Argentina (1945–1967)." Ph.D., diss., University of Illinois, 1968.

Borges, Jorge Luis. "Sylvina Bullrich Palenque: *La redoma del primer ángel.*" *Sur* 111 (1944): 74–76.

Brunton, Rosanne. "A Note on Contemporary Argentine Women's Writing: A Discussion of *The Web.*" *International Fiction Review* 15 (1988): 9–13.

Carlson, Marifran. *Feminismo! The Woman's Movement in Argentina From Its Beginnings to Eva Perón.* Chicago: Academy Chicago Publishers, 1988.

Carrera, Héctor Iñigo. *La mujer argentina.* Buenos Aires: Centro Editor de América Latina, 1972.

Carrera, Julieta. *La mujer en América escribe.* Mexico City: Semblanzas, 1956.

Castedo-Ellerman, Elena. "Feminism or Femininity? Six Women Writers Answer." *Américas* 30/1 (October 1978): 19–24.

Castillo, Debra. *Talking Back: Toward a Latin American Feminist Literary Criticism.* Ithaca and London: Cornell University Press, 1992.

Castro Klaren, Sara. "La crítica literaria feminista y la escritora en América Latina." In *Lasartén por el mango: Encuentro de escritoras latinoamericanas,* edited by Patricia Elena González and Eliana Ortega. Río Piedras, P.R.: Huracán, 1984.

Chase, Kathleen. "Latin American Women Writers: Their Present Position." *Books Abroad* 33 (1959): 150–51.

Class, Bradley Mellon. "Fictional Treatment of Politics by Argentine Female Novelists." Ph.D., diss., University of New Mexico, 1974.

Correa Zapata, Celia. "One Hundred Years of Women Writers in Latin America." *Latin American Literary Review* 3 (1975): 7–16.

———. "Victoria Ocampo and Virginia Woolf: La rebeldía en el ensayo." *Ensayos Hispanoamericanos.* Buenos Aires: Corregidor, 1978.

Cortázar, Julio. "Victoria Ocampo: *Soledad sonora.*" *Sur* 192–94 (1950): 194–97.

Cortina, Lynne Rice. *Spanish American Women Writers: A Bibliographical Guide to Research.* New York: Garland, 1983.

Corvalán, Graciela N. *Latin American Women Writers in English Translation: A Bibliography.* Los Angeles: Latin American Studies Center, California State University, 1980.

Costa, Marithelma, and Adelaida López. *Las dos caras de la escritura.* San Juan: Editorial de la Universidad de Puerto Rico, 1988.

Cypess, Sandra M. "Los elementos deícticos en la poesía y la voz femenina." *Texto Crítico* 12/34–35 (1986): 214–26.

———. "Frankenstein's Monster in Argentina: Gambaro's Two Versions." *Revista Canadiense de Estudios Hispanicos* 14/2 (Winter 1990): 349–61.

———. *La Malinche in Mexican Literature: From History to Myth.* Austin: University of Texas Press, 1990.

———. "Visual and Verbal Distances: The Woman Poet in a Patriarchal Culture." *Review/Revista Interamericana* 12/1 (Spring 1982): 150–57.

Dámaso Martínez, Carlos. *Hay cenizas en el viento.* Buenos Aires: Centro Editor de América Latina, 1982.

Dauster, Frank. "Success and the Latin American Writer." In *Contemporary Women Authors of Latin America: Introductory Essays,* edited by Doris Meyer and Margarite Fernandez Olmos. Brooklyn: Brooklyn College, 1983.

Davis, Lisa. "An Invitation to Understanding Among Poor Women of the Americas: *The Color Purple* and *Hasta no verte Jesús mío.*" In *Reinventing the Americas: Comparative Studies of Literature of the United States and Spanish America,* edited by Bell Gale Chevigny and Gari Laguardia. New York: Cambridge University Press, 1986.

De la Selva, Mauricio. "Silvina Bullrich: *Los burgueses.*" *Cuadernos Americanos* 137 (1964): 287–89.

De Laurentis, Teresa. *Alice Doesn't: Feminism, Semiotics, Cinema.* Bloomington, 1984.

De Segovia, Margot. "*Mientras los demás viven de Silvina Bullrich.*" *Ficción* 19 (1959): 168.

———. "Victoria Ocampo, memorialista." In *Tres conceptos de la literatura hispanoamericana.* Buenos Aires: Losada, 1963.

Delfino, Silvia. "Mariquita Sánchez de Thompson: Una anécdota para la cultura argentina?" *Nuevo Texto Crítico* 2/4 (1989): 39–48.

Dellepiane, Angela B. "El aporte femenino a la narrativa última argentina." In *Actas de la decimotercera conferencia anual de literaturas hispánicas en Indiana University of Pennsylvania,* edited by Nora Erro Orthmann and Juan Cruz Mendizábal. Miami: Universal, 1990.

Diamond, Arlyn, and Lee R. Edwards, eds. *The Authority of Experience: Essays on Feminist Criticism.* Amherst: University of Massachusetts Press, 1977.

Dimock, Wai Chee. "Feminism, New Historicism, and the Reader." In *Readers in History: Nineteenth-Century American Literature and the Contexts of Response,* edited by James Machor. Baltimore: Johns Hopkins University Press, 1993.

Donovan, Josephine, ed. *Feminist Literary Criticism.* Lexington: University Press of Kentucky, 1975.

———. "Women and the Rise of the Novel: A Feminist Marxist Theory." *Signs: Journal of Women in Culture and Society* 16/3 (Spring 1991): 441–62.

Earle, Peter G. "The Female Persona in the Spanish American Essay: An Overview." In *Woman as Myth and Metaphor in Latin American Literature,* edited by Carmelo Virgillo and Naomi Lindstrom. Columbia: University of Missouri Press, 1985.

Eisenstein, Zillah R. *Capitalist Patriarchy and the Case for Socialist Feminism.* New York: Monthly Review Press, 1979.

Ellison, Fred P., and Naomi Lindstrom. *Woman Between Mirrors.* Austin: University of Texas Press, 1989.

Eloy Martínez, Tomás. *La novela de Perón.* Buenos Aires: Legasa, 1985.

———. *Santa Evita.* Buenos Aires, Planeta, 1995.

Elu de Leñero, María del Carmen. *La mujer en América Latina.* 2 vols. Mexico City: Secretaría de Educación Pública, 1975.

Fares, Gustavo. "La 'hipótesis represiva' en la literatura femenina actual." *Letras de Buenos Aires* 11/24 (July 1991): 63–67.

———. "This Text Which Is Not One." *Hispanic Journal* 12/2 (Fall 1991): 277–89.

Fares, Gustavo, and Eliana Hermann, eds. "Angélica Gorodischer, escritora argentina." *Hispania* 75/5 (December 1992): 1238–39.

———. *Escritoras argentinas contemporáneas.* New York: Lang, 1993.

———. "Exilios internos: El viaje en cinco escritoras argentinas." *Hispanic Journal* 15/1 (Spring 1994): 21–29.

———. "Syria Poletti: *People with Me.*" *Journal of the Midlands Conference on Language and Literature* 6 (1993): 43.

———. "¿Y ahora? Reflexiones acerca de la literatura femenina argentina actual. *Forma oculta del mundo* de María Rosa Lojo, *Metáforas y reflejos* de Jorgelina Loubet, y *Victoria Ocampo* de María Esther Vázquez." *Letras Femeninas* 19/1–2 (Spring–Fall 1993): 121–34.

Feinman, José Pablo. *El ejército de ceniza.* Buenos Aires: Legasa, 1986.

Fernandez Olmos, Margarite. "El género testimonial: Aproximaciones feministas." *Revista/Review Interamericana* 11/1 (Spring 1981): 69–75.

Ferreyra Basso, Juan G. "Silvina Bullrich Palenque: *La tercera versión.*" *Sur* 129 (1945): 11–13.

Fletcher, Lea. "El sexismo lingüístico y su uso acerca de la mujer." *Feminaria* 1/1 (June 1988): 29–32.

———. "El temor de decir." *Feminaria* 3/6 (November 1990): 14–15.

Fletcher, Lea, and Jutta Marx. "Bibliografía de/sobre la mujer argentina a partir de 1980." *Feminaria* (November 1988–April 1989).

Flori, Mónica Roy. *Streams of Silver: Six Contemporary Women Writers from Argentina.* Lewisburg, Penn.: Associated University Presses, 1995.

Foster, David William. *Alternative Voices in the Contemporary Latin American Narrative.* Columbia: University of Missouri Press, 1985.

———. "A Bibliography of Writings by and about Victoria Ocampo (1890–1979)." *Revista Iberoamericana* 30 (1980): 51–58.

———. "Narrative Persona in Eva Perón's *La razón de mi vida.*" In *Woman as Myth and Metaphor in Latin American Literature,* edited by Carmelo Virgillo and Naomi Lindstrom. Columbia: University of Missouri Press, 1985.

———. "Los parámetros de la narrativa argentina durante 'el proceso de reorganización nacional.'" *Revista Letras* 37 (1988): 152–67.

———. "Violence in Argentine Literature: Cultural Responses to Tyranny." In *Latin American Writers on Gay and Lesbian Themes: A Bio-Critical Sourcebook,* edited by David William Foster and Emmanuel S. Nelson. Columbia: University of Missouri Press, 1995.

Foucault, Michel. *The History of Sexuality.* 3 vols. New York: Pantheon, 1978.

Fox-Lockert, Lucía. *Women Novelists in Spain and South America.* Metuchen, N.J.: Scarecrow Press, 1979.

Franco, Jean. "Apuntes sobre la crítica feminista y la literatura hispanoamericana." *Hispamérica: Revista de Literatura* 4–5 (1986): 31–43.

———. *Plotting Women's Fiction: Gender and Representation in Mexico.* New York: Columbia University Press, 1991.

Frederick, Bonnie. "In Their Own Voice: The Women Writers of the Generación del '80 in Argentina." *Hispania* 74/2 (May 1991): 282–89.

———. *Women and the Journey: The Female Travel Experience.* Pullman: Washington State University Press, 1993.

Frouman-Smith, Erica M. "Entrevista con Silvina Bullrich." *Chasqui: Revista de Literatura Latinoamericana* 8 (1979): 37–46.

———. "Female Roles in the Fiction of Silvina Bullrich." *Dissertation Abstracts International* 40 (1980): 4617A.

———. "*Reunión de directorio.*" *Latin American Literary Review* 14 (1979): 76–78.

Fuss, Diana. "Getting Into History." *Arizona Quarterly* 45/4 (1989): 95–108.

Galerstein, Carolyn L. "Outside-Inside Views of Exile: Spanish Women Novelists and Younger Generation Writers." In *Latin America and the Literature of Exile,* edited by Hans-Bernhard Moeller. Heidelberg, 1983.

García Pinto, Magdalena, ed. *Historias íntimas: Conversaciones con diez escritoras latinoamericanas.* Hanover, N.H.: Ediciones del Norte, 1988.

Garrels, Elizabeth. "Sarmiento and the Woman Question: From 1839 to the Facundo." In *Sarmiento: Author of a Nation,* edited by Tulio Halperín Donghi. Berkeley: University of California Press, 1994.

Gascón Vera, Elena. "'El naufragio del deseo': Esther Tusquets y Sylvia Molloy." *Plaza: Revista de Literatura* 11 (Autumn 1986): 20–24.

Geisdorfer Feal, Rosemary. "Women Writers into the Mainstream: Contemporary Latin American Narrative." In *Philosophy and Literature in Latin America: A Critical Assessment of the Current Situation,* edited by Jorge E. García and Mireya Camurati. New York: State University of New York Press, 1989.

Ghiano, Juan Carlos. "Beatriz Guido." Suplemento Literario de *La Nación* (April 1988): 24.

Gimbernat González, Ester. *Aventuras del desacuerdo. Novelistas argentinas de los 80.* Buenos Aires: Vergara, 1992.

———. "De cómo ejercitar la libertad: Dos obras de Luisa Valenzuela." *Discurso Literario: Revista de Temas Hispánicos* 6/2 (Spring 1989): 405–21.

———. The Eloquence of Silence: Argentine Women Writers after the 'Proceso.'" *Fiction International* 19/1 (Fall 1990): 72–82.

———. "El lento rostro de la inocencia de Edna Pozzi: Como cuestionar la inocencia de la 'historia.'" In *La historia en la literatura iberoamericana: Textos del XXVI Congreso del Instituto Internacional de Literatura Iberoamericana,* edited by Raquel Chang Rodríguez and Gabriella de Beer. New York: Editions del Norte/City University of New York, 1989.

———. "Speaking through the Voices of Love: Interpretation as Emancipation." In *Feminist Perspectives on Sor Juana Inés de la Cruz,* edited by Stephanie Merrim. Detroit: Wayne State University Press, 1991.

Giusti, Roberto. "Letras argentinas: La protesta de las mujeres." *Nosotros* 10 (1937): 87–93.

Gnutzmann, Rita. "La imagen de la mujer en la literatura rioplatense." *Alba de America: Revista Literaria* 11/20–21 (July 1993): 241–61.

———. "Tres ejemplos de escritura femenina en América Latina." *Letras de Deusto* (May–August 1989): 91–104.

González, Patricia Elena, and Eliana Ortega, eds. *La sartén por el mango. Encuentro de escritoras latinoamericanas.* Río Piedras, P.R.: Huracán, 1984.

González Freire, Nati. "La mujer en la literatura de América Latina." *Cuadernos Hispanoamericanos* (December 1984): 84–92.

González Lanuza, Eduardo. "Silvina Ocampo: *Autobiografía de Irene.*" *Sur* 175 (1948): 56–58.

Guerra Cunningham, Lucía. "Algunas reflexiones teóricas sobre la novela femenina." *Hispamérica: Revista de Literatura* 28 (April 1981): 29–39.

———. "Desentrañando la polifonía de la marginalidad: Hacia un análisis de la narrativa femenina hispanoamericana." *Inti: Revista de Literatura Hispánica* 24–25 (Fall–Spring 1986–87): 39–59.

———. "Estrategias discursivas en la narrativa de la mujer latinoamericana." *Escritura: Revista de Teoría y Crítica Literarias* 16/31–32 (January–December 1991): 115–22.

———. "Identidad cultural y la problemática del ser en la narrativa femenina latino-americana." *Discurso Literario: Revista de Temas Hispánicos* 6/2 (Spring 1989): 361–89.

———. "El lenguaje como instrumento de dominio y recurso desconstructivo de la historia en *Oficio de tinieblas* de Rosario Castellanos." *Explicación de Textos Literarios* 19/2 (1990–91): 37–41.

———. "La referencialidad como negación del paraíso: Exilio y excentrismo en *La nave de los locos* de Cristina Peri Rossi." In *Mujer y sociedad en América: IV Simposio Internacional,* edited by Juana Alcira Arancibia. California: Instituto Literario y Cultural Hispánico; Universidad Autónoma de Baja, 1988.

———, ed. *Splintering Darkness: Latin American Women Writers in Search of Themselves.* Pittsburgh: Latin American Literary Review Press, 1990.

———. "Visión marginal de la historia en la narrativa de Juana Manuela Gorriti." *Ideologies and Literature: Journal of Hispanic and Lusophone Discourse Analysis* 2/2 (Fall 1987): 59–76.

Guibert, Rita. *Seven Voices.* New York: Knopf, 1973.

Hahner, June E. *Women in Latin American History: Their Lives and Views.* Los Angeles: UCLA Latin American Center, 1976.

Harss, Luis, and Barbara Dohmann. *Into the Mainstream: Conversations with Latin-American Writers.* New York: Harper and Row, 1967.

Henríquez Ureña, Pedro. "Victoria Ocampo. *Testimonios; segunda serie.*" *Sur* 89 (1942): 65–67.

Herrán, Teresa Leonardi. "Piel de mujer, máscaras de hombre." *Feminaria* 1/2 (November 1988): 20–21.

Hoberman, Louisa A. "Hispanic American Women as Portrayed in the Historical Literature: Types or Archetypes?" *Revista/Review Interamericana* 4 (1974): 136–47.

Howell, Martha C. "A Feminist Historian Looks at the New Historicism: What's So Historical About It?" *Women's Studies: An Interdisciplinary Journal* 19/2 (1991): 139–47.

Hughes, Psiche. "Women and Literature in Latin America." In *Unheard Words: Women and Literature in Africa, the Arab World, Asia, the Caribbean and Latin America,* edited by Mineke Schipper and Barbara Potter Fasting. London: Allison and Busby, 1985.

Irigaray, Luce. *Ce sexe qui n'en est pas un.* Paris: Minuit, 1977.

Jacobs, Sue Ellen. *Women in Perspective: A Guide for Cross-Cultural Studies.* Urbana: University of Illinois Press, 1974.

Jameson, Fredric. *The Political Unconscious: Narrative as a Socially Symbolic Act.* Ithaca: Cornell University Press, 1981.

Jehenson, Myriam. *Latin-American Women Writers: Class, Race, and Gender.* Albany: State University of New York Press, 1995.

Jitrik, Noe. *La nueva promoción: Seis novelistas argentinos de 1959.* Mendoza, Argentina: Biblioteca San Martín, 1959.

Kaminsky, Amy. "Marta Lynch: The Expanding Political Consciousness of an Argentine Women Writer." *Dissertation Abstracts International* 36 (1976): 4531A–32A.

———. *Reading the Body Politic: Feminist Criticism and Latin American Women Writers.* Minneapolis: University of Minnesota Press, 1993.

———. "The Real Circle of Iron: Mothers and Children, Children and Mothers, in Four Argentine Novels." *Latin American Literary Review* 9 (1976): 77–86.

Knaster, Meri. *Women in Spanish America: An Annotated Bibliography from Pre-Conquest to Contemporary Times.* Boston: G. K. Hall, 1977.

———. "Women in Latin America: The State of Research." *Latin American Research Review* 11/1 (1976): 3–74.

Kohut, Karl, and Andrea Pagni, eds. *Literatura argentina hoy: De la dictadura a la democracia.* Frankfurt: Verbuet Verlag, 1989.

Kramarae, Cheris. "A Feminist Critique of Sociolinguistics." *Journal of the Atlantic Provinces Linguistic Association* 8 (May 1986): 1–22.

Kramarae, Cheris, and Dale Spender, eds. *The Knowledge Explosion: Generations of Feminist Scholarship.* New York: Teachers College Press, 1992.

Kristeva, Julia. *The Kristeva Reader.* Edited by Toril Moi. New York: Columbia University Press, 1986.

Lakoff, Robin. *Language and Woman's Place.* New York: Harper and Row, 1975.

Lavrín, Asunción, ed. *Latin American Women: Historical Perspectives.* Westport: Greenwood, 1978.

Lewald, H. Ernest, ed. *The Web: Stories by Argentine Women.* Washington, D.C.: Three Continents Press, 1983.

———. "Two Generations of River Plate Women Writers." *Latin American Research Review* 15 (1980): 231–36.

Lewis, Jane. "Women's History, Gender History, and Feminist Politics." In *The Knowledge Explosion: Generations of Feminist Scholarship,* edited by Cheris Kramarae and Dale Spender. New York: Teachers College Press, 1992.

Lindstrom, Naomi. "Feminist Criticism of Latin American Literature." *Latin American Research Review* 15/1 (1980): 151–59.

Lindstrom, Naomi, and Carmen Naranjo. *Women of Smoke/Mujeres de humo.* Pittsburgh: Latin American Library Review Press, 1988.

Loveluck, Juan. *Novelistas hispanoamericanos de hoy.* Madrid, 1976.

Machin, Barbara. *South of the Border.* East Haven: InBook, 1987.

MacKinnon, Catherine. *Feminism Unmodified.* Cambridge, Mass.: Harvard University Press, 1987.

Magnarelli, Sharon. *The Lost Rib: Female Characters in the Spanish-American Novel.* Lewisburg, Penn.: Bucknell University Press, 1985.

Manzur, Jorge. *Tinta roja.* Madrid: Legasa, 1981.

Marting, Diane, ed. *Women Writers of Spanish America: An Annotated Bio-Bibliographical Guide.* New York: Greenwood, 1987.

Masiello, Francine. *Between Civilization and Barbarism: Women, Nation, and Literary Culture in Modern Argentina.* Lincoln: University of Nebraska Press, 1992.

———. "Cuerpo/presencia: Mujer y estado social en la narrativa argentina durante el proceso militar." *Nuevo Texto Crítico* 2/4 (1989): 155–71.

———. "Sara de Etcheverts: The Contradictions of Literary Feminism." In *Women in Hispanic Literature: Icons and Fallen Idols,* edited by Beth Miller. Berkeley: University of California Press, 1983.

———. "Subversions of Authority: Feminist Literary Culture in the River Plate Region." *Chasqui: Revista de Literatura Latinoamericana* 21/1 (May 1992): 39–48.

Mathieu, Corina S. "Argentine Women in the Novels of Silvina Bullrich." In *Latin American Women Writers,* edited by Ivette E. Miller and Charles M. Tatum. Pittsburgh: Latin American Literary Review Press, 1975.

McGraw, Betty R. "Jean-Francois Lyotard's Postmodernism: Feminism, History, and the Question of Justice." *Women's Studies: An Interdisciplinary Journal* 20/3–4 (1992): 259–72.

Meehan, Thomas C. "Una olvidada precursora de la literatura fantástica argentina: Juana Manuela Gorriti." *Chasqui: Revista de Literatura Latinoamericana* 10/2–3 (February–May 1981): 3–19.

Meyer, Doris, and Margarite Fernandez Olmos, eds. *Contemporary Women Authors of Latin America.* Brooklyn: Brooklyn College Press, 1983.

Meyer Spacks, Patricia. *The Female Imagination.* New York: Knopf, 1975.

Miller, Beth. *Mujeres en la literatura.* Mexico City: Fleischer Editora, 1978.

———, ed. *Women in Hispanic Literature: Icons and Fallen Idols.* Berkeley: University of California Press, 1983.

Miller, Ivette E., and Charles M. Tatum, eds. *Latin American Women Writers: Yesterday and Today.* Pittsburgh: Latin American Literary Review Press, 1977.

Minc, Rose, ed. *El Cono Sur: Dinámica y dimensiones de su literatura.* Upper Montclair, N.J.: Montclair State College, 1985.

Modeski, Tania. *Loving with a Vengeance: Mass-Produced Fantasies for Women.* Hamden, Conn.: Archon Books, 1982.

Mohanty, Chandra Talpade, Ann Russo, and Lourdes Torres, eds. *Third World Women and the Politics of Feminism.* Bloomington: Indiana University Press, 1991.

Moi, Toril. *Sexual/Textual Politics: Feminist Literary Theory.* New York: Methuen, 1985.

Molloy, Sylvia. *At Face Value: Autobiographical Writing in Spanish America.* Cambridge: Cambridge University Press, 1991.

———. "Dos proyectos de vida: *Cuadernos de infancia* de Norah Lange y *El archipiélago* de Victoria Ocampo." *Filología* (1985): 279–93.

———. *En breve cárcel.* Barcelona: Seix Barral, 1981.

Montero, Oscar. "*En breve cárcel:* La Diana, la violencia y la mujer que escribe." In *La sartén por el mango: Encuentro de escritoras latinoamericanas,* edited by Patricia Elena González and Eliana Ortega. Río Piedras, P.R.: Huracán, 1984.

Montes-Huidobro, Matías, and Naomi Lindstrom. "Recovering the Lost Erotic Priestess of Caribbean Tradition." In *Woman as Myth and Metaphor in Latin American Literature,* edited by Carmelo Virgillo and Naomi Lindstrom. Columbia: University of Missouri Press, 1985.

Mora, Gabriela, and Karen S. Van Hooft, eds. *Theory and Practice of Feminist Literary Criticism.* Ypsilanti, Mich.: Bilingual Press, 1982.

Mosier, Mary Patricia. "An Ideological Study of the Novels of Marta Lynch, 1962–1974." *Dissertation Abstracts International* 40 (1979): 3335A.

———. "Recuerdo, historia, ficción." In *La historia en la literatura iberoamericana: Textos del XXVI Congreso del Instituto Internacional de Literatura Iberoamericana,* edited by Raquel Chang-Rodríguez and Gabriella de Beer. New York: Ediciones del Norte, 1989.

———. "Tierras de la memoria: La entreapertura del texto." *Escritura* (1982) 7: 13–14.

———. "Women in Power in Gorodischer's *Kalpa imperial.*" In *Spectrum of the Fantastic,* edited by Donald Palumbo. Westport: Greenwood, 1988.

Newman, Kathleen Elizabeth. "The Argentine Political Novel: Determinations in Discourse." Ph.D. diss., Stanford University, 1983.

———. "Cultural Democratization: Argentina, 1978–89." In *On Edge: The Crisis of Contemporary Latin American Culture,* edited by George Yudice, Jean Franco, and Juan Flores. Minneapolis: University of Minnesota Press, 1992.

Nunca más: The Report of the Argentine National Commission on the Disappeared. New York: Farrar, Strauss and Giroux, 1986.

Ordonez, Montserrat. "Escritoras latinoamericanas: Encuentros tras desencuentros." *Boletín Americanista* 36 (1987): 135–55.

Pescatello, Ann, ed. *Female and Male in Latin America: Essays.* Pittsburgh: University of Pittsburgh Press, 1973.

Picón Garfield, Evelyn. *Women's Voices from Latin America: Interviews with Six Contemporary Authors.* Detroit: Wayne State University Press, 1985.

Picón Garfield, Evelyn, and Iván A. Schulman. *Women's Fiction from Latin America: Selections from Twelve Contemporary Authors.* Detroit: Wayne State University Press, 1988.

Piedrahita, Carmen. "Literatura sobre la problemática femenina en Latinoamerica." *Cuadernos Americanos* 236/3 (1981): 222–38.

Piglia, Ricardo. *Respiración artificial.* Buenos Aires: Pomaire, 1980.

Poniatowska, Elena. "Mujer y literatura en América Latina." *Eco* 42/257 (March 1983): 462–72.

Reati, Fernando. *Nombrar lo innombrable: Violencia política y novela argentina 1975–1985.* Buenos Aires: Legasa, 1992.

Redondo, Susana. "Proceso de la literatura femenina hispanoamericana." *Cuadernos* 6 (1954): 34–38.

Riley, Denise. *"Am I That Name?" Feminism and the Category of 'Women' in History.* Minneapolis: University of Minnesota Press, 1988.

Rivera, Andrés. *Nada que perder*. Buenos Aires: Centro Editor de América Latina, 1982.

Roffé, Reina. "Omnipresencia de la censura an la escritora argentina." *Revista Ibero-americana* 51/132–33 (July–December 1985): 909–15.

Rojer, Olga Elaine. *Exile in Argentina, 1933–1945: A Historical and Literary Introduction.* New York: Lang, 1989.

Roses, Lorraine Elena. "Las musas no escriben, inspiran." *Third Woman* 3 (1986): 99–105.

Ross, Kathleen, and Yvette E. Miller, eds. *New World, New Voices: Short Stories by Latin American Women Writers.* Pittsburgh: Latin American Literary Review Press, 1991.

Ruiz, Elida, ed. *Las escritoras: 1840–1940.* Buenos Aires: Centro Editor de América Latina, 1980.

Saer, Juan José. *El entenado.* Buenos Aires: Folios, 1983.

Sarlo, Beatriz. "Política, ideología y figuración literaria." In *Ficción y política: La narrativa argentina durante el proceso militar,* edited by René Jara y Hernán Vidal. Buenos Aires and Minneapolis: Institute for the Study of Ideologies and Alianza Editorial, 1987.

Scott, Joan W. "Gender: A Useful Category for Historical Analysis." *American Historical Review* 91 (1986): 1053–75.

Shea, Maureen. "A Growing Awareness of Sexual Oppression in the Novels of Contemporary Latin American Women Writers." *Confluencia* (Fall 1988): 53–59.

———. "Latin American Women Writers and the Growing Potential of Political Consciousness." *Dissertation Abstracts International* 49 (1988): 515A.

Smith, Paul Julian. *The Body Hispanic: Gender and Sexuality in Spanish and Spanish American Literature.* New York: Oxford University Press, 1989.

Somers, Joseph. "Madness." In *The Eye of the Heart: Short Stories from Latin America,* edited by Barbara Howes. Indianapolis and New York: Avon, 1973.

Sosa de Newton, Lily. *Las argentinas de ayer a hoy.* Buenos Aires: L.V. Zanetti, 1967.

———. *Diccionario biográfico de mujeres argentinas.* Buenos Aires: Plus Ultra, 1980.

Sosnowski, Saúl. "La dispersión de las palabras: Novelas y novelistas argentinos en la década del setenta." *Revista Iberoamericana* 49/125 (October–December 1983): 955–63.

———, ed. *Represión y reconstrucción de una cultura: El caso argentino.* Buenos Aires: EUdeBA, 1988.

Spender, Dale. *The Writing or the Sex? or Why You Don't Have to Read Women's Writing to Know It's No Good.* New York: Pergamon, 1989.

Tierney-Tello, Mary Beth. *Allegories of Transgression and Transformation: Experimental Fiction by Women Writing under Dictatorship.* Albany: State Uiversity of New York Press, 1996.

Torres, Lourdes. "Women and Language: From Sex Differences to Power Dynamics." In *The Knowledge Explosion: Generations of Feminist Scholarship,* edited by Cheris Kramarae and Dale Spender. New York: Teachers College Press, 1992.

Ugarte, Manuel. "Women Writers of South America." *Books Abroad* 5 (1931): 238–41.

Valis, Noel, and Carol Maier, eds. *In the Feminine Mode: Essays on Hispanic Women Writers.* Lewisburg, Penn.: Bucknell University Press 1988.

Virgillo, Carmelo, and Naomi Lindstrom, eds. *Woman as Myth and Metaphor in Latin American Literature.* Columbia: University of Missouri Press, 1985.

White, Hayden. "Getting Out of History." *Diacritics* 12/3 (1982): 2–13.

Witte, Ann Barbara. "Politics, Feminism, and Democratic Transition: A Study of Selected Women Playwrights in Spain and Argentina (1963–1989)." *Dissertation Abstracts International* (June 1992).

Zapata, Cecilia Correas de. *Breve historia de la mujer en la narrativa hispanoamericana.* Toronto: University of Toronto Press, 1980.